Adobe® Flash® Professional CS5

ILLUSTRATED

Barbara M. Waxer

COURSE TECHNOLOGY
CENGAGE Learning™

Australia • Brazil • Japan • Korea • Mexico • United States

COURSE TECHNOLOGY
CENGAGE Learning™

Adobe® Flash® Professional CS5—Illustrated
Barbara M. Waxer

Vice President, Publisher: Nicole Jones Pinard

Executive Editor: Marjorie Hunt

Associate Acquisitions Editor: Brandi Shailer

Senior Product Manager: Christina Kling Garrett

Product Manager: Karen Stevens

Associate Product Manager: Michelle Camisa

Editorial Assistant: Kim Klasner

Director of Marketing: Cheryl Costantini

Senior Marketing Manager: Ryan DeGrote

Marketing Coordinator: Kristen Panciocco

Developmental Editor: Katherine C. Russillo

Senior Content Project Manager: Jill Braiewa

Print Buyer: Fola Orekoya

Art Director: GEX Publishing Services

Copyeditor: Mark Goodin

Proofreader: Chris Clark

Indexer: Rich Carlson

QA Manuscript Reviewers: John Frietas, Jeff Schwartz, Marianne Snow, Susan Whalen

Cover Artist: Mark Hunt

Compositor: GEX Publishing Services

Library of Congress Control Number: 2010930162

International Edition:

ISBN-13: 978-0-538-47756-7

ISBN-10: 0-538-47756-3

Cengage Learning International Offices

Asia
www.cengageasia.com
tel: (65) 6410 1200

Australia/New Zealand
www.cengage.com.au
tel: (61) 3 9685 4111

Brazil
www.cengage.com.br
tel: (55) 11 3665 9900

India
www.cengage.co.in
tel: (91) 11 4364 1111

Latin America
www.cengage.com.mx
tel: (52) 55 1500 6000

UK/Europe/Middle East/Africa
www.cengage.co.uk
tel: (44) 0 1264 332 424

Represented in Canada by
Nelson Education, Ltd.
tel: (416) 752 9100 / (800) 668 0671
www.nelson.com

Cengage Learning is a leading provider of customized learning solutions with office locations around the globe, including Singapore, the United Kingdom, Australia, Mexico, Brazil, and Japan. Locate your local office at: **www.cengage.com/global**

For product information: **www.cengage.com/international**
Visit your local office: **www.cengage.com/global**
Visit our corporate website: **www.cengage.com**

Adobe product screen shot(s) reprinted with permission from Adobe Systems.

Adobe®, Dreamweaver®, Flash®, InDesign®, Illustrator®, and Photoshop® are either registered trademarks or trademarks of Adobe Systems Incorporated in the United States and/or other countries. THIS PRODUCT IS NOT ENDORSED OR SPONSORED BY ADOBE SYSTEMS INCORPORATED, PUBLISHER OF ADOBE® DREAMWEAVER®, FLASH®, INDESIGN®, ILLUSTRATOR®, AND PHOTOSHOP®.

CREDITS: Fig B-33 archives.gov; Fig C-26 Electronic Frontier Foundation: licensed under a Creative Commons Attribution-NonCommercial-ShareAlike 2.5 license; Fig D-43 memory. loc.gov/ammem/oahtml/oahome.html; Fig E-1 http://www2.ed.gov/policy/gen/guid/ assistivetech.html; Fig E-2 Adobe product screen shot reprinted with permission from Adobe Systems Incorporated; Fig E-27 Courtesy NASA/JPL-Caltech; Fig F-32 Courtesy The International Spy Museum (www.spymuseum.org); Fig G-19 academic.cengage.com/ coursetechnology; Fig G-32 mono-1.com/monoface/main.html; Fig H-1 Courtesy NASA and STScI; Fig H-22 copyright.gov; Fig H-23 & H-31 Courtesy Creative Commons

AVAILABILITY OF RESOURCES MAY DIFFER BY REGION. Check with your local Cengage Learning representative for details.

Printed in the United States of America
1 2 3 4 5 6 7 16 15 14 13 12 11 10

Brief Contents

Contents

Preface

Welcome to *Adobe® Flash® Professional CS5—Illustrated*. The unique page design of the book makes it a great learning tool for both new and experienced users. Each skill is presented on two facing pages so that you don't have to turn the page to find a screen shot or finish a paragraph. See the illustration on the right to learn more about the pedagogical and design elements of a typical lesson.

This book is an ideal learning tool for a wide range of learners—the "rookies" will find the clean design easy to follow and focused with only essential information presented, and the "hotshots" will appreciate being able to move quickly through the lessons to find the information they need without reading a lot of text. The design also makes this a great reference after the course is over!

Coverage

Eight units offer thorough coverage of essential skills for working with Adobe Flash Professional CS5, including including several ways of animating objects; incorporating video; creating graphics and text; adding interactivity; using using basic ActionScript 3.0, including code hints; and integrating Flash with other Adobe CS5 programs.

Written by Barbara Waxer, a professional writer, media instructor, and copyright educator, this text offers a real-world perspective with exercises designed to develop the practical skills and techniques necessary to work effectively in a professional interactive or animation environment.

Each two-page spread focuses on a single skill.

Introduction briefly explains why the lesson skill is important.

A case scenario motivates the the steps and puts learning in context.

UNIT B — Flash CS5

Copying and Transforming an Object

As you work in Flash, you save time if you copy objects and **transform**, or reconfigure, the copies instead of re-creating each object from scratch. You can transform an object by scaling, rotating, skewing, and distorting it. Flash offers a few different ways to copy an object from outside or within the program. You can reconfigure objects using options for the Free Transform tool. Options for the Free Transform tool are described in Table B-3. Now that you have set the colors for the design element, you are ready to finalize it by copying and transforming the triangle.

STEPS

1. Adjust the magnification so that less of the Stage is visible; approximately by half
2. Click the Selection tool on the Tools panel if necessary, then drag a bounding box around the triangle to select both the stroke and the fill
3. Click Edit on the Application bar, click Copy, click Edit on the Application bar, then click Paste in Center
   A duplicate of the triangle is pasted in the center of the visible Stage, as shown in Figure B-15. You want to rotate the copied object to create a design.

   TROUBLE
   Depending on your monitor and zoom level, your pasted object may not appear in the same location as the one shown in the figure.

4. Click the Free Transform tool on the Tools panel, then move the mouse pointer near the lower-right sizing handle of the copied triangle until the rotate pointer appears
   When you select the Free Transform tool, sizing handles appear around the object, as shown in Figure B-16. By default, you can scale, rotate, and skew an object. The position of the mouse pointer on or near the object determines which option pointer is active. To limit the tool to a single function, click an option at the bottom of the Tools panel.

   QUICK TIP
   To flip objects horizontally or vertically or to rotate objects 90°, click Modify on the Application bar, point to Transform, then click a flip or rotate command.

5. Press and hold [Shift], drag the mouse pointer counterclockwise until the shape rotates 90°, then release the mouse button
   The triangle rotates and snaps into place. Pressing and holding [Shift] constrains the rotation to 45° increments; you can rotate an object from any corner. You decide to reposition the rotated object to form the completed design element.

   TROUBLE
   You may need to drag slowly or increase magnification to see the line.

6. Drag the rotated triangle to the position shown in Figure B-17
   When the rotated triangle is left-aligned with the original, a dotted alignment line appears along the objects' left edges.

7. Save the document

TABLE B-3: Options for the Free Transform tool

tool option	name	description
	Snap to Objects	Aligns objects
	Rotate and Skew	Slants an object horizontally or vertically
	Scale	Resizes an object by side or proportionately
	Distort	Repositions corners to create perspective
	Envelope	Adds anchor points to allow for extreme distortion in lines and curves

Flash 36 — Creating Graphics and Text

Tips and troubleshooting advice, right where you need it—next to the step itself.

Tables provide helpful summaries of key terms, buttons, or keyboard shortcuts.

Assignments

The lessons use GreenWinds Eco-Cruise, an ecologically friendly travel agency, as the case study. The assignments on the light yellow pages at the end of each unit increase in difficulty. Additional case studies provide a variety of interesting and relevant exercises for students to practice skills.

Assignments include:

- **Concepts Reviews** consist of multiple choice, matching, and screen identification questions.

- **Skills Reviews** provide additional hands-on, step-by-step reinforcement.

- **Independent Challenges** are case projects requiring critical thinking and application of the unit skills. The Independent Challenges increase in difficulty, with the first one in each unit being the easiest. Independent Challenges 2 and 3 become increasingly open-ended, requiring more independent problem solving.

- **Real Life Independent Challenges** are practical exercises to help students with their everyday lives by developing their Flash project. Students work on this project throughout the text, using the skills they learn in each unit.

- **Advanced Challenge Exercises** set within the Independent Challenges provide optional steps for more advanced students.

- **Visual Workshops** direct students to the Internet to visit Web sites and view Flash movies for critical review and inspiration.

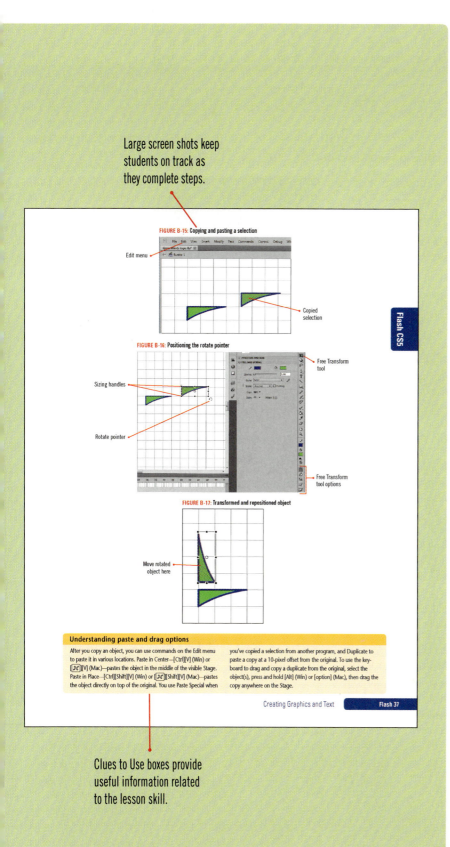

Large screen shots keep students on track as they complete steps.

Clues to Use boxes provide useful information related to the lesson skill.

Flash CS5

FIGURE B-15: Copying and pasting a selection

Edit menu

Copied selection

FIGURE B-16: Positioning the rotate pointer

Sizing handles

Rotate pointer

Free Transform tool

Free Transform tool options

FIGURE B-17: Transformed and repositioned object

Move rotated object here

Understanding paste and drag options

After you copy an object, you can use commands on the Edit menu to paste it in various locations. Paste in Center—[Ctrl][V] (Win) or [⌘][V] (Mac)—pastes the object in the middle of the visible Stage. Paste in Place—[Ctrl][Shift][V] (Win) or [⌘][Shift][V] (Mac)—pastes the object directly on top of the original. You use Paste Special when you've copied a selection from another program, and Duplicate to paste a copy at a 10-pixel offset from the original. To use the keyboard to drag and copy a duplicate from the original, select the object(s), press and hold [Alt] (Win) or [option] (Mac), then drag the copy anywhere on the Stage.

Creating Graphics and Text   Flash 37

Assessment & Training

SAM 2010: SKILLS ASSESSMENT MANAGER

SAM 2010 is designed to help bring students from the classroom to the real world. It allows students to train and test on important computer skills in an active, hands-on environment.

SAM's easy-to-use system includes powerful interactive exams, training and projects on the most commonly used Microsoft® Office applications. SAM simulates the Office 2010 application environment, allowing students to demonstrate their knowledge and think through the skills by performing real-world tasks such as bolding word text or setting up slide transitions. Add in live-in-the-application projects and students are on their way to truly learning and applying skills to business-centric document.

Designed to be used with the Illustrated Series, SAM includes handy page references, so students can print helpful study guides that match the Illustrated Series textbooks used in class. For instructors, SAM also includes robust scheduling and reporting features.

STUDENT EDITION LABS

Our Web-based interactive labs help students master hundreds of computer concepts, including input and output devices, file management and desktop applications, computer ethics, virus protection, and much more. Featuring up-to-the-minute content, eye-popping graphics, and rich animation, the highly interactive Student Edition Labs offer students an alternative way to learn through dynamic observation, step-by-step practice, and challenging review questions.

COURSENOTES

Course Technology's CourseNotes are six-panel quick reference cards that reinforce the most important and widely used features of a software application in a visual and user-friendly format. CourseNotes serve as a great reference tool during and after the student completes the course. CourseNotes for Microsoft Office 2010, Word 2010, Excel 2010, Access 2010, PowerPoint 2010, Windows 7, and more are available now!

COURSECASTS Learning on the Go. Always Available…Always Relevant.

Our fast-paced world is driven by technology. You know because you are an active participant—always on the go, always keeping up with technological trends, and always learning new ways to embrace technology to power your life. Let CourseCasts, hosted by Ken Baldauf of Florida State University, be your guide into weekly updates in this ever-changing space. These timely, relevant podcasts are produced weekly and are available for download at http://coursecasts.course.com or directly from iTunes (search by CourseCasts). CourseCasts are a perfect solution to getting students (and even instructors) to learn on the go!

Instructor Resources

The Instructor Resources CD is Course Technology's way of putting the resources and information needed to teach and learn effectively into your hands. With an integrated array of teaching and learning tools that offer you and your students a broad range of technology-based instructional options, we believe this CD represents the highest quality and most cutting edge resources available to instructors today. Many of these resources are available at www.cengage.com/coursetechnology. The resources available with this book are:

- **Instructor's Manual**—Available as an electronic file, the Instructor's Manual includes detailed lecture topics with teaching tips for each unit.

- **Sample Syllabus**—Prepare and customize your course easily using this sample course outline.

- **PowerPoint Presentations**—Each unit has a corresponding PowerPoint presentation that you can use in lecture, distribute to your students, or customize to suit your course.

- **Figure Files**—The figures in the text are provided on the Instructor Resources CD to help you illustrate key topics or concepts. You can create traditional overhead transparencies by printing the figure files. Or you can create electronic slide shows by using the figures in a presentation program such as PowerPoint.

- **Solutions to Exercises**—Solutions to Exercises contains every file students are asked to create or modify in the lessons and end-of-unit material. Also provided in this section, there is a document outlining the solutions for the end-of-unit Concepts Review, Skills Review, and Independent Challenges.

- **Data Files for Students**—To complete most of the units in this book, your students will need Data Files. You can post the Data Files on a file server for students to copy. The Data Files available on the Instructor Resources CD are also included on a CD located at the front of the textbook.

Instruct students to use the Data Files List included on the CD found at the front of the book and the Instructor Resources CD. This list gives instructions on copying and organizing files.

- **ExamView**—ExamView is a powerful testing software package that allows you to create and administer printed, computer (LAN-based), and Internet exams. ExamView includes hundreds of questions that correspond to the topics covered in this text, enabling students to generate detailed study guides that include page references for further review. The computer-based and Internet testing components allow students to take exams at their computers, and also saves you time by grading each exam automatically.

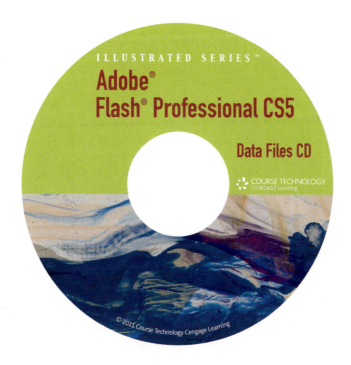

Read This Before You Begin

What are Data Files?

A Data File is a partially completed animation, graphic, video, or ActionScript 3.0 code file that you use to complete the steps in the units and exercises to create the final document that you submit to your instructor. The Data Files that you need for each unit are listed on the opening page of each unit.

Where are the Data Files?

Your instructor will provide the Data Files to you or direct you to a location on a network drive from which you can download them. The Data Files are also included on a CD located at the front of the textbook. As you download the files, select where to store them, such as a hard drive, a network server, or a USB storage device. The instructions in the lessons refer to "the location where you store your Data Files" when referring to the Data Files for the book.

What software was used to write and test this book?

This book was written and tested on a computer with a typical installation of Microsoft Windows 7. The browsers used for any steps that require a browser are Mozilla Firefox 3 and Internet Explorer 8. If you are using this book on Windows Vista, your dialog box title bars will look slightly different, but will work essentially the same.

This book is written and tested on both the Windows version and the Macintosh version of Adobe Flash Professional CS5. The two versions of the software are virtually the same, but there are a few platform differences. When there are differences between the two versions of the software, steps written specifically for the Windows version end with the notation (Win) and steps for the Macintosh version end with the notation (Mac). In instances when the lessons are split between the two operating systems, a line divides the page and is accompanied by Mac and Win icons.

Also, in this book, Macintosh commands instruct users to press the [return] key to enter information. On some newer Macintosh keyboards, this key may be named [enter] or the keyboard may include both [return] and [enter].

Do I need to be connected to the Internet to complete the steps and exercises in this book?

Some of the exercises in this book assume that your computer is connected to the Internet. If you are not connected to the Internet, see your instructor for information on how to complete the exercises.

What do I do if my screen is different from the figures shown in this book?

This book was written and tested on computers with monitors set at a resolution of 1024 × 768. If your screen shows more or less information than the figures in the book, your monitor is probably set at a higher or lower resolution. If you don't see something on your screen, you might have to scroll down or up to see the object identified in the figures. In some cases, the figures will not match your screen because the Flash windows have been resized or moved in an effort to make the figures as easy to read as possible. Mac users should be aware that the tops of dialog boxes and windows may appear to slip beneath the menu bar when you drag them near the top of the screen. Note that the appearance of commands on menus and in dialog boxes will vary.

What do I do if I see an Adobe Flash Player security warning?

Beginning with solution files created in Unit G, you will encounter the Adobe Flash Player Security warning dialog box when you click a button in a SWF or HTML file that links to a URL. This is a Flash security feature that requires you to allow access to the URL in the Global Security Settings Panel. Although you access the Panel through Flash Player Help online, the security settings affect your local computer. To allow access to a URL, click Settings in the Adobe Flash Player Security dialog box. On the Flash Player Help, Global security settings for content creators page, click Edit locations. Next, click Add location, click Browse for Files, navigate to where you store the SWF, select it, click Open, then reopen the SWF file in your browser. Instructors should confirm with their IT departments that institutional policy will allow access. To adjust security settings, navigate to http://www.macromedia.com/support/documentation/en/flashplayer/help/settings_manager.html, then click the Global Security Settings Panel link at the left.

How do I use Flash with other Adobe CS5 programs?

The lessons in Unit H assume students have access to Adobe Fireworks, Adobe Photoshop, and Adobe Dreamweaver. To take full advantage of these lessons, set your file association for PNG files to Fireworks. Users whose PSD file associations are set to Photoshop Elements 8 can perform the same steps in Full Edit mode in the Editor workspace.

What if I can't find some of the information in the exercises on the Internet?

This book uses the Internet to provide real-life examples in the lessons and end-of-unit exercises. Because the Internet is constantly changing to display current information, some of the links used and described in the book may be deleted or modified before the book is even published. If this happens, searching the referenced Web sites will usually locate similar information in a slightly modified form. In some cases, entire Web sites may move. Technical problems with Web servers may also prevent access to Web sites or Web pages temporarily. Patience, critical thinking, and creativity are necessary whenever the Internet is being used in the classroom.

What if my icons look different?

Symbols for icons, buttons, and pointers are shown in the steps each time they are used. Icons may look different in the Files panel depending on the file association settings on your computer.

What if I can't see my file extensions?

The learning process will be easier if you can see the file extensions for the files you will use in the lessons. To do this in Windows 7, open an Explorer window, click Organize, click Folder and search options, click the View tab, uncheck the box Hide extensions for known file types, then click OK. To do this on a Macintosh, go to the Finder, click the Finder menu, then click Preferences. Click the Advanced tab, then select the Show all file name extensions check box.

Other Adobe CS5 Titles

Adobe® Dreamweaver® CS5—Illustrated
Sherry Bishop (0538478691)

Ten units provide essential training on using Dreamweaver CS5 to create Web sites. Coverage includes creating a Web site, developing Web pages, formatting text, using and managing images, creating links and navigation bars, using CSS to layout pages, and collecting data with forms.

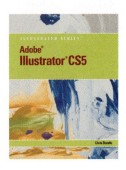

Adobe® Illustrator® CS5—Illustrated
Chris Botello (1111221960)

Eight units cover essential skills for working with Adobe Illustrator CS5 including drawing basic and complex shapes, using the Pen tool, working with blends, compound paths and clipping masks, creating pattern fills and gradient fills for objects, and designing stunning 3D effects.

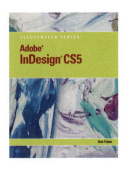

Adobe® InDesign® CS5—Illustrated
Ann Fisher (0538477873)

Eight units provide essential training on using Adobe InDesign CS5 for designing simple layouts, combining text, graphics, and color, as well as multi-page documents, layered documents, tables, and InDesign libraries.

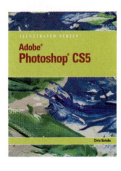

Adobe® Photoshop® CS5—Illustrated
Chris Botello (0538477814)

Eight units offer thorough coverage of essential skills for working with Adobe Photoshop from both the design and production perspective, including creating and managing layer masks, creating color effects and improving images with adjustment layers, working with text and combining text and imagery, and using filters and layer styles to create eye-popping special effects.

For more information on the Illustrated Series, please visit:
www.cengage.com/ct/illustrated

Acknowledgements

Author Acknowledgements

I am fortunate to be surrounded by a cadre of talented and dedicated colleagues who strive for a more perfect printing and suffer my humor, mostly of their own volition. My thanks to Nicole Pinard, Vice President, Publisher at Course Technology, Marjorie Hunt, Executive Editor, and Associate Acquisitions Editor Brandi Shailer for adding Flash to the Illustrated repertoire and inviting me to write the book. Our Product Manager Karen Stevens guided us with a deft touch, and always foresaw incoming meteors on a collision course. Project Managers Jill Braiewa and Louise Capulli kept us spot-on through production. Many thanks to our ace quality assurance testers John Freitas, Jeff Schwartz, and especially to Marianne Snow and Susan Whalen, who shot the Macintosh figures. Big thanks also to Senior Product Manager Christina Kling-Garrett and her sons Jack and Keith, on whom itzyBotz is modeled, and to Associate Product Manager Michelle Camisa. I am very grateful for always-positive interactions with my Developmental Editor, Kate Rusillo, whose support and good humor were endless.

Kudos to Anita Quintana, my friend and colleague at Santa Fe Community College, for translating my babblings and scribbles into such amazing art for the Data Files.

Finally, the warmest of acknowledgement always to my partner, Lindy, who waved gamely as I disappeared into my office and marveled at my alleged ability to write with cats ensconced around my keyboard and person.

Barbara Waxer

Getting Started with Adobe Flash Professional

Adobe Flash Professional CS5 is a multimedia program used to create animations, games, Web interfaces, and other user experiences. Its tools let you create content and control whether and how users interact with it. Flash is a powerful program. By learning and applying the essential skills presented in these units, your projects will stand out with impressive Flash content. To work productively in Flash, you need to know some basic multimedia concepts, how to navigate in the program, how to play a movie, and how to get help when you need it. You have just started working at GreenWinds Eco-Cruise, an ecologically friendly travel agency specializing in oceanic vacations. Marketing Director Marta Diaz has selected you as an intern, and you'll use Flash to create content for an online ad. You prepare for your first project by familiarizing yourself with Flash.

OBJECTIVES

Understand Adobe Flash

Start Adobe Flash Professional CS5

View the Flash workspace

Arrange the workspace

Open a document and play a movie

Understand the Timeline

Add a layer and element

Explore Help and exit Flash

Understanding Adobe Flash

Adobe Flash is a multimedia program that lets you create and organize media and then apply animation and other effects to them. **Multimedia** refers to content that integrates different types of elements such as text, graphics, video, animation, and sound. You can use Flash tools to arrange how media elements appear and function to create animated movies that let users view and even interact with them. You want to learn how Flash can help you in your work as a marketing intern.

DETAILS

You can use Adobe Flash to:

• ### Add movies to Web pages

Flash lets you create Web page components. Flash is commonly used to create Web page animations, often referred to as movies or video. An **animation** is a series of still images that are played rapidly in a sequence, creating the illusion of movement. An animation can be one part of a Web page or it can be a stand-alone file, such as an e-card, advertisement, game, or simulation. You can also use Flash to create an entire Web page. Figure A-1 shows a simple animation open in Flash.

Flash videos typically contain many graphics. They often use streaming video and audio as well as vector graphics, a type of graphic that reduces file size. **Streaming** is an online method of playing media in your browser before it has downloaded completely, thus saving time and storage space. You'll learn more about vector graphic files in Unit B.

> **QUICK TIP**
> To ensure your content is accessible to all users, your design must plan for consistent design and navigation elements, mouse and keyboard controls, labels, audio, and visual captions.

• ### Create interactive content

Flash lets you create **interactive content** that accepts and responds to human actions using multimedia elements. One type of interactive content includes **navigational components** such as icons, menus, and similar items that help you navigate a Web page or another application. You can use and reuse such elements to create a consistent **user interface**, which consists of items that help users interact with a program. Other interactive content can include large amounts of user interaction, such as that seen in Figure A-2, which shows the result of a user changing a variety of facial features by clicking parts of the face.

> **QUICK TIP**
> When planning an RIA application, your team needs to know the functional requirements, how the RIA will be used and by whom, and whether you should concentrate on design or data.

• ### Create self-running programs

You can use advanced features in Flash to create **Rich Internet Applications (RIA)**, which are Web programs that work like desktop application programs, but the user doesn't need to install any software to run them. Instead, the Flash content contains the necessary functionality that allows the program to run. Examples of RIAs could include a Web buying guide to help you select the features you want in a particular product, such as a digital camera, or a map that displays directions, or data, such as demographic or voting information. RIAs often include interactive content as well, and they can be delivered on a mobile device, on your desktop, or on the Web. RIAs are characterized by a consistent user interface (buttons, colors, menus, and fonts), which shortens the development time and improves the usability of your project or site. You'll learn more about creating consistent and reusable elements in a later unit.

> **QUICK TIP**
> The Flash Player comes standard in the browser software installed in most new computers and is downloaded and installed millions of times each day around the world.

• ### Develop content to create playable files

Flash is an **authoring tool**, which is a program that creators use to develop and package content for users. In a program such as a word processor, you create a document file that end users see or use. In Flash, however, the authoring files you work on in the program are never opened or viewed by the users. Instead, when you are ready to deliver a movie to end users, you change it to a different file type.

Flash files that you create are known as **documents**, and they have the **.fla** file extension. To create an output file for users, you save your document in the **.swf** file format. To play a SWF file in a Web page, users must have the **Flash Player plug-in**, a free, easily downloadable program, installed in their browser. Other programs can also play SWF files.

FIGURE A-1: Viewing a Flash movie

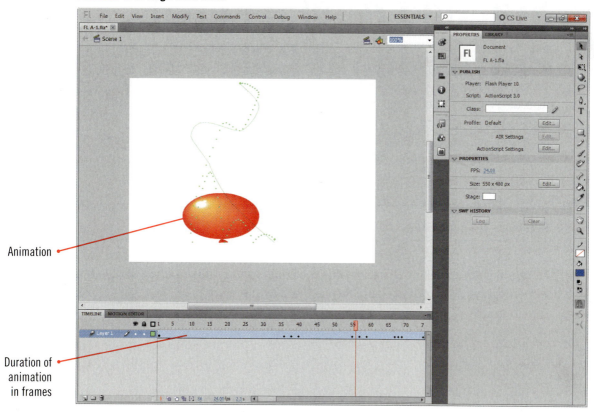

Animation

Duration of
animation
in frames

FIGURE A-2: Viewing a Web site created in Flash

monoface™

happy new year from all of us.

what do i do?
shuffle face
view gallery
screensaver

mono-1.com
©2007 mono LLC

Design Matters

Understanding animation

Translating light into sight involves a nearly instantaneous exchange between our eyes and brain. Depending on the brightness of an image, we can retain its impression for less than 1/10th of a second. Our capacity to retain an image, even as a new image is "burned" on top of it, is known as **persistence of vision**. This overlap between images creates the illusion of movement. Because our eyes keep an image in our mind as it processes each new one, our brains are "tricked" into seeing smooth motion. Theatrical release and digital movies play at 24 frames per second. At this speed, persistence of vision ensures that we never see that a film is essentially dark for much of the time. If you watch a silent movie from the early twentieth century, however, which runs at only 16 frames per second, you will see a noticeable flickering. At this speed, you can actually perceive individual frames flashing on the screen.

Starting Adobe Flash Professional CS5

Depending on the type of computer you own and its operating system, you can start Flash in several ways. When you install Flash, the installation program may place a Flash shortcut icon on your desktop (Win) or in the dock (Mac). You can double-click the icon to open the program. However, you can always start the program using the Start menu. You are ready to start Flash and begin familiarizing yourself with the workspace.

STEPS

WIN

1. **Click the Start button 🔵 on the Windows taskbar, point to All Programs, then click the Adobe Web Premium CS5 folder (or the name of the Adobe CS5 folder loaded on your computer), as shown in Figure A-4**

   The Start menu opens on the desktop. The left pane of the Start menu includes shortcuts to the most frequently used programs on the computer. The programs and items on your Start menu and desktop will differ from those shown in the figure.

> **TROUBLE**
> If this is the first time you are using Flash, or if you are using a trial version, you might receive a prompt to register the program.

2. **Click Adobe Flash Professional CS5 🔴**

   The Adobe Flash Professional CS5 Welcome Screen appears in the program window.

MAC

1. **Open the Finder, click the hard drive icon, if necessary, double-click Applications, then double-click the Adobe Web Premium CS5 folder (or the name of the Adobe CS5 folder loaded on your computer). If there isn't an Adobe folder present, then click the Adobe Flash CS5 folder, as shown in Figure A-4**

   The items in your Finder window will differ from those shown in the figure.

> **TROUBLE**
> If this is the first time you are using Flash, or if you are using a trial version, you might receive a prompt to register the program.

2. **Double-click Adobe Flash CS5 🔴**

   The Adobe Flash Professional CS5 Welcome Screen appears.

Understanding the Welcome Screen

In the top three panes of the Welcome Screen, you can create a file from several templates, open existing or recently used files, create new files of various file types, and link to Flash training. You can also access a link to the Flash Exchange Web site, where you can download extensions, plug-ins, and other components.

The lower-left corner of the Welcome Screen contains links to sites where you can learn about new features in Flash Professional CS5 and access other specific information and tutorials. The Macintosh Welcome screen also has a link for a feature tour in the lower-right corner. To turn off the Welcome Screen so it does not open when you start Flash, click the Don't show again check box in the lower-left corner of the window. See Figure A-3.

FIGURE A-3: Welcome Screen

Flash CS5

Viewing the Flash Workspace

The Flash interface consists of several components arranged into a workspace. The **workspace** is the screen area where you work with the elements of your movie. You use Flash to create movies, and you, as the director and producer, interact with the workspace elements to create them. A movie naturally includes characters; in Flash that means controlling the appearance of various media elements, such as objects, images, text, sound, and video. In a movie, you also control actions over time, determining how, when, and what actions occur. You decide to examine the Flash workspace to familiarize yourself with it.

Refer to Figure A-5 to find the Flash workspace elements described below:

- The most commonly used workspace components are the Stage, Timeline, panels, and Application bar. The main area is the **Stage**, which contains the movie's elements—text, images, graphics, drawings, video, and sound—that you will work with as you create your movies. The Stage shows how these elements interact with each other and how the action plays in the movie overall. As you work in a Flash file, you are working on a **project**, which is the source Flash .fla file you create and modify. You can work on multiple Flash projects at one time; each file opens in its own Document window, represented by a tab at the top of the Stage. The gray area surrounding the Stage is known as the Pasteboard, where you can place or store objects that do not yet appear in the movie. Objects that enter or exit the movie from offstage also appear on the Pasteboard.

- The **Timeline** controls and organizes the movie elements by using layers and frames. **Layers** are individual rows that contain content in your project. A **frame** is a single point in a movie. When you play a document in Flash, a red translucent bar called the **playhead** moves through the frames, displaying them on the Stage.

- You use individual windows called **panels** to control crucial aspects of a project. You use them to display information and options for selected objects, select tools for creating and modifying objects, and store media objects for your project. In the default view, panels are docked in the right half of the workspace. A **panel group** is a bundle of related panels that open as one.
  - The **Properties panel** displays the attributes and available options for the selected element on the Stage or in the Timeline.
  - The **Library panel** contains the media that you'll use in a project, including video, sound, photos, and other graphics. You can import media elements to the Library panel and then drag them to the Stage.
  - The **Tools panel** contains tools to draw, select, modify, and view graphics and text. The Tools panel is divided into sections: selection tools; drawing, painting, and text tools; retouching tools; navigation tools; color tools; and tool options. Tool options vary based on the tool selected.

- The **Application bar** contains Flash commands on the left and workspace and Help options on the right. You can click the **workspace switcher** to switch to a different preset workspace configuration. The currently selected workspace name appears on the workspace switcher, and the Essentials workspace is the default workspace. Other choices include Animator, Designer, and Developer, and Small Screen. Most are tailored to a specific task, while Classic emulates the layout from older versions of Flash, and Small Screen minimizes all panels for working on smaller monitors. To select a workspace, click the workspace switcher on the Application bar, then click a workspace name.

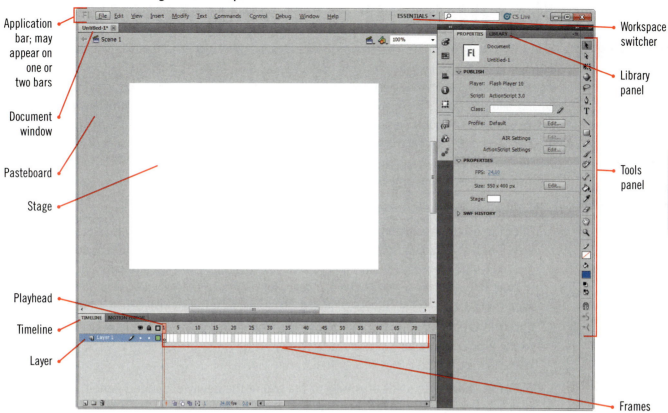

FIGURE A-5: Viewing the Flash workspace

- Application bar; may appear on one or two bars
- Document window
- Pasteboard
- Stage
- Playhead
- Timeline
- Layer
- Workspace switcher
- Library panel
- Tools panel
- Frames

Planning and managing a project

Developing a Flash project or Web site can easily become a complex process. Typically, a team consists of designers, developers, artists, managers, and, of course, the client. It is essential to have clear, seamless communication about design and content. Investing a little bit of time to develop a project plan can help streamline your workflow, keep the focus on your goals, and troubleshoot problems. The process chart shown in Figure A-6 outlines the steps that can save you time and help you avoid errors that are difficult or time consuming to fix. Project management provides a methodical approach that guides a project from start to finish. It controls the scope, resources, budget, and schedule, and it identifies the milestones through five phases: initiation, planning, executing, testing, and closing. Good project management will detect common problems early, such as when the project scope begins to creep or when the addition of features results in unplanned changes.

Planning also helps manage expectations; you should identify what your client receives in the final package, known as the **deliverable**. It starts with the goals of the project and the content that supports the goals. It could include all the specifications, prototypes and preparatory documents, copy writing, identity and content design, image selection and editing, deployment on multiple devices, maintenance, actual files (HTML, SWF, planning), and so on. Your contract should also specify change control charges (to manage scope creep), who owns all the design and content elements, and whether you can use them in your portfolio. Building in a common workflow and communication process ensures that everyone shares common assumptions, evaluation criteria, and accountability.

FIGURE A-6: Flash project planning process

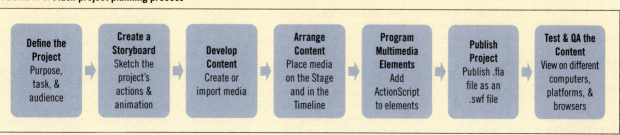

Define the Project	Create a Storyboard	Develop Content	Arrange Content	Program Multimedia Elements	Publish Project	Test & QA the Content
Purpose, task, & audience	Sketch the project's actions & animation	Create or import media	Place media on the Stage and in the Timeline	Add ActionScript to elements	Publish .fla file as an .swf file	View on different computers, platforms, & browsers

UNIT A
Flash CS5

Arranging the Workspace

Panels open by default in the selected workspace when you start Flash. See Table A-1 for a summary of the different workspace configurations you can select. You can think of panels as floating windows that you can arrange to maximize your on-screen "real estate." Flash lets you dock (group), undock, regroup, collapse, expand, and close panels or panel groups. You can collapse panels completely to **iconic view**. To open or close a panel, click Window on the Application bar, then click the panel's name. To expand or collapse a panel or panel group, click the gray panel next to the tab or the panel title bar. To undock a panel group, drag the panel title bar; to undock a single panel, drag the panel name in the tab. You create a new file, then explore and modify the Flash workspace.

STEPS

1. **Click File on the Application bar, click New, verify that ActionScript 3.0 is selected in the New Document dialog box, then click OK**

    A new blank document named Untitled-1 opens in the Document window. **ActionScript** is a programming language in Flash that lets you control interactivity and actions in a movie or Web site. You'll learn more about creating new files and ActionScript in a later unit. You explore collapsed panels in the workspace.

2. **Click the Expand Panels arrow ◄◄ above the iconic view panel on the Panel title bar next to the Properties panel**

    Several panels and panel groups expand, as shown in Figure A-7.

3. **Click the Collapse to Icons arrow ►► at the top of the newly expanded panels, then click ►► at the top of the Properties panel**

    The panels are collapsed to icons, although the Properties and Library icons have labels identifying them. You can move a panel in the workspace.

4. **Drag the light gray panel title bar at the top of the Tools panel to the left side of the Document window, as shown in Figure A-8**

    The Tools panel is undocked, and the tools are arranged in a square panel. You can also open or close individual panels by clicking Window on the Application bar and then clicking a panel name, by clicking the Panel title bar on a collapsed panel, or by clicking a collapsed panel icon.

5. **Click the Align panel icon ▦ in the iconic panel group**

    The Align panel opens on top of its panel group, as shown in Figure A-9. In the Window menu, open panels have a check mark next to their name. To close an open panel, click the Close button on the panel or click its name in the Window menu.

6. **Click the workspace switcher in the Application bar, then click Reset 'Essentials'**

    The Essentials workspace appears in its original configuration.

7. **Click File on the Application bar, then click Close to close the file**

> **QUICK TIP**
> To increase the width of a panel, place the mouse pointer along its edge, then drag ⟺ left or right.

> **TROUBLE**
> Mac arrows differ.

> **QUICK TIP**
> You can move undocked panels anywhere on the screen, even if the Flash program window is in Restore Down view.

> **QUICK TIP**
> To dock a panel, drag a gray panel title bar to an area of the workspace. Then when a blue bar or rectangle is visible and the panel appears translucent, release the title bar.

TABLE A-1: Flash workspaces

workspace	function
Animator	Create and edit animation
Classic	Default configuration from previous Flash versions
Debug	Analyze object properties, the Timeline, and ActionScript code
Designer	Create artwork
Developer	Write ActionScript code and programs
Essentials	Default all-purpose configuration
Small Screen	Minimized panels for working in a small viewing area

FIGURE A-7: Viewing expanded panels

Panel title bar

Collapse to Icons arrow

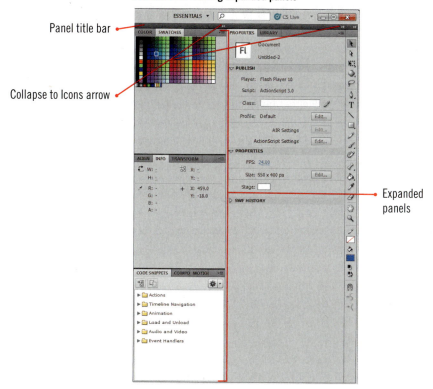

Expanded panels

FIGURE A-8: Undocked Tools panel

Drag light gray panel title bar to move an undocked panel

Drag name tab to undock a panel

Iconic panels

Tools panel undocked; your exact arrangement might differ

FIGURE A-9: Panel opened from collapsed icon

Iconic view of panels

Align panel   Align panel icon

Getting Started with Adobe Flash Professional

UNIT A

Flash CS5

Opening a Document and Playing a Movie

When you work in Flash, you'll either be creating a new document or opening an existing one. It is always good practice to save a file with a different file name to protect the original. As you continue getting acquainted with Flash, you open a sample file, save it with a new name, then play and test the movie.

STEPS

QUICK TIP

You can also click Open in the Welcome Screen, then press [Ctrl][O] (Win) or [⌘][O] (Mac) to open a file.

1. **Click File on the Application bar, click Open, then navigate to the location where you store your Data Files**

   The Open dialog box opens, and the list of available files appears in the file list, as shown in Figure A-10.

2. **Click FL A-1.fla, then click Open**

   The document opens. A balloon object and its animation path are visible on the Stage.

3. **Click File on the Application bar, click Save As to open the Save As dialog box, type balloon-bounce in the File name text box (Win) or Save As text box (Mac), then click Save**

   The document is renamed, and the new name appears in the Document window.

4. **Click View on the Application bar, point to Magnification, then click Fit in Window**

   The Stage is scaled to fit in the Document window. Objects off the Stage, such as the balloon, may not be visible. You can also click the View arrow at the top of the Document window to select a view option.

QUICK TIP

Based on your work preferences, you can use commands on the Control menu, keyboard shortcuts shown on the Control menu, or the Controller to preview a movie.

5. **Click Control on the Application bar, then click Play**

   The balloon floats in and bounces a couple times. As the movie plays on the Stage, the playhead moves through the Timeline. Several commands on the Control menu are similar to playback buttons, such as Rewind or Step Forward One Frame. To quickly play or stop a movie, you can press [Enter] (Win) or [return] (Mac). You explore ways to control how to view a movie.

6. **Click Window on the Application bar, point to Toolbars, then click Controller**

   The Controller opens, displaying a set of playback buttons, as shown in Figure A-11.

7. **Click the Step back one frame button ◀ in the Controller, drag the playhead in the Timeline to frame 1, then drag it to frame 75**

   The playhead moves back one frame, then to the beginning of the movie, and then to the end. Playing a movie in Flash presents a general preview of a movie, but does not provide a way to fully test it, which is critical if the movie contains interactivity such as buttons. You preview and test the movie using the Flash Player.

QUICK TIP

You can turn off looping by clicking Control on the Application bar (Win) or menu application bar (Mac) in the Flash Player window, and then clicking Loop (Win) or Loop Playback (Mac).

8. **Click Control on the Application bar, point to Test Movie, then click in Flash Professional**

   The movie plays in a Flash Player window, as shown in Figure A-12. You can increase the size of the Flash Player window as needed by clicking and dragging a corner of the window. By default, the movie plays repeatedly, or **loops**. You can also press [Ctrl][Enter] (Win) or [⌘][return] (Mac) to test a movie. When you test a movie, Flash automatically creates an .swf file, which you can see if you open the file management utility for your computer, then navigate to where you store your Data Files.

9. **Click the Close button on the Flash Player and the Controller to close them**

Getting Started with Adobe Flash Professional

FIGURE A-10: Open dialog box

Your location might differ

Your view and details might differ

Click to open selected file

FIGURE A-11: Viewing the Controller

Control menu

Window menu

Controller; your location might differ

Playback buttons

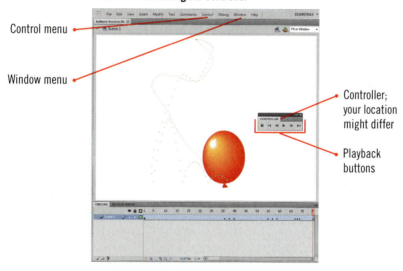

FIGURE A-12: Testing a movie in Flash Player

Flash Player window (Win)

Flash Player menu (Mac menus differ)

Movie playing

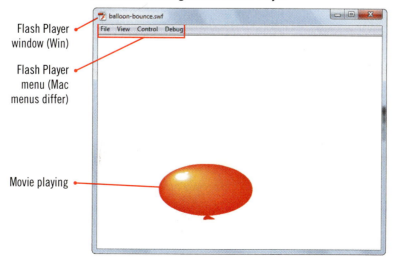

Understanding the Timeline

The Timeline is a multipurpose tool divided into two main areas. On the left are layers, which appear in a column. Layers contain the elements of a movie and determine their position. On the right are frames, which appear in a row and show the elements in your project over time. As you continue to familiarize yourself with the Flash interface, you review the functions of the Timeline.

As you get acquainted with the Timeline, you review the features listed below:

- **Layers section** Layers let you build depth and dimension into a project. In the Timeline, layers are arranged in a stack as they appear on the Stage, from front to back: The layer at the top of the stack is in front in the movie, and the layer at the bottom of the stack is in back in the movie. You can see this in Figure A-13, where the orange balloon is the object in front, followed by the Happy Birthday text, and finally the cake. In the Timeline, the layers correspond to their appearance on the Stage: The balloon layer is at the top of the Timeline, the text layer is in the middle, and the cake layer is at the bottom.

  The Timeline offers several ways to manipulate layers. For existing layers, you can use buttons at the top of the layers section to show or hide a layer, lock it from editing, or display it as an outline. At the bottom of the layers section are buttons to add and delete layers or create a folder, where you can move related layers. Flash projects can become complex, and folders can be a useful organizing tool for your layers, just as they are with file management on your computer. See Figure A-14.

  You may also find it useful to move layers in the Timeline to affect their appearance on the Stage. You can use buttons at the bottom of the layers portion of the Timeline to add or delete a layer and create a folder, where you can store related layers.

- **Frames section** You use frames to create animation; you create different effects by using different frame types, which you'll learn more about in a later unit. Each frame is a snapshot in time of an event on the Stage. Time in Flash is measured in frames, known as a **frame rate**, or frames per second—**fps**.

  You can view the status of a movie—the current frame, frame rate, and total elapsed time up to the selected frame—using indicators at the bottom of the Timeline, as shown in Figure A-14. The playhead shows you the current frame playing in the movie. You can manually drag the playhead in the Timeline to play a group of frames on the Stage, in a process known as **scrubbing**.

- **Changing appearance** You can modify the Timeline as you can other panels: You can undock, move, resize, or close it. You can also adjust your view of frames by clicking the Panel options button and selecting a frame size. Figure A-15 shows a Timeline modified to show large frames and an expanded layer.

Creating a custom workspace

You can arrange panels in a workspace to suit your individual work preferences, such as moving the Tools panel to the left side of the window. You can modify any preset workspace and then save that layout as a new workspace. To create a custom workspace, arrange the workspace as you wish, click the workspace switcher on the Application bar, then click New Workspace. In the New Workspace dialog box, type a new name in the Name text box, then click OK. The new name appears on the workspace switcher and at the top of the Workspace menu. To delete or rename a workspace, click the workspace switcher on the Application bar, click Manage Workspaces, select a workspace, then click Rename or Delete. Click Yes to confirm a deletion or OK to rename, then click OK.

FIGURE A-13: Viewing layers

Scene

Selected object

Objects on Stage

Layers in Timeline

Selected layer

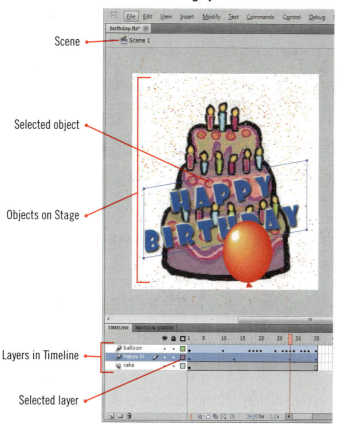

FIGURE A-14: Viewing the Timeline

Show All Layers as Outlines icon

Show or Hide All Layers icon

Lock or Unlock All Layers Icon

New Layer button

New folder button

Delete button

Current Frame indicator

Frame Rate indicator

Elapsed Time indicator

Drag playhead to display one or more frames

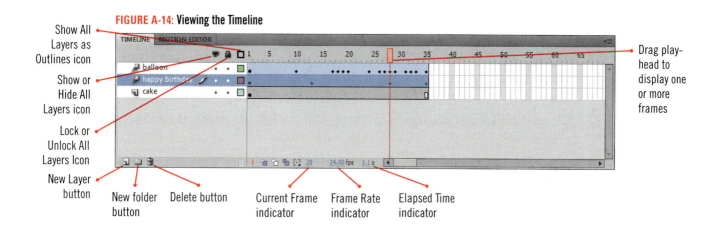

FIGURE A-15: Modified Timeline

Expanded layer

Large frames

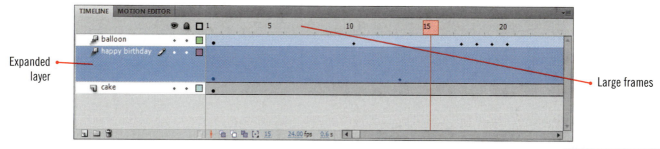

Getting Started with Adobe Flash Professional

Flash 13

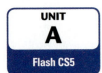

Adding a Layer and Element

Working with layers is an important skill to develop for working with projects. By default, each document has one layer that you add elements to. You add elements to a project by importing them or by dragging them from the Library panel to the Stage. Renaming layers is an organizing technique that makes it easy to find a specific layer. You add a layer to the Timeline, add an element to the movie, and then modify layers.

STEPS

1. **Verify that the document balloon-bounce.fla is open, then click the New Layer button at the bottom of the Timeline**

   A new layer, Layer 2, appears at the top of the Timeline. You add content to the layer using the Library panel.

2. **Click the Library panel, click park.jpg to select it, then drag park.jpg to the Stage, as shown in Figure A-16**

   The new element is on top of the balloon, obscuring it from view. You hide the layer temporarily.

3. **Click the Show or Hide All Layers icon at the top of the Timeline, then click the red X in the visibility column next to Layer 1**

   All the layers are hidden when they all have a red "X," and Layer 2 is hidden after you display Layer 1. Although you can now see the balloon, you can't work with the new content, so you decide to show Layer 2 and move it down in the Timeline to change its stacking order.

4. **Click the red X in the visibility column on Layer 2, click and hold Layer 2 in the Timeline, drag the layer beneath Layer 1, then when a black bar appears below Layer 1, as shown in Figure A-17, release the mouse button**

   Layer 2 is stacked beneath Layer 1, and both layers are visible on the Stage. The layer names do not describe the layers very well, so you rename the layers to something more descriptive.

5. **Double-click the Layer 2 name label in the Timeline, type background, then press [Enter] (Win) or [return] (Mac)**

   You renamed the layer "background."

6. **Double-click the Layer 1 name label in the Timeline, type balloon, press [Enter] (Win) or [return] (Mac), then compare your screen to Figure A-18**

7. **Press [Ctrl][Enter] (Win) or [⌘][return] (Mac) to test the movie, then close the Flash Player**

8. **Click File on the Application bar, click Close, then click Yes (Win) or Save (Mac) to save changes in the Adobe Flash CS5 dialog box**

FIGURE A-16: Adding content to a new layer

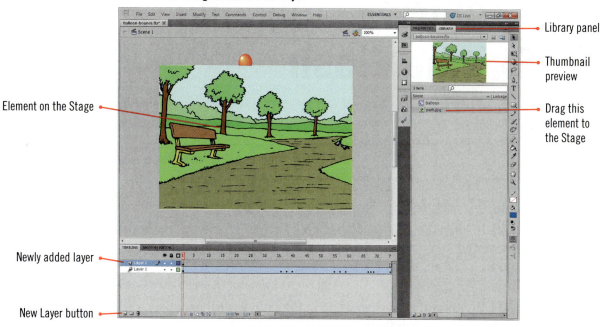

Library panel

Thumbnail preview

Drag this element to the Stage

Element on the Stage

Newly added layer

New Layer button

FIGURE A-17: Moving a layer in the Timeline

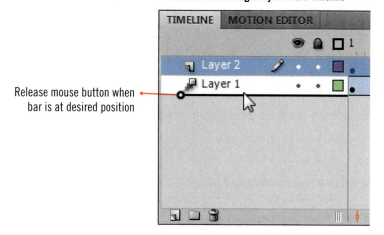

Release mouse button when bar is at desired position

FIGURE A-18: Viewing renamed layers

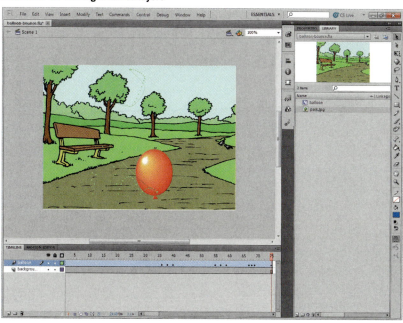

Exploring Help and Exiting Flash

Flash has an extensive Help system that supplies information quickly and easily. Help is organized so that you can find whatever you need, whether you want to look up a subject by topic or search for specific keywords. You can access Help from the program window by typing a search term in the Search text box on the Application bar, or you can open Help from the Window menu. You examine Flash Help so you'll know how to get help when you need it.

STEPS

QUICK TIP

You can also press [F1] to open Help or type a keyword or phrase in the Search text box on the Application bar.

1. **Click Help on the Application bar, click Flash Help, then follow updating instructions if prompted**
   The Flash Help window opens in your browser, as shown in Figure A-19. You can search for topics by typing a keyword in the Search Flash Content text box, or by expanding topics under Adobe Flash Professional CS5.

2. **Click Using Flash Professional CS5 in the right pane if necessary, click the Workspace plus sign ⊞ under Using Flash Professional CS5 (Win), then click The Timeline**
   Specific information about the Timeline appears in the right pane, as shown in Figure A-20. At the top of the right pane, you can click the Home button to view Adobe Community Help, and the Help system for each program in Creative Suite 5 and other associated programs.

3. **Click the Adobe reference only check box, click in the Search Flash content text box, type panels, then press [Enter] (Win) or [return] (Mac)**
   A list of topics that include the word "panels" appears in the search results, as shown in Figure A-21.

4. **Scroll down the list, click a link of interest, then read the topic**

5. **Close the Adobe Community Help window**
   The Help window closes, and you return to Flash. You are ready to exit the program.

QUICK TIP

You can also press [Ctrl][Q] (Win) or [⌘][Q] (Mac) to close the program.

6. **Click the Close button on the Application bar**
   Flash closes.

Using additional Help features

In addition to the main Help system, you may find other commands on the Help menu useful. You can download tutorials and extensions (user-created software that enhances Flash capabilities), access forums, and find additional support and training by clicking the Flash Exchange, Manage Extensions, Flash Support Center, and Adobe Online Forums links on the Help menu. Much of the support is free.

FIGURE A-19: Adobe Flash Professional CS5 Help

Type keyword or phrase here

Click to search in Adobe-created content only

Click to expand topic

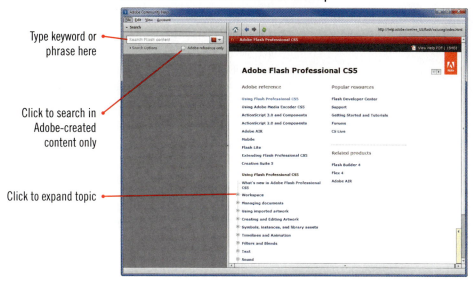

FIGURE A-20: Viewing a Help topic

Click to go to Adobe Community Help screen

Click to return to previous or next screens

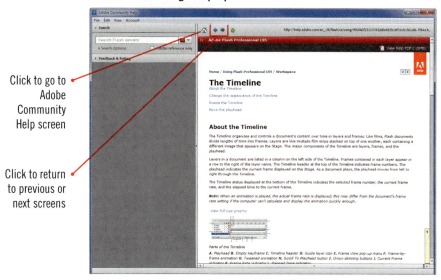

FIGURE A-21: Searching for help on a keyword

Keyword

Search results

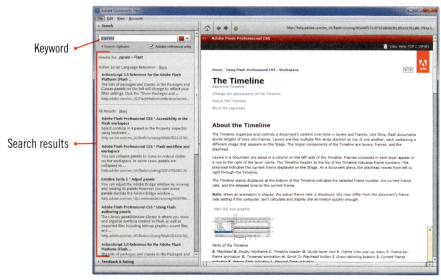

Practice

Concepts Review

For current SAM information, including versions and content details, visit SAM Central (http://www.cengage.com/samcentral). If you have a SAM user profile, you may have access to hands-on instruction, practice, and assessment of the skills covered in this unit. Since various versions of SAM are supported throughout the life of this text, check with your instructor for the correct instructions and URL/Web site for accessing assignments.

Label the elements of the Flash workspace shown in Figure A-22.

FIGURE A-22

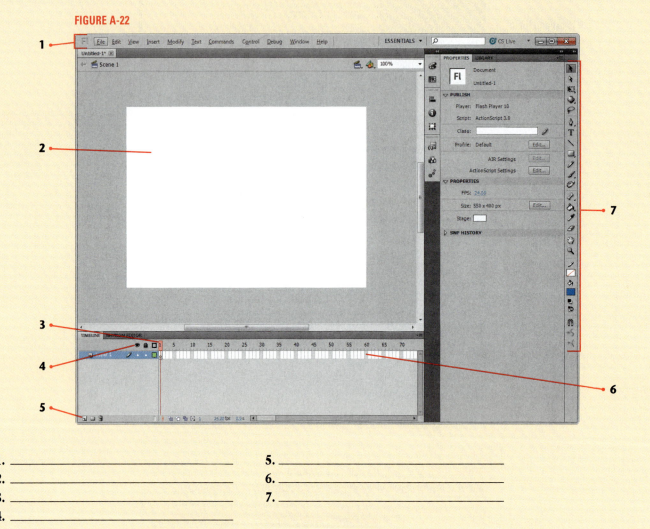

1. _____
2. _____
3. _____
4. _____
5. _____
6. _____
7. _____

Match each term with the statement that best describes it.

8. **.fla**	**a.**	Area containing movie's elements
9. **Stage**	**b.**	Rapidly moving sequence of images creating the illusion of movement
10. **Workspace**	**c.**	The output file of a Flash project for viewing on the Web
11. **Frame rate**	**d.**	Native Flash file type
12. **Animation**	**e.**	Measurement in time of a movie or Flash project
13. **Layer**	**f.**	A row containing content for a Flash project
14. **.swf**	**g.**	A configuration of the components in the Flash program window

Select the best answer from the list of choices.

15. Which component shows a snapshot of an event in a movie?

  a. Library panel

  b. Frame

  c. Layer

  d. Pasteboard

16. What happens when you reset a workspace?

  a. You can name a custom workspace.

  b. You can no longer move components around.

  c. The currently open file closes.

  d. Components return to their default size and location.

17. Which key can you press to open Help?

  a. [H]

  b. [F10]

  c. [F1]

  d. [F12]

18. Which command do you use to preview a movie in the Flash Player?

  a. Preview Movie

  b. Test Movie

  c. Play Movie

  d. Watch Movie

19. What best describes what happens on the Stage when you move a layer to the top of the Timeline?

  a. The layer may be completely visible.

  b. You should add animation to it.

  c. The first frame is selected.

  d. The layer may be partially visible.

20. Which of the following is *not* available in the Help system?

  a. Preferences

  b. Topic search

  c. Keyword search

  d. Community help

Skills Review

1. Understand Adobe Flash.

  a. Describe animation and how it can constitute a multimedia file.

  b. Explain the difference between the Flash program and the Flash Player.

2. Start Adobe Flash Professional CS5.

  a. Start Flash.

  b. Describe two things you can do in the Welcome Screen.

  c. Open a new document.

3. View the Flash workspace.

  a. Identify the Stage.

  b. Identify the Timeline.

  c. Identify expanded and collapsed panels.

  d. Identify the Tools panel.

4. Arrange the workspace.

  a. Collapse the Tools panel to iconic view.

  b. Collapse the Properties panel and Library panel to iconic view.

  c. Undock the Tools panel from the other panels.

  d. Reset the Essentials workspace.

  e. Display the Small Screen workspace.

  f. Display the Essentials workspace, then close the open document.

5. Open a document and play a movie.

  a. Open the document FL A-2.fla from the location where you store your Data Files.

  b. Save the document as **abduction.fla**.

  c. Change the view so the Stage fits in the window, if necessary.

  d. Play the movie on the Stage.

  e. Open the Controller, use a button to rewind the movie, then move the playhead to frame 3. (*Hint*: Use a command on the Window menu to open the Controller.)

  f. Test the movie.

  g. Close the Flash Player but do not close the Controller.

Skills Review (continued)

6. Understand the Timeline.

   a. Describe the two main sections of the Timeline.

7. Add a layer and element.

   a. Verify that the document abduction.fla is open, then add a new layer.

   b. Display the Library panel, then drag saturn.jpg to the right side of the Stage.

   c. Play the movie.

   d. Hide and then show Layer 1.

   e. Rename Layer 1 **saturn**.

   f. Move the saturn layer to the bottom of the Timeline, use buttons on the Controller to move the playhead to frame 30, then compare your screen to Figure A-23.

   g. Test the movie, then close the Flash Player.

   h. Save and close the document abduction.fla.

8. Use Help and exit Flash.

   a. Open the Help system.

   b. Expand the topic Using imported artwork, then select Placing artwork into Flash.

   c. Select the Adobe reference only check box (Win), if necessary click the Search Flash content text box, then search for information by typing the word **timeline** in the Search text box and pressing [Enter] (Win) or [return] (Mac).

   d. Display Help information on one of the topics concerning the Timeline.

   e. Close the Help window.

   f. Exit Flash.

FIGURE A-23

Independent Challenge 1

You're helping a toy store develop an online presence and persona for its line of robotic toys. The owners want to build interest in the toys with a subtle animation. You begin with one of the newest additions.

   a. Start Flash, open the file FL A-3.fla from the location where you store your Data Files, then save it as **robocat.fla**.

   b. Show Layer 2 and Layer 3 in the Timeline.

   c. Move the playhead to frame 1, if necessary, then play the movie on the Stage.

   d. Rename Layer 2 **left eye**.

   e. Rename Layer 3 **right eye**.

   f. Add a new layer, then name it **mouse**.

   g. Display the Library panel, if necessary, undock it, then drag the moving_mouse from the Library panel to the lower-right corner of the Stage.

   h. Move the mouse layer above the catbody layer in the Timeline.

   i. Test the movie, then close the Flash Player.

   j. Drag the playhead to frame 29, click the Pasteboard, then compare your screen to Figure A-24.

   k. Reset the workspace, save your work, close the document, then exit Flash.

FIGURE A-24

Independent Challenge 2

A friend is starting a blog about using music to heal from a broken heart. You take over this project from the person who created it. The previous author was experimenting with a couple of different effects, so you decide to keep the one that best fits the theme.

a. Start Flash, open the file FL A-4.fla from the location where you store your Data Files, then save it as **heart2heart.fla**. (*Hint*: Click OK if you receive a prompt about a missing font.)

b. Show all layers.

c. Play the movie on the Stage.

d. Move Layer 2 above Layer 1.

e. Hide Layer 3, then play the movie on the Stage, noting that the hidden layer is not visible.

f. Test the movie. Compare playing the animation in the Flash Player to playing the movie on the Stage. (*Hint*: Layers hidden in the Timeline still play when the movie is tested in the Flash Player.)

g. Delete Layer 3. (*Hint*: Click the Delete button on the bottom of the Timeline.)

h. Rename Layer 1 **beating heart**, then rename Layer 2 **text**.

i. Drag the playhead to frame 37, click the Pasteboard, then compare your screen to Figure A-25.

j. Save the file, test the movie, then close the Flash Player.

FIGURE A-25

Advanced Challenge Exercise

- Create a new layer named static heart, then move it beneath the text layer.
- Show the Library, then drag Symbol 1 to the Stage and arrange the heart on the Stage as desired.
- Lock the beating heart layer. (*Hint*: Click the circle under the Lock or Unlock All Layers button column in the layer.)
- Test the movie, close the Flash Player, then save the document.

k. Close the document heart2heart.fla.

l. Exit Flash.

Independent Challenge 3

Adobe's online support can help answer a question, provide troubleshooting tips, and direct you to more advanced techniques. You decide to go online and examine some of its features.

a. Start Flash.

b. Select Flash Support Center from the Help menu.

c. View or read an item that interests you. (*Hint*: Some features might be advanced.)

d. Print a page, then add your name to the printout.

Advanced Challenge Exercise

- Select Adobe Online Forums on the Help menu.
- Select at least one topic.
- Scroll through a couple pages of the forum, then print a topic that interests you. (*Hint*: You can also type a keyword in the Search Forums text box if you wish.)

e. Close the Help window and exit Flash.

Real Life Independent Challenge

You're interested in learning more about controlling movies and modifying panels in Flash. You begin by exploring different workspaces and features.

a. Start Flash, then open any of the saved documents you worked on in this unit.

b. Switch to the Designer workspace, then examine the open panels.

c. Use Help to look up the function of panels you are unfamiliar with.

d. Undock the Tools panel, then redock it on the right side of the program window. (*Hint*: Drag the panel to the right until a blue vertical line is visible, then release the mouse button.)

e. Reset the Designer workspace, then display the Essentials workspace.

f. In the Timeline, change the frame size to Tiny. (*Hint*: Use the Panel options button.)

g. Open the Controller, then play, stop, rewind, and move the movie frame by frame for a couple of frames.

h. Use commands on the Control menu to replicate the instructions in Step g.

i. Test the movie. Then in the Flash Player window, click Control on the Application bar (Win) or application menu bar (Mac) to replicate the instructions in Step g, then close the Flash Player.

j. Reset the frame size to Normal in the Timeline, reset the Essentials workspace, then close the document.

k. Exit Flash.

Visual Workshop

When you work in Flash, you can customize your workspace so that you can view and access the information you need. Start Flash, then arrange the elements in the workspace so that it matches the one shown in Figure A-26. When you are finished, press [Print Screen] (Win) or [⌘][Shift][4] to select the window using the mouse (Mac), paste the image into a word-processing program, add your name at the top of the document, then print or post the document. Please check with your instructor for assignment submission instructions. Close the word processor without saving changes, then exit Flash.

FIGURE A-26

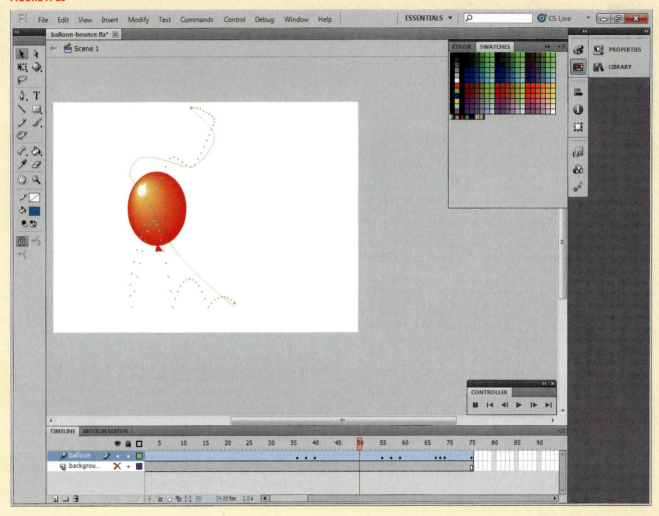

Getting Started with Adobe Flash Professional

Creating Graphics and Text

Files You Will Need:

FL B-1.fla

Creating objects in Flash is often the first step to creating dazzling animation or Web elements. You use drawing tools such as the Rectangle tool, Oval tool, and PolyStar tool to create shapes, and the Pencil tool and Line tool to create lines. You use these tools to create vector graphics. Along with bitmap graphics, which designers usually use to display photographs, vector graphics are prominent on the Web. Designers use vector graphics to display illustrations. You use the Text tool to create text. Because text and shapes are vector objects, you can modify their attributes without affecting the quality of the image. You begin work on the GreenWinds Eco-Cruise logo using vector shapes and text.

OBJECTIVES

Understand vector and bitmap graphics

Create a new document

Set tool options and create a shape

Reshape an object

Select and modify a shape

Copy and transform an object

Use design panels

Create text

Modify text

Understanding Vector and Bitmap Graphics

Graphics are the core of your animations. Generally, two types of graphics are used on the Web: vector and bitmap. Although you can import bitmap images into a Flash document, bitmap images are usually best used as a static design element or for limited animation. Most often in Flash, you work with vector graphics and create them using drawing tools on the Tools panel. Once you select a shape tool, you can choose between two types of drawing modes: merge drawing and object drawing. Before drawing in Flash, you want to learn more about graphics and Flash drawing modes.

DETAILS

Review the following graphic types:

- ### Vector graphics

  A **vector graphic** is a mathematically calculated object composed of **anchor points** and straight or curved line segments, which collectively form a **path**. You can fill a path with a color, gradient, or pattern and outline it with a line known as a **stroke**. Vector graphics appear smooth, which makes them perfect for illustrations.

  Because they retain their appearance regardless of how you edit them, vector graphics offer far more flexibility than bitmap images. They keep their sharp, crisp-looking edges no matter how much you enlarge them. Figure B-1 compares the image quality of enlarged vector and bitmap images.

- ### Bitmap graphics

  A **bitmap graphic** displays a picture image as a matrix of dots, or pixels, on a grid. A **pixel** is the smallest square of color used to display an image on a computer screen. This is why most of the photographs and other images on a Web page are bitmap images (also known as **raster images**). Pixels allow your computer screen to depict colors realistically in a photographic image. A bitmap image consists of a finite number of pixels. Therefore, when you resize the image, the existing pixels are stretched over a larger area, which causes distortion and loss of image quality. The shell image on the right side of Figure B-1 shows the jagged edges and blurry appearance typical of an enlarged bitmap graphic.

- ### Resolution

  Resolution describes the degree of clarity, detail, and sharpness of a displayed or printed image. Resolution is expressed by the number of pixels in a square inch of an image. The higher the resolution, the better the picture. On-screen resolution is usually 72 or 96 pixels per inch (ppi); print graphics require higher resolution, typically starting around 220 ppi.

- ### Flash drawing modes

  Flash has two drawing modes: Merge Drawing mode and Object Drawing mode. Determining which drawing mode to use depends on your design goals and how you want objects to interact as you draw or arrange them. **Merge Drawing mode** assumes that the objects' paths (their strokes and fills) will combine in some fashion, such as using the outline of one object to create a shape in another. You can select, move, or delete an object's fill or stroke, or overlap multiple objects and then move the top one to punch or cut its shape through the bottom shape. **Object Drawing mode** treats the object as a whole. You can modify an object's attributes, such as fill or stroke color, and you can overlap multiple objects without affecting either object. The top object may obscure the bottom object, just as a top layer obscures a lower layer in the Timeline. Figure B-2 compares some of the features of Merge Drawing and Object Drawing.

FIGURE B-1: Comparing vector and bitmap images

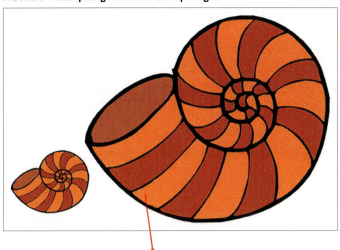

Vector images remain
crisp when enlarged

Bitmap images become blurry
and jagged when enlarged

FIGURE B-2: Comparing objects in Merge Drawing and Object Drawing modes

Object selected
in Merge
Drawing mode

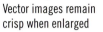

Moving the shape
fill leaves stroke
"punched" through
bottom star

Overlapped
shapes

Object selected
in Object
Drawing mode

Moving the
shape moves
entire shape

Creating a New Document

You can create a new document in Flash and then modify document settings, such as size or color. Flash provides several methods to precisely measure and position objects on the Stage: You can display rulers, create guides, or display a grid. ▰▰▰ Your boss, Vanessa Mayes, wants you to begin developing the GreenWinds Eco-Cruise logo by creating the document, modifying the Stage size, and displaying the grid.

1. **Start Flash, click File on the Application bar, click New, then click OK in the New Document dialog box**

   A new untitled document opens.

2. **Click File on the Application bar, click Save As to open the Save As dialog box, navigate to the location where you store your Data Files, type GreenWinds logo in the File name text box (Win) or Save As text box (Mac), then click Save**

   You begin by setting the size of the document.

3. **Click Modify on the Application bar, then click Document**

   The Document Settings dialog box opens, as shown in Figure B-3. Here you can modify the document's Stage size, color, frame rate, and unit of measurement for rulers. **Rulers** appear along the top and left sides of the Stage using pixels as their unit of measurement. To show rulers, click View on the Application bar, then click Rulers. To align objects at an exact measurement, you can drag a **guide** from the ruler onto the Stage, where it appears as a solid line to help align objects. To adjust Guide properties, click View on the Application bar, point to Guides, then click Edit Guides. In the Guides dialog box, you can adjust guide color and visibility, clear or lock guides, and how accurately objects snap to guides: close, normal, or distant.

4. **Type 200 px in the (width) text box, press [Tab], type 200 px in the (height) text box, then click OK to resize the Stage**

   QUICK TIP

   You can also press [Ctrl][2] (Win) or [⌘][2] (Mac) to fit the Stage in the window.

5. **Click the View list arrow at the top of the Document window, then click Fit in Window (Win)**

   The Stage fills the Document window. You turn on the grid to help align objects on the Stage.

6. **Click View on the Application bar, point to Grid, then click Show Grid**

   A **grid** of squares appears on the Stage, as shown in Figure B-4. The grid and guides are alignment and measurement tools only and do not appear in a published movie. You want to ensure that objects will align to the grid for a consistent look. You also want objects to automatically align to the grid.

   QUICK TIP

   Objects will snap to the grid or guides even if they are not displayed; objects will snap to guide first if it falls between grid lines.

7. **Click View on the Application bar, point to Grid, click Edit Grid, click the Snap to grid check box to select it as shown in Figure B-5, then click OK to close the Grid dialog box**

   Turning on Snap to Grid automatically aligns objects when you create or move them. The object snaps to the closest intersection on the grid.

8. **Click View on the Application bar, point to Snapping, click Snap Align if necessary to select it, then save the document**

   With Snap Align selected, dotted lines will appear on the Stage when you align objects.

Understanding view tools

In addition to adjusting magnification on the Stage using the View list arrow in the Document window, you can use the Zoom tool 🔍. You can zoom in or zoom out by selecting one of the zoom buttons that appears at the bottom of the Tools panel and then clicking the Stage. To focus in on a particular area, you can select the Zoom tool and drag a zoom bounding box around an area on the Stage and the magnification will increase based on the size of the selection box. To resize to 100% quickly, double-click the Zoom tool on the Tools panel. You can use the Hand tool 🖐 to move a particular part of a large or magnified object into view if the object is too large to fit completely in the current magnification. To switch to the Hand tool temporarily when another tool is selected, press [Spacebar]. Neither tool affects the actual size of objects in your document; they simply allow you to manipulate your view of the Stage.

FIGURE B-3: Document Settings dialog box

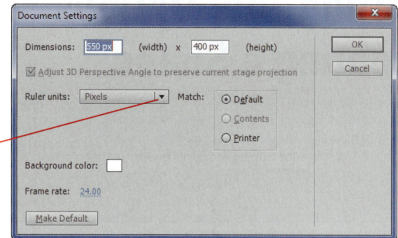

Click to adjust unit of
measurement of ruler

FIGURE B-4: Viewing the grid turned on in a document

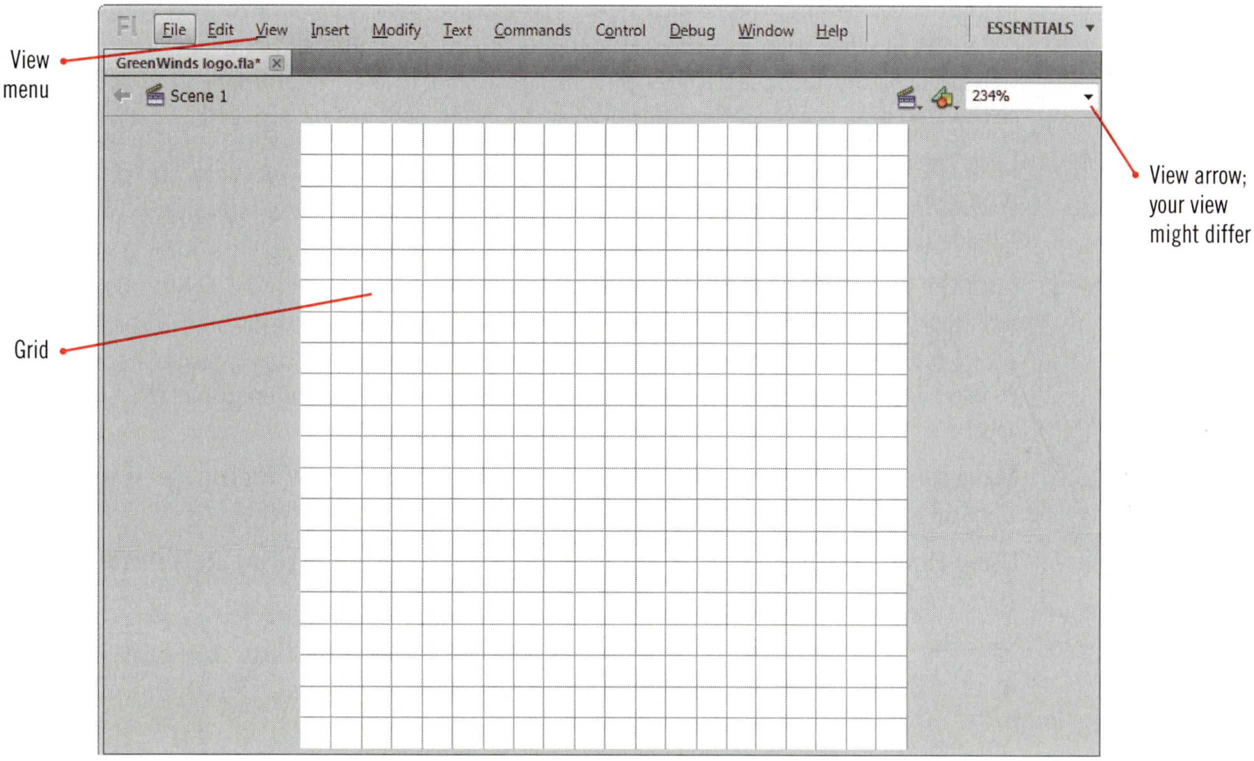

View
menu

View arrow;
your view
might differ

Grid

FIGURE B-5: Grid dialog box

Click to align
objects to the grid

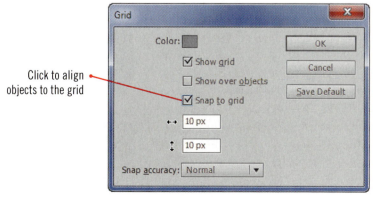

Setting Tool Options and Creating a Shape

You use Flash tools to create the artwork for your movies. The Tools panel is separated into sections, each containing related tools, such as drawing, view, and selection. The drawing section contains tools for drawing or painting lines, shapes, and patterns. Many tools have tool options at the bottom of the Tools panel. Table B-1 describes the drawing and painting tools. You select colors for strokes and fills using the color pop-up window. You start work on the logo by setting the stroke and fill color and then creating a shape.

STEPS

QUICK TIP
You can adjust the transparency of a color by decreasing the percentage of the Alpha setting, or not set any color by clicking the No Color icon ⊘.

1. **Click the Stroke Color control tool on the Tools panel to open the color pop-up window, then click the blue color swatch (#3300FF) shown in Figure B-7**
   The stroke color is set to blue. The color pop-up window contains solid and gradient color swatches. You can select a color by clicking a color swatch, typing a hexadecimal color value, or clicking the System Color Picker button and then selecting a color. **Hexadecimal** is an alphanumeric system for defining color on the Web that designates each color by a set of six numbers and/or letters. You can set the stroke and fill colors to black and white in one click by selecting the Black and white button. Next, you set the fill color.

2. **Click the Fill Color control tool on the Tools panel, click the hexadecimal text box, type #FFCC00, then press [Enter] (Win) or [return] (Mac)**
   A yellow fill color is set.

TROUBLE
If the Rectangle tool is not visible on the Tools panel, click and hold the visible tool, then click the Rectangle tool.

3. **Click the Rectangle tool on the Tools panel**
   Some tools, such as the Rectangle tool, have multiple tools associated with them on the Tools panel. A small arrow ◢ in the lower-right corner of the tool icon indicates that other tools are available in that tool group. To select additional tools, click and hold the tool, then click the tool you want from the tool menu that appears.

4. **Make sure the Object Drawing button at the bottom of the Tools panel is not selected**
   You want to draw the shape in Merge Drawing mode.

QUICK TIP
To create a perfect square or circle, select the Rectangle tool or Oval tool, and then press and hold [Shift] as you draw the shape on the Stage.

5. **Using Figure B-8 as a guide, drag the pointer + on the Stage to create a rectangle**
   The rectangle appears in the blue stroke and yellow fill colors you set.

6. **Save the document**

Aligning objects on the Stage

Flash provides several options for aligning objects, shown in Figure B-6. Snap Align displays a dotted line when you drag an object within a defined distance of another object or the Stage edge. Snap to Grid aligns an object's center or edge to a grid intersection. Snap to Guides aligns an object's center or edge to a guide dragged from the ruler. Snap to Objects snaps an object along another object's edge. Snap to Pixels moves objects one pixel at a time. To turn a snapping option on or off, click View on the Application bar, then click an option. To adjust snapping options, click View on the Application bar, point to Snapping, click Edit Snapping, then adjust options in the Edit Snapping dialog box.

FIGURE B-6: Viewing rulers, guides, and alignment lines

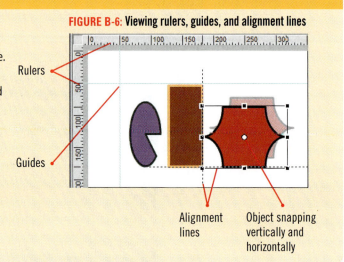

Rulers

Guides

Alignment lines

Object snapping vertically and horizontally

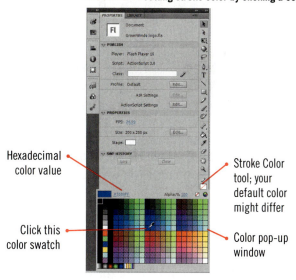

Hexadecimal
color value

Stroke Color
tool; your
default color
might differ

Click this
color swatch

Color pop-up
window

FIGURE B-8: Creating a shape

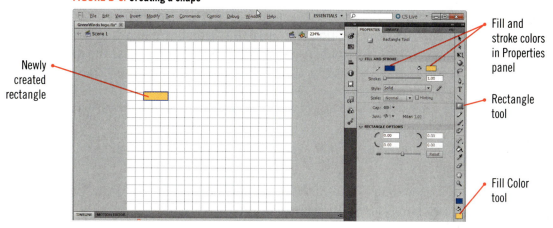

Fill and
stroke colors
in Properties
panel

Newly
created
rectangle

Rectangle
tool

Fill Color
tool

TABLE B-1: Drawing and painting tools

tool	tool name	description
	Pen tool	Creates paths and anchor points
	Text tool	Creates text
	Line tool	Creates straight lines
	Pencil tool	Creates freehand lines
	Brush tool	Paints fill shapes
	Spray Brush tool	Sprays in a specific fill pattern or shape
	Deco tool	Creates geometric patterns
Shape tools		
	Rectangle tool	Creates squares and rectangles
	Oval tool	Creates circles and ellipses
	Rectangle Primitive tool	Creates squares and rectangles with extra modifiable properties
	Oval Primitive tool	Creates circles and ellipses with extra modifiable properties
	PolyStar tool	Creates multisided shapes or multipointed shapes, such as stars

Flash CS5

Reshaping an Object

Flash offers unique ways to change an object's shape. The Selection tool allows you to manipulate the object's shape directly by dragging its border into a different contour. When you need to adjust your view of an object, you can use the Zoom tool to zoom in or out of the image. 🎨 You work on the design elements of the logo by changing the rectangle to a triangle and then creating a curve.

STEPS

1. **Click the Zoom tool 🔍 on the Tools panel, move the Zoom In pointer ⊕ near the rectangle, then click the Stage until the object and grid are clearly visible on your screen, if necessary**

   The plus sign in ⊕ indicates that you are zooming in, or enlarging, your view of the object. To zoom out of an object, press and hold [Alt] (Win) or [option] (Mac), then click the Stage.

QUICK TIP

You can deselect objects on the Stage by pressing [Ctrl][Shift][A] (Win) or [⌘][Shift][A] (Mac).

2. **Click the Selection tool ▶ on the Tools panel, then position the mouse pointer over the lower-right corner of the rectangle until the corner pointer ↳ is visible**

   Depending on where you place the Selection tool pointer, a different pointer appears. The corner pointer allows you to adjust corners.

3. **Drag ↳ to the upper-right corner of the rectangle, then when the dragged corner snaps and becomes a straight line, as shown in Figure B-9, release the mouse button**

   The rectangle is now a triangle. A snap ring is visible as you reshape the object. A **snap ring** is an alignment aide; the ring becomes larger as it nears a snapping point, in this case, a grid intersection. You want to move the lower-right point on top of the upper-right point to have one smooth line. Next, you add a curve to an edge of the triangle.

TROUBLE

If the curve pointer is not visible as you point to the edge of the triangle, redo Step 3 to create a perfectly straight line.

4. **Move the mouse pointer over the bottom edge of the triangle until the curve pointer ↳ appears**

5. **Click and drag ↳ toward the upper-left corner of the rectangle, then when the curve resembles Figure B-10, release the mouse button**

   The bottom edge of the triangle is now curved.

6. **Save the document**

Understanding guide layers

A **guide layer** is a layer that contains a shape you can use to trace or align objects, or to create a motion path for an animated object. First you create the shape or path on the guide layer, then you use it as a template for objects in the layers above it. For example, say you want to show the unusual path a spaceship takes before entering faster-than-light speed. You could draw and modify an oval shape on a guide layer and then use it to create the motion path of a spaceship graphic "flying" in another layer. You can also import or copy a graphic to a layer and then convert it to a guide layer. To create a guide layer, right-click (Win) or [control]-click (Mac) a layer in the Timeline, then click Guide. A guide layer icon 🔨 appears on the layer. Because a guide layer appears in the Timeline but is not visible in a published movie, it is an efficient design tool.

FIGURE B-9: Modifying a shape

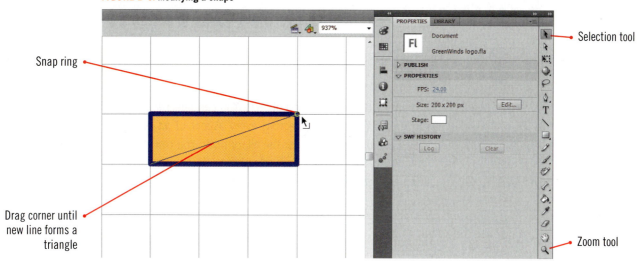

Snap ring

Selection tool

Drag corner until
new line forms a
triangle

Zoom tool

FIGURE B-10: Creating a curve

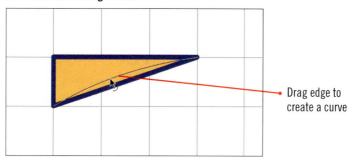

Drag edge to
create a curve

Understanding primitive tools

You can create the same shapes using Rectangle Primitive and Rectangle tools or the Oval Primitive and Oval tools. The difference lies in their shape type and editability after you create them. The shapes you draw with the primitive tools are separate objects, similar to objects you draw in Object Drawing mode using regular shape tools. With the regular shape tools, you set the shape options before you create the shape. After you create the shape, you cannot alter

shape options, such as corner radius value for a rectangle, and start and end angles and inner radius values for an oval. In contrast, you can edit any of these settings with a primitive shape, and reset the shape to default settings. See Figure B-11. With the Rectangle Primitive tool, you can even change a corner radius as you are creating it by dragging the mouse on the Stage. To so do, press the Up or Down arrow keys on the keyboard.

FIGURE B-11: Comparing primitive and regular shape tools options

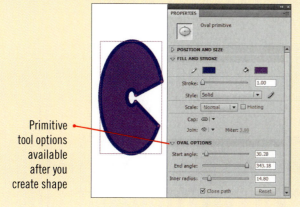

Primitive
tool options
available
after you
create shape

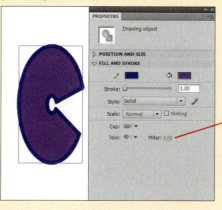

Regular
shape tool
options
unavailable
after you
create shape

Selecting and Modifying a Shape

As you create your animations, you select drawing objects. You can select an entire object or just a part of it. The Selection tool is your go-to tool for selecting every aspect of an object. With Merge Drawing objects, you can select part or all of the stroke, just the fill, or both. You can change the fill or stroke using the Properties panel. Table B-2 describes the other selection tools, the Subselection tool, and the Lasso tool. You select and change the stroke and fill of the logo object.

STEPS

QUICK TIP
To quickly select an entire object or multiple objects, click the Selection tool, then drag a selection bounding box around the objects you want to select.

1. **Click the Selection tool on the Tools panel if necessary, then click the yellow fill in the triangle to select it**
   The selection has a dot pattern over it, indicating it is selected, and properties for the shape appear on the Properties panel, as shown in Figure B-12. The word "Shape" appears at the top of the Properties panel, indicating that you are editing a shape.

2. **Click the top edge of the triangle**
   Only the top stroke of the triangle is selected. The Stroke color icon and other stroke attributes settings are active on the Properties panel, as shown in Figure B-13.

3. **Double-click the top edge of the triangle**
   The entire stroke that surrounds the shape is selected. You are ready to change the color of the stroke.

QUICK TIP
You can double-click any part of the stroke to select it in its entirety.

4. **Click the Stroke color icon on the Properties panel, click the hexadecimal text box, type #0000BA, press [Enter] (Win) or [return] (Mac), then click the Pasteboard or a blank part of the Stage to deselect it**
   The stroke color changes to a darker blue. Next, you decide to change the fill color.

QUICK TIP
For objects created in Object Drawing mode, you can double-click the object and then individually select a fill or stroke.

5. **Click the yellow fill in the triangle, click the Fill color icon on the Properties panel, click the hexadecimal text box, type #03CC03, then press [Enter] (Win) or [return] (Mac)**
   The fill color changes to a bright green.

6. **Deselect the object, then compare your screen to Figure B-14**
   The new stroke and fill colors also appear on the Tools panel.

7. **Save the document**

TABLE B-2: Selection tools

tool	name	tool option	name	description
	Selection tool			Selects by clicking or dragging
			Snap to Objects	Aligns objects
			Smooth	Smoothes a straight line
			Straighten	Straightens a curved line
	Subselection tool			Manipulates anchor points
	Lasso tool			Selects objects freehand
			Magic Wand	Selects pixels based on color
			Magic Wand Settings	Sets how Magic Wand selects pixels
			Polygon Mode	Selects objects in straight lines

FIGURE B-12: Selecting a fill

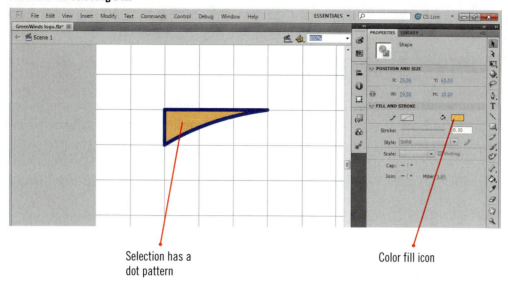

Selection has a
dot pattern

Color fill icon

FIGURE B-13: Selecting part of a stroke

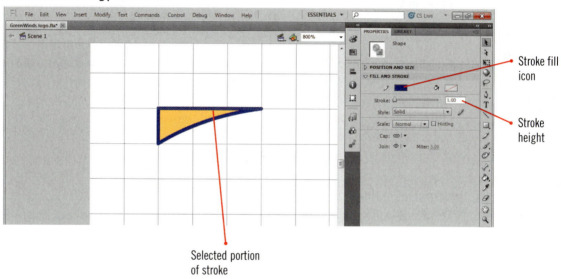

Stroke fill
icon

Stroke
height

Selected portion
of stroke

FIGURE B-14: Viewing edited colors in an object

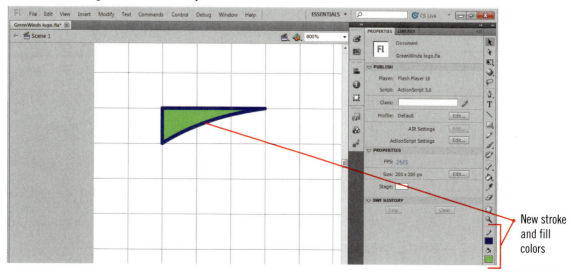

New stroke
and fill
colors

Copying and Transforming an Object

As you work in Flash, you save time if you copy objects and **transform**, or reconfigure, the copies instead of re-creating each object from scratch. You can transform an object by scaling, rotating, skewing, and distorting it. Flash offers a few different ways to copy an object from outside or within the program. You can reconfigure objects using options for the Free Transform tool. Options for the Free Transform tool are described in Table B-3. Now that you have set the colors for the design element, you are ready to finalize it by copying and transforming the triangle.

STEPS

1. Adjust the magnification so that less of the Stage is visible; approximately by half

2. Click the Selection tool ▶ on the Tools panel if necessary, then drag a bounding box around the triangle to select both the stroke and the fill

TROUBLE
Depending on your monitor and zoom level, your pasted object may not appear in the same location as the one shown in the figure.

▶ 3. Click Edit on the Application bar, click Copy, click Edit on the Application bar, then click Paste in Center

A duplicate of the triangle is pasted in the center of the visible Stage, as shown in Figure B-15. You want to rotate the copied object to create a design.

4. Click the Free Transform tool ▦ on the Tools panel, then move the mouse pointer near the lower-right sizing handle of the copied triangle until the rotate pointer ↻ appears

When you select the Free Transform tool, sizing handles appear around the object, as shown in Figure B-16. By default, you can scale, rotate, and skew an object. The position of the mouse pointer on or near the object determines which option pointer is active. To limit the tool to a single function, click an option at the bottom of the Tools panel.

QUICK TIP
To flip objects horizontally or vertically or to rotate objects 90°, click Modify on the Application bar, point to Transform, then click a flip or rotate command.

▶ 5. Press and hold [Shift], drag the mouse pointer counterclockwise until the shape rotates 90°, then release the mouse button

The triangle rotates and snaps into place. Pressing and holding [Shift] constrains the rotation to 45° increments; you can rotate an object from any corner. You decide to reposition the rotated object to form the completed design element.

TROUBLE
You may need to drag slowly or increase magnification to see the line.

▶ 6. Drag the rotated triangle to the position shown in Figure B-17

When the rotated triangle is left-aligned with the original, a dotted alignment line appears along the objects' left edges.

7. Save the document

TABLE B-3: Options for the Free Transform tool

tool option	name	description
🧲	Snap to Objects	Aligns objects
↻	Rotate and Skew	Slants an object horizontally or vertically
◰	Scale	Resizes an object by side or proportionately
◹	Distort	Repositions corners to create perspective
▨	Envelope	Adds anchor points to allow for extreme distortion in lines and curves

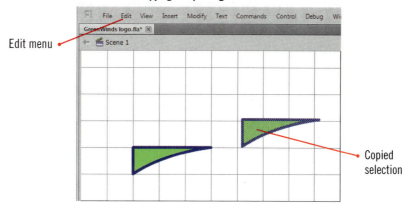

FIGURE B-15: Copying and pasting a selection

Edit menu

Copied selection

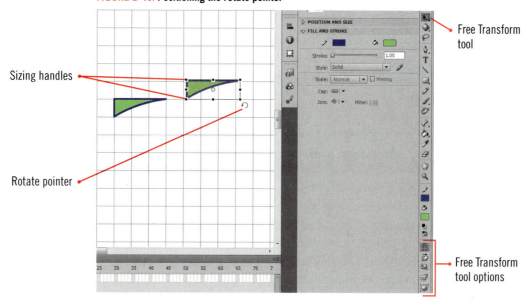

FIGURE B-16: Positioning the rotate pointer

Sizing handles

Rotate pointer

Free Transform tool

Free Transform tool options

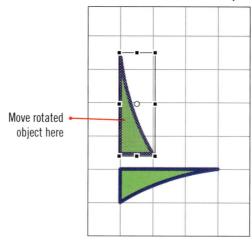

FIGURE B-17: Transformed and repositioned object

Move rotated object here

Understanding paste and drag options

After you copy an object, you can use commands on the Edit menu to paste it in various locations. Paste in Center—[Ctrl][V] (Win) or [⌘][V] (Mac)—pastes the object in the middle of the visible Stage. Paste in Place—[Ctrl][Shift][V] (Win) or [⌘][Shift][V] (Mac)—pastes the object directly on top of the original. You use Paste Special when you've copied a selection from another program, and Duplicate to paste a copy at a 10-pixel offset from the original. To use the keyboard to drag and copy a duplicate from the original, select the object(s), press and hold [Alt] (Win) or [option] (Mac), then drag the copy anywhere on the Stage.

Using Design Panels

Now that you're familiar with the basic Flash interface, this is a good time to learn about several other panels that perform specific design functions as you create your animations: the Info, Align, Transform, Color, and Swatches panels. You open a panel by clicking its icon or by clicking its name on the Window menu. If you find you use a panel frequently, you can dock it in an existing panel group, or create a new panel group. To do so, click the Panel options button, then select a command. You have already noticed the abundance of features in Flash. You explore the design panels to see how they can improve your efficiency when working with movie elements.

DETAILS

- The **Info panel** shows information based on where the pointer is on the Stage, such as the color beneath the pointer, and the size, location, and color of a selected object, as shown in Figure B-18. You view coordinates for an object in the X (horizontal) and Y (vertical) axes. The Info panel displays the same information as the Position and Size section of the Properties panel.

- You use the **Align panel** to size, align, or distribute multiple objects to the Stage or to each other. You can quickly resize an object to match the Stage's width, height, or both. To align objects to the Stage, click the Align/Distribute to Stage check box. Otherwise, objects will be aligned relative to each other. Figure B-18 compares several objects aligned and distributed to each other and to the Stage. Options on the Align panel are also available as commands on the Modify, Align menu.

- You can use the **Transform panel** to perform the functions of the Free Transform tool, and more. The sample in Figure B-19 shows how you can set values to skew an object. In addition to using transform options, you can use the Duplicate Selection and Transform button to copy and transform a new object in one step. For example, if your design required duplicate but slightly modified objects, you could rotate an object 25° and then click the Duplicate Selection and Transform button. The pasted object would be rotated an additional 25° from the original. If you want to undo the size transformations you've made to an object, click the Reset button at the top of the panel. To undo all transformations, click the Remove Transform button. Many options on the Transform panel are also available as commands on the Modify, Transform menu.

- The **Color panel** contains features for adjusting an object's stroke and fill colors, many of which are also available on the Properties panel. You can select solid or gradient color, hue, brightness, and **alpha** (transparency) of an object. The **Swatches panel** contains colors from the active color palette, or set, of available colors. You can add colors to the Swatches panel, and save a palette to share with other Flash users or in a format usable by other Adobe programs, such as Photoshop. Figure B-20 shows the Color and Swatches panels.

Using Web-safe colors

The pop-up color window that appears when you change text, stroke, or fill color displays the colors included with your document. The default Flash color palette is the **Web-safe color palette**, a set of 216 colors that appear consistent in Web browsers and across computer platforms. Many consider the limited Web-safe color palette a moot issue for most computers, given the improvement in standard video cards. However, Web-safe colors are still relevant when developing content to be viewed on a portable device, such as a mobile phone.

FIGURE B-18: Viewing the Info and Align panels

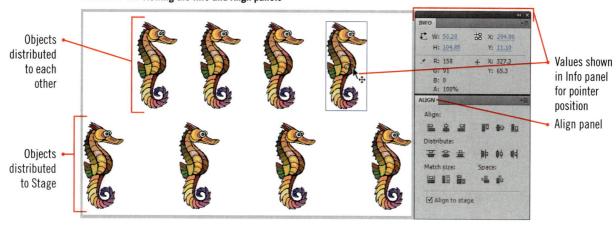

Objects distributed to each other

Objects distributed to Stage

Values shown in Info panel for pointer position

Align panel

FIGURE B-19: Skewing an object using the Transform panel

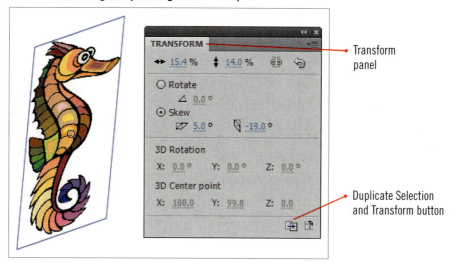

Transform panel

Duplicate Selection and Transform button

FIGURE B-20: Viewing the Color panel and Swatches panel

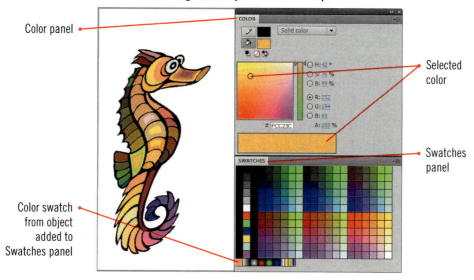

Color panel

Selected color

Swatches panel

Color swatch from object added to Swatches panel

Resizing objects

To adjust a shape's size proportionately, make sure the Lock Constrain icon 🔗 on the Properties panel is active. To adjust a width or height size individually, click 🔗 to make the Unlock Constrain icon 🔗 active. The ScreenTip for both the Lock Constrain and Unlock Constrain icons is Lock width and height values together.

Creating Text

Using the Text tool, you can create text to use in movies by creating a **text block**, which is an object containing text that you can move and modify. You can modify a host of text attributes, including font, size, style, color, alignment, orientation, and spacing. You can create **variable-width text**, in which the text block continues to expand as long as you type, or **fixed-width text**, whose width is limited by the size of the text block. You experiment with both text modes to see the advantages of each in your logo.

STEPS

1. **Click the Text tool** T **on the Tools panel, then verify that TLF Text is selected as the Text engine on the Properties panel**

   The default text engine, **Text Layout Framework (TLF)** text, provides flexible formatting features that can accommodate complex typographic requirements. You can create columns, wrap text around any object, and link text blocks. The text types are **Read Only** (cannot select or edit text), **Selectable** (can select but not edit text), or **Editable** (can both select and edit text). For this project, you want Read Only text.

2. **Click the Text type list arrow in the Text Tool section of the Properties panel, then click Read Only**

   Users will not be able to select or edit the text.

TROUBLE
If a section in the Properties panel is not expanded, click the expand section arrow ▷ on the section's title bar.

3. **Click the Set the font family list arrow in the Character section of the Properties panel, click Times New Roman, click the Set the font style list arrow, then if necessary, click Regular, click the Select point size text box, then type 12**

   You decide to set a new text color.

4. **Click the Text (fill) color box in the Character section of the Properties panel, click the hexadecimal text box, type #006600, then press [Enter] (Win) or [return] (Mac)**

   A new dark green text color is set. You create a fixed-width text block to limit how much text fits on one line.

5. **Using Figure B-21 as a guide, drag a text block beneath the shapes on the Stage three grid squares tall and six grid squares wide, then type GreenWinds ecocruise** (*Note: The name of the company is deliberately misspelled*)

   The fixed-width text block is not quite wide enough to accommodate the word "GreenWinds." See Figure B-22, but do not worry about the precise size of your text block. You can adjust the size so the word fits on one line. (You'll correct the lowercase "e" and "c" on "ecocruise" and add a hyphen in the next lesson.)

TROUBLE
If you inadvertently deselect the text, click it with the Text tool.

6. **Position the mouse pointer over the small black square sizing handle ↔ on the right side of the text block, then drag ↔ to the right until the word "ecocruise" fits on the top line**

   All the letters in the word "GreenWinds" are together, but you would have to continue to adjust the text block to get it to fit precisely. Instead, you delete this text and create variable-width text.

7. **Click the Selection tool ▶ on the Tools panel, then press [Delete]**

QUICK TIP
To manually insert a line break in variable-width text, press [Enter] (Win) or [return] (Mac).

8. **Click** T **on the Tools panel, click the Stage beneath the shapes, then type GreenWinds ecocruise**

   The words fit precisely in the text block on one line, as shown in Figure B-23.

9. **Save the document**

FIGURE B-21: Creating a fixed-width text box

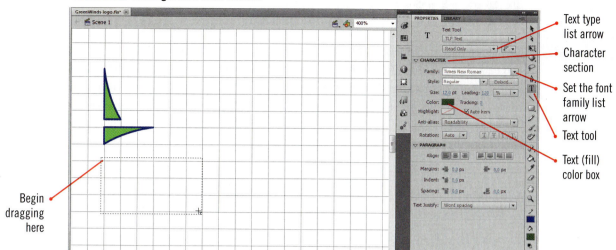

Begin
dragging
here

Text type
list arrow

Character
section

Set the font
family list
arrow

Text tool

Text (fill)
color box

FIGURE B-22: Viewing fixed-width text

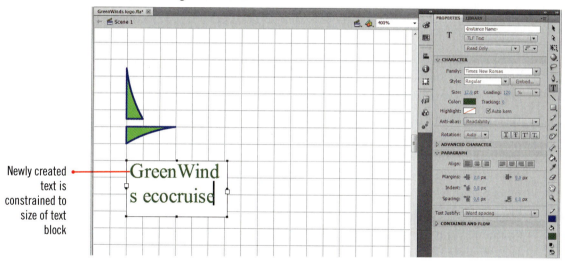

Newly created
text is
constrained to
size of text
block

FIGURE B-23: Creating variable-width text

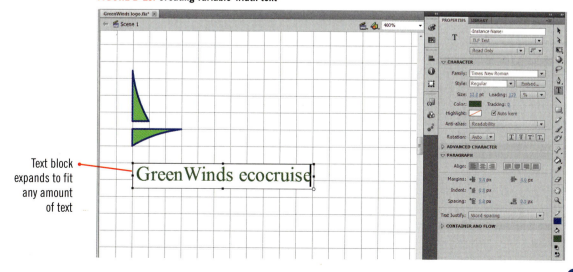

Text block
expands to fit
any amount
of text

Creating Graphics and Text

Modifying Text

You can modify any aspect of text using features on the Properties panel. Many features on the Character and Paragraph sections are similar to options offered in word-processing programs, such as font attributes, indent, and alignment options. You can take a sample of an existing color in a document and then apply it to another element. The Filters section offers text effects such as drop shadow, bevel, and glow. To add a filter, click the Add filter button, then click a filter in the list. You conclude your work on the GreenWinds Eco-Cruise logo by adjusting the text's attributes, spelling, and final position.

STEPS

1. Click in the text box if necessary, then press [Ctrl][A] (Win) or [⌘][A] (Mac) to select the text

TROUBLE

You may need to scroll down the list to the "G" section to locate the font, or if this font is not available, select another font. Some fonts might not have a bold option.

2. Click the Set the font family list arrow on the Properties panel, click Adobe Garamond Pro, click the Set the font style list arrow, then click Bold

   The font changes to Adobe Garamond Pro, bold style.

3. Click the Select point size text box, type 13, then press [Enter] (Win) or [return] (Mac)

   The font size increases, as shown in Figure B-24. When you create text, the current set of fonts installed on your computer is available to you in Flash. A **font** or **font family** is the entire array of letters, numbers, and symbols created in the same shape, known as a **typeface**. You notice that the company name, "ecocruise," needs some editing.

4. Drag the pointer over the word "ecocruise" to select it, then type Eco-Cruise

   The company name is correct. You want the text color to be the same as the fill color of the triangles. The easiest way to accomplish this is to pick up, or **sample**, the fill color directly.

5. Click the Selection tool on the Tools panel, click the Text (fill) color box on the Properties panel, move the eyedropper pointer over the fill in the bottom triangle in the logo, as shown in Figure B-25, then click once

   The font color changes to the bright green of the triangle fill. The eyedropper pointer samples color anywhere in the program window.

QUICK TIP

Your text block might snap to a slightly different location.

6. Click the text block above the "G," when the pointer changes to ▸₊, drag the text block to the location shown in Figure B-26, notice a snap ring appears, then click outside the text block to deselect it

7. Save and close the document, then exit Flash

Understanding Flash text engines

In the TLF text engine, you can access advanced text features, add a link to text and set advanced properties in the Advanced Character section, or set columns in the Container and Flow section. TLF text uses containers, which are similar to text blocks, to support text flowing across and around columns and images. You can resize and link containers and add borders and a background color to create professional-looking text flows. TLF also provides typographical control for kerning (the space between adjacent letters), ligatures (two or more letters, such as "fl," that appear as a single symbol), typographic and digit case, proportional width, baseline shift, and hyphenation, among others.

In addition to TLF text, you can select the Classic Text engine, which provides three text types. **Static text** is the default type and is best used for basic content. For movies that contain interactivity, you can select **Input text** for obtaining user information, and **dynamic text** for displays that constantly update.

Both text engines share aliasing properties to ensure the best font appearance: Use Device Fonts (common ones installed on your computer are best), Readability (improve legibility at small sizes), and Animation (designed to create smooth movement).

FIGURE B-24: Editing text attributes

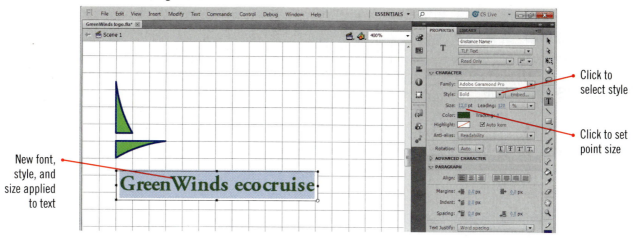

New font, style, and size applied to text

Click to select style

Click to set point size

FIGURE B-25: Sampling a color

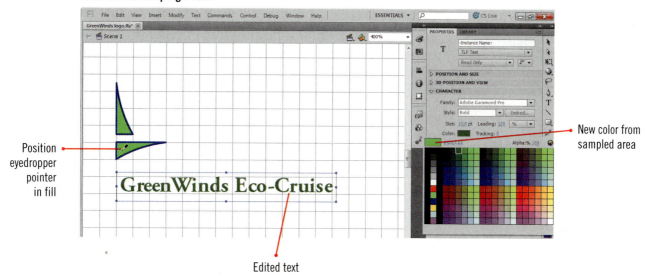

Position eyedropper pointer in fill

New color from sampled area

Edited text

FIGURE B-26: Aligning text

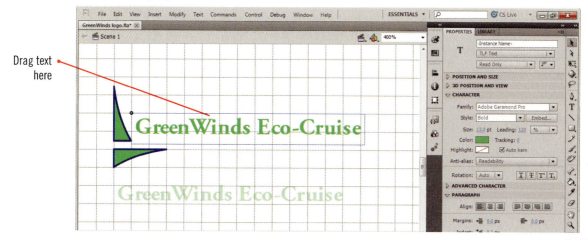

Drag text here

Creating Graphics and Text

Practice

Concepts Review

Label the elements of the Flash screen shown in Figure B-27.

FIGURE B-27

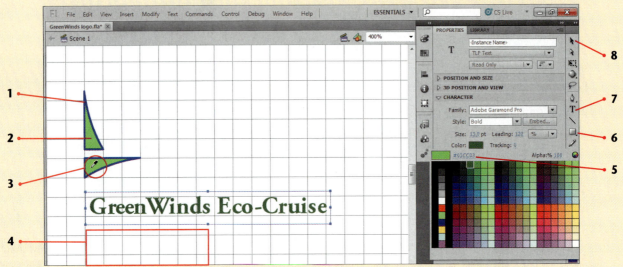

1. _____
2. _____
3. _____
4. _____

5. _____
6. _____
7. _____
8. _____

Match each term with the statement that best describes it.

9. **Free Transform tool**
10. **Anchor point**
11. **Sampling**
12. **Fixed-width text**
13. **Grid**
14. **Merge Drawing mode**
15. **Hexadecimal**

a. Text block created in a set size
b. Used to scale, skew, or rotate an object
c. Can merge new strokes and fills into existing ones
d. Used to define color in an alphanumeric system
e. Component of vector objects
f. A layout of horizontal and vertical squares used to align objects
g. To select a color by clicking an object

Select the best answer from the list of choices.

16. From which menu can you open the Transform, Info, and Color panels?

  a. Window   **c.** Edit

  b. Modify   **d.** View

17. Which of the following are drawing modes in Flash?

  a. Fixed-width Drawing and Merge Drawing   **c.** Merge Drawing and Bitmap Drawing

  b. Merge Drawing and Object Drawing   **d.** Bitmap Drawing and Vector Drawing

18. What is the typical resolution for Web images?

  a. 72 or 96 ppi   **c.** 150 or 200 ppi

  b. 24 or 72 ppi   **d.** 150 or 96 ppi

19. Which key(s) do you press to constrain a rotation to 45° increments?

  a. [Alt] (Win) or [option] (Mac)   **c.** [Shift][Tab]

  b. [Ctrl] (Win) or [⌘] (Mac)   **d.** [Shift]

20. Which of the following is *not* true when describing the grid?

  a. You can adjust the size.   **c.** Objects will snap to the grid if it is not displayed.

  b. You can adjust the grid color.   **d.** You can view the grid in the published movie.

Skills Review

1. Understand vector and bitmap graphics.

  a. Describe the difference between vector and bitmap graphics.

  b. Give an example of how vector and bitmap graphics are used on the Web.

  c. Explain what a pixel is in relation to a bitmap image.

  d. Describe one difference between Merge Drawing mode and Object Drawing mode.

2. Create a new document.

  a. Start Flash, then create a new document named **LightFootRecycling.fla**.

  b. Open the Document Settings dialog box, then make the width **300** px and leave the height at **400** px.

  c. Show the grid and turn on Snap to Grid.

  d. Save the document.

3. Set tool options and create a shape.

  a. Select the Stroke Color control tool, then set the color to none. (*Hint*: Click the No color icon.)

  b. Select the Fill Color control tool, click the hexadecimal text box, then set the color to **#0033CC**.

  c. Select the Rectangle tool, make sure that you are drawing in Merge Drawing mode, create a rectangle of any size, select it, then adjust the size on the Properties panel to approximately W: **98**, H: **38**. (*Hints*: If necessary, expand the Position and Size section on the Properties panel. To size dimensions independently, click the Link icon, then enter each value separately. The ScreenTip for both the Link and Break Link icons is Lock width and height values together.)

  d. Press and hold [Shift], create a square elsewhere on the Stage, select it, then adjust its size to W: **48**, H: **48**.

  e. Save the document.

4. Reshape an object.

  a. Zoom in the Stage as needed.

  b. Select the Subselection tool, then drag the upper-right corner of the square inward until it snaps to form a triangle. (*Hint*: The Subselection tool is located beneath the Selection tool on the Tools panel.)

  c. Select the Free Transform tool, click the triangle, press and hold [Shift], then rotate the triangle 45° clockwise.

  d. Drag the rotated triangle to the left side of the rectangle, use the arrow keys to align it so it forms an arrowhead, then click a blank area of the Stage, as shown in Figure B-28. (*Hint*: Be sure to align the triangle to the rectangle before deselecting it, as it will merge with the rectangle to form an arrow.)

  e. Save the document.

FIGURE B-28

Skills Review (continued)

5. **Select and modify a shape.**
   a. Select the arrow's fill.
   b. Change the fill color to **#000099**.
   c. Save the document.

6. **Copy and transform an object.**
   a. Select the arrow if necessary, move it lower on the Stage, then copy and paste it anywhere on the Stage.
   b. Open the Transform panel, then use the Rotate control to rotate the arrow **120°**. (*Hint*: Click the icon in the iconic panels next to the Properties panel or use the Window menu to open the panel.)
   c. Move the arrow to the position shown in Figure B-28.
   d. Press and hold [Alt] (Win) or [option] (Mac), drag and copy the copied arrow to create a third arrow, rotate it **120°**, then move the arrow to the position shown in Figure B-28.
   e. Save the document.

7. **Use design panels.**
   a. List two pieces of information contained on the Info panel.
   b. Describe how selecting the Align/Distribute to stage button on the Align panel affects objects.

8. **Create text.**
   a. Select the Text tool, then if necessary, set the Text type to Read Only, the font to Times New Roman (or a similar font) and the font size to 40 pt.
   b. Create a fixed-width text block beneath the arrows that is the width of the bottom arrow, then type **recycle**.
   c. Fit the text in the text block, then delete the text block.
   d. Click the Stage, then type **recycle**.
   e. Save the document.

9. **Modify text.**
   a. Select the text, then change the font to Arial or a similar font, the font style to Black, the font size to 50, and the text fill color to black. (*Hint*: Click a color swatch in the first column.)
   b. Select the first letter, then type **R**.
   c. Position the text in the location shown in Figure B-28.
   d. Turn off the grid; deselect all objects, then save the document.
   e. Exit Flash.

Independent Challenge 1

You work at CoasterWoop, an online source of news by, for, and about roller coaster enthusiasts. Your boss has asked you to redo the logo to something modern and minimalist. You begin by creating three circles in Flash and then transforming them in a creative way.

   a. Start Flash, open a new file, then save it as **CoasterWoop.fla**.
   b. Make sure that Snap to Grid is turned off and that Snap Align and Snap to Guides are turned on.
   c. Select the Oval tool on the tools panel, then select the Object Drawing option. (*Hint*: The Oval tool is in the Rectangle tool group.)
   d. Set the stroke color to black with no fill color, then set a stroke height of 1 px.
   e. Draw a perfectly round circle, then modify it as follows: size 40 px, stroke color #FF0000, stroke height 5 px.
   f. Open the Transform panel, select the Skew option, then change the Skew Horizontal value to 10.0°.
   g. Draw a second perfect circle, then modify it as follows: size 65 px, stroke color #FFCC00, stroke height 7 px, skew horizontal 4.0°.

Independent Challenge 1 (continued)

h. Draw a third perfect circle, then modify it as follows: size 85 px, stroke color #0000FF, stroke height 9 px, skew horizontal –17°.

i. Select the circles, then use a command on the Modify, Align menu to bottom-align them. (*Hint*: Be sure that the Align to Stage is not selected.)

j. Zoom in the Stage as necessary, then drag the circles to the positions shown in Figure B-29. (*Hint*: Be sure to first create a selection box around the circles; otherwise, you will modify the shape border when you drag.)

k. Select the Text tool, then if necessary, set the Text type to Read Only, set the font to Myriad Pro or another font, bold, 24 pt, black, then type **CoasterWoop** beneath the circles.

l. Drag the text to center it, deselect the text, then compare your image to Figure B-29. (*Hint*: Use the arrow keys to center the text.)

m. Save and close the document, then exit Flash.

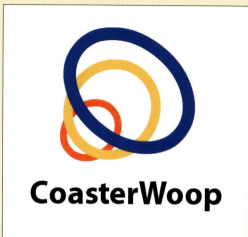

Independent Challenge 2

As the new Program Director at Lingoroots, an educational Web site specializing in linguistics, you're constantly looking for exciting ways to engage new visitors. For the next feature, you'll compare the evolution of written Chinese across its 4,000-year history. The earliest written Chinese characters were pictures, which evolved to a more stylized and artistic writing form. You begin by using artwork a colleague sent you to trace a mountain.

a. Start Flash, open the file FL B-1.fla from the location where you store your Data Files, then save it as **lingoroots.fla**. (*Hint*: The document contains a guide layer named mountain trace that you'll use to trace an object.)

b. Zoom in the Stage as necessary, then make sure that Layer 1 is selected in the Timeline.

c. Select the Line tool on the Tools panel, make sure you are in Merge Drawing mode, change the fill color to none, then change the stroke color to #CC0000 and stroke height to 1 px.

d. Using Figure B-30 and the guide layer, draw a series of lines to form the mountain range and horizon. (*Hint*: To use the Line tool, drag in any direction on the Stage. Draw the left side of each mountain a little higher than the right side.)

e. Select the Selection tool, then use the curve pointer to adjust the sides of the first and third peaks, as shown in Figure B-30.

f. Select the entire object, change the stroke height to 4.5 px, deselect the object, select just the left side (stroke) of each mountain, then change the stroke height to 6 px. (*Hint*: To repeat the previous action or command, press [Ctrl][Y] (Win) or [⌘][Y] (Mac).)

g. Select the Text tool, set the Text type to Read Only, the font to Adobe Garamond Pro, 14 pt, color #66666, then type **Mountain-Ancient**.

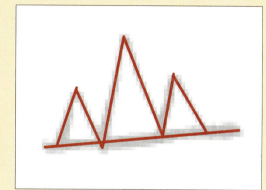

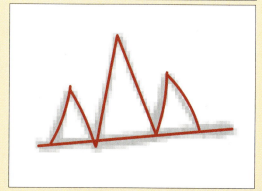

Independent Challenge 2 (continued)

h. Select the text, then change the font style to italic and move it beneath the object.

i. Align the text with the right side of the object, hide the guide layer, then compare your screen to Figure B-31.

Advanced Challenge Exercise

- Make a copy of the object, then move it away from the original.
- Resize the copied object, change the color, then change the stroke height.
- Align the copied object on the Stage.

j. Save and close the document.

k. Exit Flash.

FIGURE B-31

Mountain-Ancient

Independent Challenge 3

You work for ibRobotz, an online entertainment site. Users can download ibRobotz characters or create their own to insert in stories. You've been assigned to develop a character for younger users, so you begin building one using various Flash drawing tools.

a. Start Flash, create a new document, then save it as **ibrobotz.fla**.

b. Change the background color to #0066FF. (*Hint*: Use the Document Settings dialog box.)

c. On the Tools panel, set the stroke and fill colors to default black and white, select the Oval tool, set the stroke height to 4.5 px, then make sure you are in Merge Drawing mode.

d. Create a perfectly round circle that is 100 px round. (*Hint*: Be sure to select the entire object.)

e. Create a rectangle with the following dimensions: W: 100 px and H: 80 px. (*Hint*: Make sure the Break Link icon appears on the Properties panel.)

f. Using Figure B-32 as a guide, select the rectangle, then drag it to the middle of the circle, so that the circle looks like a dome when the rectangle intersects it.

g. Create two rectangles with the dimensions W: 100 px and H: 17 px, and W: 100 px and H: 15 px, then stack them beneath the first rectangle.

h. Color the strokes and fills of the objects as you wish, then use the Align panel to align the horizontal centers of all the objects, or show the grid and align them manually.

i. Select the Pencil tool, set the color to black and the stroke to 4.5 px, draw arms and legs, then reshape the appendages as you wish or as shown in Figure B-32 if desired.

j. Create eyes, hands, feet, and a mouth using the drawing tools of your choice, then reshape, transform, and color them.

k. Select the Text tool, set the font to Arial, regular, size 16 pt, position the cursor in the middle rectangle, then type **ibROBOTZ**.

l. Change the color of the letters "ib" to a different color than the rest of the text.

m. Create an antenna using the drawing tools of your choice, then align, reshape, transform, and color it as you wish.

n. Compare your screen to the sample shown in Figure B-32.

FIGURE B-32

Independent Challenge 3 (continued)

Advanced Challenge Exercise

- Embellish the antenna using additional tools in the drawing section.
- Using one or more tools described in Table B-1, change the shape and stroke of the hands.
- Transform or reshape at least one object.

o. Save and close the document, then exit Flash.

Real Life Independent Challenge

You're interested in developing your own Flash project. You can pick the theme of your choice, such as something about friends, family, interests, and so on.

a. Begin planning your Flash project. (*Hint*: Use the planning chart in Unit A as a template.)

b. Start Flash, create a new document, then save it as **myproject.fla**.

c. Set document settings as desired.

d. Use a minimum of three drawing tools to create multiple objects, set stroke and fill, and transform at least two of them. Identify the tools and tool options you used.

e. Show the grid, set snapping options, and/or use the Align panel to align objects. Identify which align options you found most useful.

f. Check your document for proper alignment and design consistency.

g. Save and close the document myproject.fla, then exit Flash.

Visual Workshop

Visiting Web sites is a great way to get inspired for your own projects. Figure B-33 shows the site for the National Archives. Go to www.archives.gov or study the figure below and answer the following questions. For each question, include why or how you reached a conclusion. You can open a word processor or use the Text tool in Flash to complete this exercise. When you are finished, add your name to the document, save it, print it, then close the word processor or exit Flash.

a. What is the Web site's purpose and goal?

b. Who is the target audience? How does the design (look and feel) of the Web site fit the target audience?

c. Looking at the banner and navigation bar at the top of the page:

- How are vector and bitmap shapes used?
- Are there obviously drawn shapes? Which elements appear to have been created in Merge Drawing mode or Object Drawing mode?
- Do objects have clear strokes and fills?
- How do objects appear to have been modified or transformed?
- How is text used on this page? How many fonts are there?

d. What is animated on this page?

e. What is your overall opinion of the design, organization, and function of this page? How would you improve it?

f. Close your browser.

FIGURE B-33

Using Symbols and the Library Panel

Files You Will Need:

FL C-1.fla
FL C-2.fla
FL C-3.fla
FL C-4.fla
FL C-5.fla

In any creative project, you begin by considering the purpose of the piece. For example, in a print piece, you want photographs to have the highest visual quality. But for the Web or mobile devices, where users interact with Flash movies and performance is often critical, you need to strike a balance between visual quality and file size. Symbols are the key to creative and successful animation in Flash because they allow you to keep file size small. Flash stores symbols on the Library panel. You can create clones of symbols without adding to file size, and edit them as desired.  Your boss, Vanessa, wants you to work on an animation for the GreenWinds Eco-Cruise Web site. To prepare a document for animation, you convert objects to symbols, create symbols, and generate instances.

OBJECTIVES

Understand symbols and instances

Understand the Library panel

Create a symbol

Add instances to the Stage

Edit an instance

Edit a symbol

Organize the Library panel

Understanding Symbols and Instances

A Flash movie can quickly accumulate many elements, each of which increases file size. Some elements, such as video, can take up more space than others, such as simple text. Because elements appear in multiple frames, a movie's file size can grow even more. Fortunately, Flash allows you to reuse elements by creating symbols, which you can copy and edit. You can create any number of instances from a single symbol, which eliminates the need to copy Flash elements individually. You examine the way symbols operate in Flash so you can use them to save file space in the GreenWinds movie.

DETAILS

Before creating design elements, you review information about symbols and instances:

- **Symbols and instances**

  A **symbol** is a copy of an object, such as a graphic, that you can reuse in a movie. You can convert an existing object to a symbol or create a new one from scratch. The advantage of using symbols is that you can use them multiple times in any movie while keeping file size at a minimum. You must first create a copy of the symbol. A copied symbol is known as an **instance**; you create an instance by dragging a symbol from the Library to the Stage. As soon as the copy of the symbol reaches the Stage, it becomes an instance and is linked to the symbol. Flash stores and manages symbols on the Library panel, and instances on the Stage. To preview a symbol, click the symbol's name in the Library. You can adjust the size of the preview pane as needed.

  You can modify the properties of an individual instance, although you are limited to editing its transformation and color effect properties. Editing instance properties does not affect the symbol's properties. However, if you edit the properties of a symbol, each instance is updated instantly on the Stage. Figure C-1 shows a shark symbol on the Library panel and several modified instances of the symbol on the Stage.

- **Symbol types**

  When you create a symbol, you can choose one of three types: graphic, movie clip, or button. Each serves a specific purpose and has a unique icon to help identify it in the Library panel, as shown in Table C-1. A **graphic symbol** is a static object usually used to create an animation spanning across frames in the Timeline. A **movie clip symbol** is a minimovie or animation within a Flash movie. It has its own Timeline and plays independently of the main movie's Timeline. You place it into a single frame of the main movie. A **button symbol** responds to users clicking or rolling over it, which activates a different part of the movie, such as playing a movie clip. You'll learn about movie clips and buttons in later units. Figure C-2 shows the Convert to Symbol dialog box, where you can name a symbol and select its type.

- **How symbols help reduce file size**

  While an instance is an accurate representation of a symbol, only the symbol on the Library panel contributes to a document's file size, no matter how many instances you create. Flash adds the instance's properties to the file, but the amount of actual data added is minor.

TABLE C-1: Symbol icons

icon	type	description
	Movie clip	Use for animations within a movie
	Button	Use for interactivity
	Graphic	Use for static objects

FIGURE C-1: Viewing a symbol and its instances

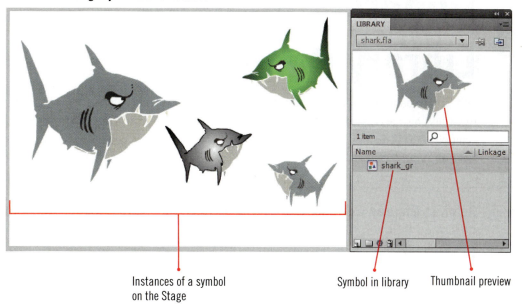

Instances of a symbol on the Stage

Symbol in library

Thumbnail preview

FIGURE C-2: Using the Convert to Symbol dialog box to create a symbol

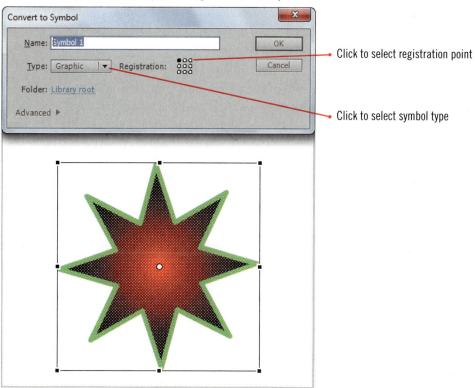

Click to select registration point

Click to select symbol type

Using the Break Apart command

In addition to using the Break Apart command to sever an instance from its symbol, you can break apart text to divide a word into its individual characters, and then break apart a character to convert it to an editable path.

If you break apart a bitmap, you can modify individual segments of the image. Depending on the source image, breaking apart an image can also reduce overall file size and load time.

Understanding the Library Panel

The Library panel lets you manage symbols and media elements, such as sounds, in the current document and also access libraries in other open documents. You can create, edit, preview, and organize symbols. ▨▨▨ You review the main components of the Library panel and the importance of naming symbols properly.

DETAILS

Refer to Figures C-3 and C-4 as you review the Library panel tools and functions described below:

QUICK TIP
Expand the width of the Library panel to view additional information such as the number of instances used and the date the symbol was modified.

- ### Using the Library panel

  Flash automatically adds symbols to the Library panel as soon as you create or import them. You can access libraries from other open documents by clicking the Library panel list arrow and then clicking a document. To share an element or symbol from another movie, display the library that contains the element, then drag it to the Stage, to the Library panel, or copy and paste it.

  The Library panel is also a management tool you can use to organize symbols and other elements. For example, you can create a folder where you place related symbols. See Figure C-3.

  Flash provides three sample libraries, known as Common Libraries, where you can access preset buttons and sounds. To open a common library panel, click Window on the Application bar, point to Common Libraries, then click a library panel.

QUICK TIP
You do not have to use an underscore to separate a symbol type from the symbol name; for example, you could name a symbol *namegr* or *grname* instead of *name_gr* or *gr_name*.

- ### Naming symbols on the Library panel

  As you construct animations, you will create symbols—lots of them. When you create a symbol, you can name it whatever you wish. In practice, however, you should follow an effective naming convention. A symbol name should convey what it is and identify it as a graphic, a movie clip, or a button. Flash assigns unique icons to symbols, but it can also be helpful to indicate their type in your symbol names using short abbreviations. You can add a symbol type abbreviation as a prefix or a suffix. For example, by adding the suffix "_gr" to the name, you can also tell immediately that this is a graphic symbol.

  Remember, too, that the more precise a symbol name is, the easier it will be to find it later. For example, the Library panel in Figure C-3 contains several symbols relating to sharks. It may be tempting to name related symbols in a sequence, such as shark-1, shark-2, and so on, but that would not help much if you're looking for the great white shark symbol. So, you would want to indicate the shark type in the symbol name.

  In addition to naming a symbol for convenience and accuracy, you must also follow file-naming conventions for Web elements, such as using only lowercase letters. Just as a Web browser cannot display a file it cannot read, the Flash Player cannot play a symbol it cannot read. Do not include spaces, tabs, brackets, slashes, punctuation, or the characters above the number keys. But you can add hyphens and underscores to make it easier to read the symbol name.

- ### Understanding hyphens and underscores in names

  Hyphens and underscores are great for making a long file name easier to read, but it's important to know that Flash sorts them differently. Flash sees a hyphen as a space separating the words, so it sorts by the first word. In contrast, Flash sees underscores as being a part of the word and sorts the entire name string. It doesn't matter which you use in a symbol, as long as you are consistent. Figure C-4 compares how Flash sorts symbols with hyphens and underscores. If you use underscores or hyphens consistently, the list is—and will appear to be—in alphabetical order. If you alternate using underscores or hyphens when you name related symbols, they will not appear to be in alphabetical order because Flash sorts underscores first.

FIGURE C-3: Viewing symbols in the Library

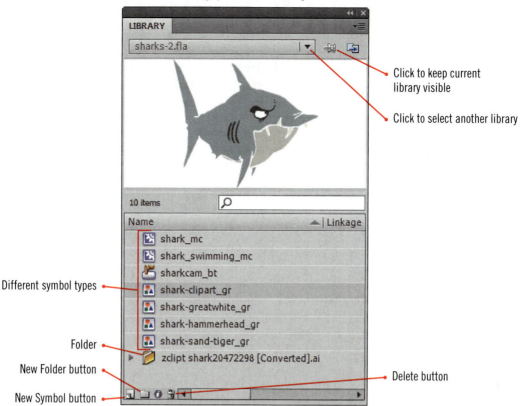

Click to keep current library visible

Click to select another library

Different symbol types

Folder

New Folder button

New Symbol button

Delete button

FIGURE C-4: Comparing the sort order of symbol names with underscores and hyphens

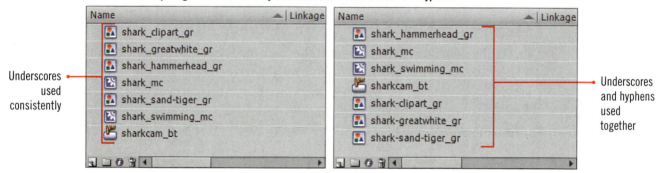

Underscores used consistently

Underscores and hyphens used together

Understanding transformation and registration points

Symbols and other objects have a **transformation point**, a small hollow circle that appears on an object when it is selected, which Flash uses to orient the object every time you transform or animate it. For example, when you rotate an object, it pivots around the transformation point. You can move the transformation point by selecting the Free Transform tool, dragging the transformation point to a new location, and then selecting the Transformation point button 🔲 on the Info panel.

The **registration point** appears as a small plus sign and is the default point that positions an object on the Stage. You can adjust an object's registration point—and its position on the Stage—by adjusting its X and Y values in the Properties panel or Info panel 🔲. For symbols, text, and other objects, the default registration point is the upper-left corner, which corresponds to the X and Y values. The registration point is visible when you edit a symbol, and it is crucial

when using ActionScript to move instances. Figure C-5 shows the transformation and registration points in a selected object.

FIGURE C-5: Transformation and registration points

Registration point

Transformation point

Flash CS5

Creating a Symbol

Flash offers different ways to create a symbol and add it to the Library panel. You can convert an existing object, create a new symbol, or add a preset symbol (buttons and sounds, primarily) from the Common Libraries. Usually, you'll convert an object to a symbol.  Vanessa has informed you that GreenWinds Eco-Cruise wants several elements in its movie. You begin by converting one of the key elements, a dolphin graphic, to a symbol.

STEPS

1. **Start Flash, open the file FL C-1.fla from the location where you store your Data Files, then save it as GreenWinds_symbols.fla**

   The document contains objects on two layers. The light blue wave layer is locked to prevent accidental editing.

   > **QUICK TIP**
   > You may still need to select an object to display properties on the Properties panel.

2. **Click Layer 1 to select it if necessary, click the Selection tool ▸ on the Tools panel, then draw a bounding box around the dolphin to select it**

   The object is selected, and properties for a Shape appear on the Properties panel.

3. **Show the Library panel**

   The Library panel contains two symbols that are already inserted as instances in the light blue wave layer.

   > **QUICK TIP**
   > You can also press [F8] to open the Convert to Symbol dialog box.

4. **Click Modify on the Application bar, then click Convert to Symbol**

   The Convert to Symbol dialog box opens, as shown in Figure C-6. You name the symbol and set the type.

   > **TROUBLE**
   > Expand the height of the preview area by dragging the bottom of the window, if necessary.

5. **Type dolphin_gr in the Name text box, click the Type list arrow, click Graphic, if necessary, then click OK**

   Flash converts the drawing to a symbol, and it appears on the Library panel, as shown in Figure C-7. Flash also automatically converts the dolphin object on the Stage to an instance of the dolphin symbol.

6. **Change the name of Layer 1 in the Timeline to dolphins**

7. **Click the dolphin instance on the Stage, click the Properties panel, expand the Color Effect section, if necessary, then compare your screen to Figure C-8**

   Properties for the instance of the symbol appear on the Properties panel. The Color Effect section replaces the Fill and Stroke section that appears when a shape is selected.

8. **Save the document**

FIGURE C-6: Convert to Symbol dialog box

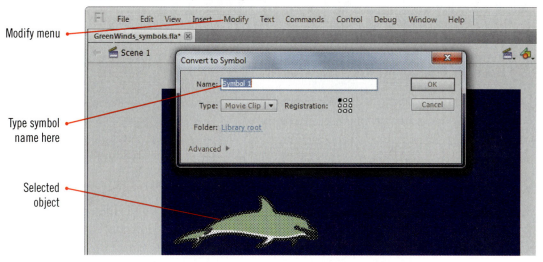

Modify menu

Type symbol name here

Selected object

FIGURE C-7: Viewing a new symbol in the Library panel

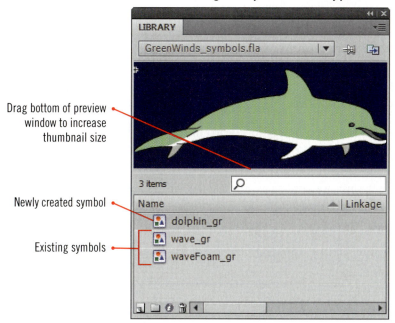

Drag bottom of preview window to increase thumbnail size

Newly created symbol

Existing symbols

FIGURE C-8: Viewing instance properties

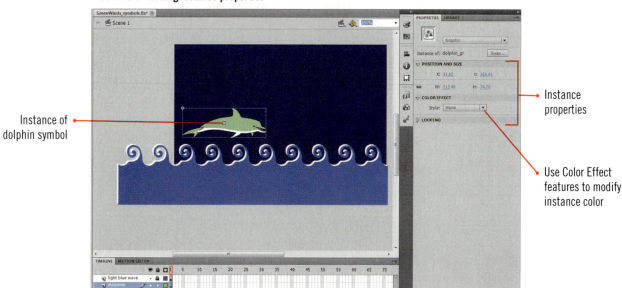

Instance of dolphin symbol

Instance properties

Use Color Effect features to modify instance color

Using Symbols and the Library Panel

Adding Instances to the Stage

Once you create symbols, the next step is to bring instances of them into your movie. To add an instance, you drag the symbol's preview thumbnail or symbol name on the Library panel to the Stage. You begin building the movie by adding another instance of the dolphin symbol and constructing a wave. You'll adjust the final position and colors of the instances in later lessons.

STEPS

1. **Make sure the dolphins layer is selected in the Timeline, show the Library panel, then drag an instance of the dolphin_gr symbol on the Stage, as shown in Figure C-9**

   The dolphins layer now contains two instances of the dolphin_gr symbol.

2. **Create a new layer in the Timeline, then name it dark blue wave**

QUICK TIP

If necessary, drag the layers section of the Timeline to the right to make the layer name visible.

3. **With the dark blue wave layer still selected, drag an instance of the waveFoam_gr symbol from the Library panel to the middle of the Stage**

   The instance of waveFoam_gr is a white wave pattern, which you will use to add dimension to the waves. To position the instance, you open the Info panel, so you can keep the Library panel accessible.

4. **Click the Info panel icon ⓘ in the iconic panels to open the Info panel, then make sure the Registration point button ⊞ is visible on the panel**

TROUBLE

If the Registration point button ⊞ is not visible on the panel, click the Transformation point button ⊞ on the Info panel to show it.

5. **Type –110 in the Selection X position (Win) or X position (Mac) text box, press [Tab], type 220 in the Selection Y (Win) or Y position (Mac) position text box, then press [Enter] (Win) or [return] (Mac)**

   Flash repositions the instance based on its registration point, as shown in Figure C-10. The wave extends into the Pasteboard, which will be useful when you animate the waves in a later unit.

6. **Drag an instance of the wave_gr symbol to the Stage**

7. **On the Info panel, set the X value to –107, set the Y value to 222, then press [Enter] (Win) or [return] (Mac)**

   You constructed the dark blue wave shown in Figure C-11. You will change its color in the next lesson.

8. **Save the document**

Understanding the Elements and Principles of Design

The **Elements of Design** are the basic ingredients that the artist uses separately or in combination to produce artistic imagery. *Lines* serve to illustrate or provide information. *Shapes* are areas that are contained within an implied line, or are identified because of color or value changes. Shapes have length and width, and can be geometric or free form. *Form* describes the volume and mass, or the three-dimensional aspects of objects that take up space. *Value* or color tone, refers to dark and light. *Color* communicates feeling and can make a statement. *Texture* influences the mood of the design and consequently that of the reader. *Space*, whether white or negative, binds sections, frames the design, and focuses attention.

The **Principles of Design** determine how the Elements of Design are used in a composition. *Balance* consists of how two different elements, such as type and shape, can offset each other to be perfectly formatted. It relates to symmetry, an even placement of visual weight in the design; asymmetry, the psychological or "felt" balance even if space and shapes are not evenly distributed; and radial balance, where images emit from a point like spokes on a wheel. Balance also covers the *rule of thirds*, where you divide an image area into thirds using two vertical and two horizontal lines so you have nine equal parts. You place important compositional elements along these lines. In addition, design should have *repetition* of visual movement, such as colors, shapes, or lines. *Pattern* uses the art elements in planned or random repetitions. *Movement* is used to direct the viewer's eye through the work, often to a focal area. *Contrast* is the difference in values, colors, textures, shapes, and other elements. *Emphasis* is also known as dominance in graphic design—the first thing the eye sees. Finally, there should be *unity*, the cohesive quality that makes an artwork feel complete and finished.

FIGURE C-9: Adding a second instance to a layer

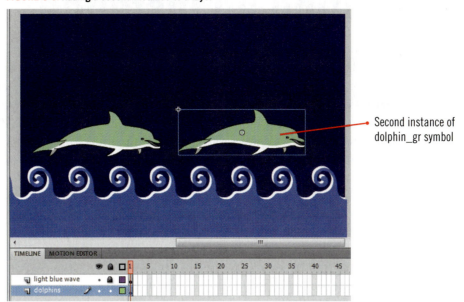

Second instance of dolphin_gr symbol

FIGURE C-10: Positioning the waveFoam_gr instance

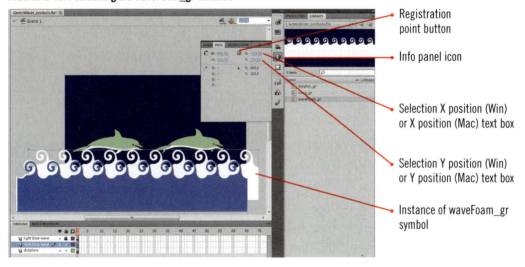

Registration point button

Info panel icon

Selection X position (Win) or X position (Mac) text box

Selection Y position (Win) or Y position (Mac) text box

Instance of waveFoam_gr symbol

FIGURE C-11: Constructing an element using multiple instances

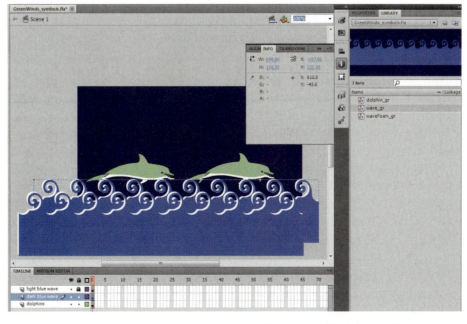

Editing an Instance

Once you have placed the instances for your animation on the Stage, you often want to change their color and position. You can edit instances using the Properties panel and the Transform panel (or by selecting options for the Free Transform tool). You change the color of an instance by applying an effect to it on the Properties panel. Each instance can have individual coloring, which you set in the Color Effect section. You can adjust brightness, tint, transparency, and advanced color options.  Vanessa thinks the design would have more depth if the wave in the back were a darker blue. You decide to do this by applying a color effect. You also rotate and position the dolphin instances to heighten the effect.

STEPS

1. **With the second wave_gr instance still selected on the dark blue layer, show the Properties panel, click the Styles list arrow in the Color Effect section, then click Tint**
   Options for the Tint style appear and are shown in Figure C-12. You can adjust the amount of tint by adjusting its percentage. You can change the tint color in three ways: Click the Tint color swatch to open the color pop-up window and then click a color swatch, drag an RGB slider, or enter values in the RGB text boxes. **RGB (red, green, blue)** is a color model for color produced by emitted light, such as computer monitors. You adjust how much tint is applied using the Tint slider.

2. **If necessary, change the Tint amount text box to 100%, drag the Red slider △ to the left until 0 appears in the text box, drag the Green slider △ to the left until 0 appears in the text box, then drag the Blue slider △ to the right until 255 appears in the text box**
   The wave_gr instance on the dark blue wave layer turns dark blue.

3. **Click the left dolphin instance on the Stage**

4. **Open the Transform panel, then set the rotation to −27°**

5. **In the Position and Size section of the Properties panel, set the X value to −23.25 and the Y value to 252.60**
   The dolphin appears to be jumping from behind the waves.

6. **Select the right dolphin instance, click the Transform panel icon ⊞ in the iconic panels, then set the rotation to −30°**

7. **On the Properties panel, set the X value to 120.20 and the Y value to 242.80**
   You positioned and rotated the dolphin instances. You want the dolphins to appear to be jumping between the waves, not behind them, so you move the dolphins layer in the Timeline.

8. **Drag the dolphins layer between the light blue layer and the dark blue layer in the Timeline, then compare your screen to Figure C-13**

9. **Save the document**

FIGURE C-12: Selecting a fill

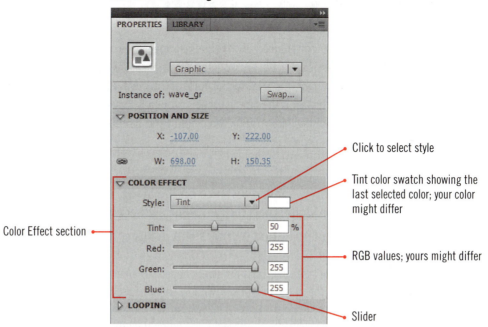

Color Effect section

Click to select style

Tint color swatch showing the last selected color; your color might differ

RGB values; yours might differ

Slider

FIGURE C-13: Repositioned and transformed instances

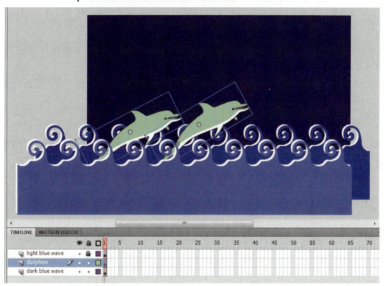

Design Matters

Understanding RGB color

RGB is the default color model used for computer monitors, cell and smart phones, television screens, and any other medium that emits the light itself. Red, green, and blue are the additive primary colors of light.

Additive primary colors combine to produce other colors, as shown in Figure C-14. RGB color values range from 0 to 255, representing all possible levels of red, green, or blue. Adding 100% of all three colors (255 red, 255 green, and 255 blue) produces white. A value of 0 red, 0 green, and 0 blue, which is the absence of light, produces black.

FIGURE C-14: Additive primary colors

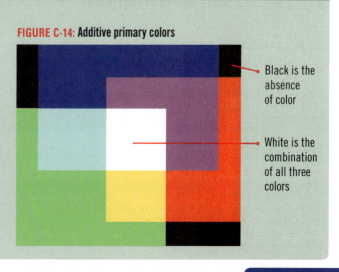

Black is the absence of color

White is the combination of all three colors

Editing a Symbol

As you work in Flash, you often need to change the appearance of multiple instances of a symbol. When you edit a symbol, the changes affect every instance automatically. Because changing a symbol can have a profound effect on a document, the Edit menu provides three ways to edit a symbol. You can also double-click an instance on the Stage or on the Library panel to open it for editing. Vanessa would like the dolphins to be a more realistic color. You fix the color in the symbol so it'll be correct when another designer uses it in a GreenWinds project.

STEPS

1. Select only the right dolphin instance on the Stage, click View on the Application bar, point to Preview Mode, then click Anti-Alias, if necessary

> **QUICK TIP**
> You can also double-click an instance on the Stage to edit it in place.

2. Click Edit on the Application bar, click Edit in Place, then compare your screen to Figure C-15

The dolphin symbol is selected, and the symbol opens in an edit window in the Document window with its own Timeline. The top of the Document window contains the Back button, which you can click to return to Scene 1, and the **breadcrumb trail**, a navigation aid you can use to keep track of an element's location in the document. Other elements on the Stage, including the other dolphin instance, are dimmed (they appear lighter in color). Additional edit symbol commands are described in Table C-2.

3. Close or collapse the Info and Transform panels, if necessary

4. Click the Selection tool ▶ on the Tools panel if necessary, deselect the dolphin, then click the green body to select it

Because you are editing the symbol, which is a drawn shape, regular Fill and Stroke options appear on the Properties panel. You select a new color for the dolphin body.

5. Click the Fill color icon ◇ ▬ on the Properties panel, click the hexadecimal text box, type #CCCCCC, compare your screen to Figure C-16, then press [Enter] (Win) or [return] (Mac)

The symbol and the other instance of dolphin_gr change to a realistic light gray, as shown in Figure C-16. You are finished editing the symbol, so you return to the Scene 1 window.

> **QUICK TIP**
> You can also click Scene 1 at the top of the Document window to return to the main Stage.

6. Click the Back button ⇦ at the top of the Document window to return to Scene 1 and the main Stage, click the Pasteboard, then compare your screen to Figure C-17

You test the movie to see how the elements look when published.

7. Save the document, then press [Ctrl][Enter] (Win) or [⌘][return] (Mac) to test the movie

Only the areas of the wave instances that are on the Stage appear in the published movie.

8. Close the Flash Player

TABLE C-2: Edit symbol commands

command	access it from	what it does
Edit Symbols, Edit Selected	Edit menu	Edits symbol within current Document window; other elements on Stage not visible
Edit	Right-click (Win) or [control]-click (Mac)	Edits symbol
Edit in Place	Edit menu or right-click (Win) or [control]-click (Mac)	Edits symbol within current Document window; other elements on Stage still visible
Edit in New Window	Right-click	Edits symbol in separate Document window

FIGURE C-15: Editing a symbol in place

Edit menu

Back button

Symbol name in menu indicates you are editing a symbol

Breadcrumb trail

Selected symbol

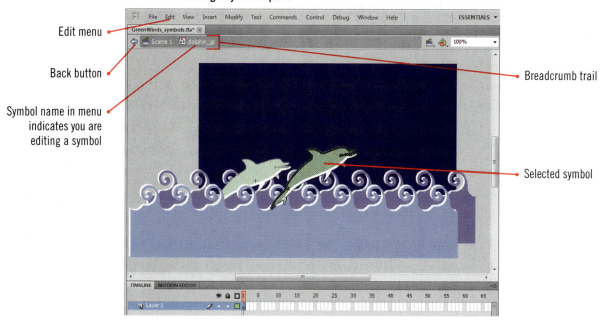

FIGURE C-16: Editing color in a symbol

New color

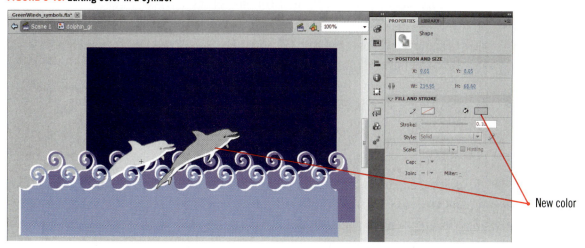

FIGURE C-17: Viewing modified instances after editing symbol

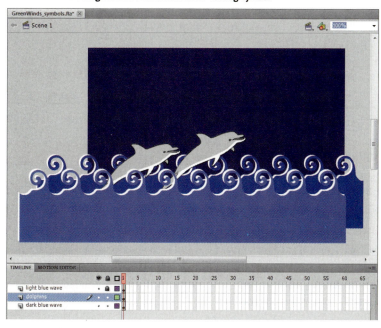

UNIT C
Flash CS5

Organizing the Library Panel

As you develop your animations, you will accumulate numerous symbols and other elements on the Library panel. You can organize them by creating folders, just as you manage files using your computer's file management system. You can **sort**, or rearrange, elements on the Library panel in ascending or descending order. If your movie contains numerous symbols and elements, you can search for one by typing its name in the Search text box. You decide to organize the symbols by acquainting yourself with the sort option on the Library panel and creating a folder for the wave symbols.

STEPS

> **QUICK TIP**
> You can also press [Ctrl][L] (Win) or [⌘][L] (Mac) to open the Library panel.

1. **Show the Library panel, then drag the left edge of the panel to the left to expand it so all columns are visible, as shown in Figure C-18**

   The columns contain information for each element, including its Name, its Use Count (the number of times you've dragged it to the Stage), the date it was modified, and the element type. (It also has information on Linkage, an advanced feature relating to ActionScript.) You can click a column title to sort elements on that column, just as you can in your operating system.

2. **Return the Library panel to its former width, click the Name column header to sort the elements alphabetically in descending order, then click the Name column header again to re-sort them alphabetically in ascending order**

   Flash sorts the symbols from Z to A and then A to Z. You can sort any column in ascending or descending order.

3. **Click the New Folder button ▭ at the bottom of the Library panel, type Waves in the text box, then press [Enter] (Win) or [return] (Mac)**

   A new folder named "Waves" appears at the bottom of the Library panel, as shown in Figure C-19. Because folder names are not Web documents, you can name them as you wish, using capital letters and nonstandard characters.

> **QUICK TIP**
> To select multiple symbols, press and hold [Shift], then click the symbols.

4. **Drag the symbols waveFoam_gr and wave_gr into the Waves folder**

   The folder is highlighted in green when you drag an element over it.

> **QUICK TIP**
> To delete a folder or element, select it, then click the Delete button 🗑 at the bottom of the Library panel.

5. **Click the Expand folder icon ▶ to show the folder contents, then compare your screen to Figure C-20**

   The symbols appear in the folder.

6. **Save the document, then exit Flash**

Grouping and ungrouping objects

Often, you may want to combine multiple shapes to form a single object. To manipulate multiple shapes or objects as one, you **group** them. To group objects, click Modify on the Application bar, then click Group, or press [Ctrl][G] (Win) or [⌘][G] (Mac).

Deciding whether you should group objects or convert them to a symbol is based on their use in the movie. For example, if the objects are not a repetitive element, or if you just need to group them together briefly, but plan to separate them later in the movie, there is no need to convert them into a symbol. However, if you are going to animate the objects, it is always best practice to convert them to a symbol.

To ungroup objects, click Modify on the Application bar, then click Ungroup, or press [Ctrl][Shift][G] (Win) or [⌘][Shift][G] (Mac). When editing a symbol that has grouped objects, first double-click the symbol to edit them, then ungroup the objects.

FIGURE C-18: Viewing columns in the Library panel

Click column to sort ascending or descending

FIGURE C-19: Creating a folder in the Library panel

Folders count as items

Newly created folder

New Folder button

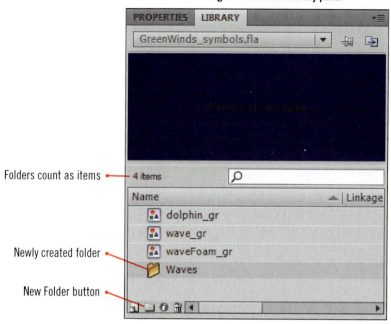

FIGURE C-20: Viewing symbols in a folder

Click to collapse folder

Symbols in folder

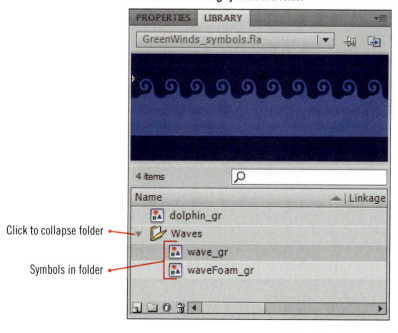

Practice

Concepts Review

For current SAM information, including versions and content details, visit SAM Central (http://www.cengage.com/samcentral). If you have a SAM user profile, you may have access to hands-on instruction, practice, and assessment of the skills covered in this unit. Since various versions of SAM are supported throughout the life of this text, check with your instructor for the correct instructions and URL/Web site for accessing assignments.

Label the elements of the Flash screen shown in Figure C-21.

FIGURE C-21

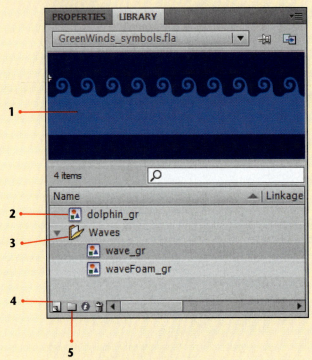

1. _____   4. _____
2. _____   5. _____
3. _____

Match each term with the statement that best describes it.

6. **Instance**   a. A color model for emitted light
7. **RGB**   b. A reusable movie element
8. **Symbol**   c. Default point that locates an object on the Stage
9. **Library panel**   d. Component where Flash stores symbols and other elements
10. **Registration point**   e. A representation of a symbol
11. **Transformation point** f. Orientation point for an object

Select the best answer from the list of choices.

12. Which of the following is *not* a way to create an instance?
    a. Break apart an instance on the Stage.
    b. Drag a symbol to the Stage.
    c. Copy an instance from another document.
    d. Convert an object to a symbol.

13. Which symbol would you use to run an animation in one frame of a movie?
    a. Graphic
    b. Break Apart
    c. Button
    d. Movie clip

14. Which of the following is *not* a way to return to the main Stage after editing a symbol?
    a. Click the Back button.
    b. Double-click the symbol.
    c. Click Scene 1 or the Back button.
    d. Click Scene 1.

15. When adding a type to a symbol name, where is a good place to add the type?
    a. Anywhere
    b. At the beginning or the end
    c. Only at the end
    d. Only at the beginning

16. When editing the color of an instance, which option do you use to change its color?
    a. Tint
    b. Stroke color icon
    c. Fill color icon
    d. Either the Fill color or Stroke color icon

Skills Review

1. **Understand symbols and instances.**
    a. Describe the difference between a symbol and an instance.
    b. List three types of symbols.
    c. Briefly describe how symbols help reduce file size.

2. **Understand the Library panel.**
    a. Describe the main function of the Library panel.
    b. List two requirements and one recommendation for naming symbols.
    c. Briefly describe how you could use hyphens and underscores in symbol names.
    d. Briefly describe how Flash sorts hyphens and underscores.

3. **Create a symbol.**
    a. Start Flash, open the file FL C-2.fla from the location where you store your Data Files, then save it as **LightFootRecycling_symbols.fla**.
    b. Show the Library panel.
    c. On the Stage, select the bag of newspapers object, then convert it to a graphic symbol named **bagNewspaper_gr**.
    d. In the Timeline, rename Layer 1 **newspaper**.
    e. Save the document.

4. **Add instances to the Stage.**
    a. Drag an instance of the recycleSymbol_gr symbol to the upper-right corner of the Stage. (*Hint*: You will adjust the instance later.)
    b. Create a new layer named **recycle bin back**.
    c. Drag an instance of the recycleBinBack_gr symbol to the middle of the Stage.
    d. Open the Info panel, make sure the Registration point icon appears, then set the X value to **150.8** and the Y value to **148.2**.
    e. Create a new layer named **recycle bin front**.
    f. Drag an instance of the recycleBinFront_gr symbol to the middle of the Stage, then roughly align its corners to the corners of the back of the bin.
    g. On the Info panel, set the X value to **147.9** and the Y value to **148.2**.
    h. Lock the two recycle layers, then save the document.

Skills Review (continued)

5. **Edit an instance.**
   a. Hide the two recycle bin layers, then move the instance of the recycleSymbol_gr symbol on top of the newspaper bag.
   b. Open the Transform panel, then transform the size to **40%**, and the skew horizontal to **6.0°**.
   c. On the Info panel, set the X value to **295** and the Y value to **133**.
   d. Save the document.

6. **Edit a symbol.**
   a. Select the recycleSymbol_gr symbol on the Library panel, then double-click the preview thumbnail.
   b. Change the fill color to white (#FFFFFF), then return to the Stage in Scene 1.
   c. Show the two recycle bin layers, then move the plastic bottles layer between the recycle bin front layer and the recycle bin back layer.
   d. Using Figure C-22 as a guide, drag the plastic bottles in the bin.
   e. Save the document.

FIGURE C-22

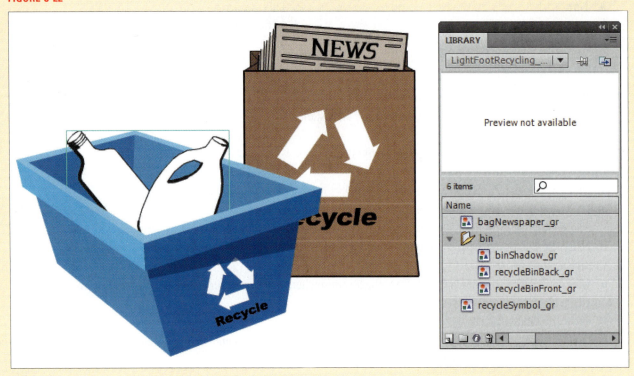

7. **Organize the Library panel.**
   a. On the Library panel, create a new folder named **bin**.
   b. Move every symbol except recycleSymbol_gr and bagNewspaper_gr into the folder.
   c. Expand the folder, then compare your screen to Figure C-22.
   d. Save the document, then exit Flash.

Independent Challenge 1

You work at CoasterWoop, an online source of news by, for, and about roller coaster enthusiasts. Your boss would like you to create an animation of a roller coaster for the Web page. You begin by creating and modifying the symbols you'll use in the movie.

a. Start Flash, open the file FL C-3.fla from the location where you store your Data Files, then save it as **CoasterWoop_symbols.fla**.

b. Make sure that Snap to Grid is turned off and that Snap Align and Snap to Objects are turned on, then open the Info panel and zoom in as needed. (*Hint*: Use the View menu.)

c. Select Layer 1, convert the shape to a graphic symbol named **foliageFront_gr**, then rename Layer 1 **foliage front**.

d. Convert the shape in Layer 2 to a graphic symbol named **foliageBack_gr**, rename Layer 2 **foliage back**, then move the layer to the bottom of the Timeline.

e. Drag an instance of the foliageBack_gr symbol to the Stage, then place it by changing the X value to **47.5** and Y value to **142.8**. (*Hint*: Use the Info panel or the Properties panel.)

f. Create a new layer named **rail1**, move it to the bottom of the Timeline, drag an instance of the rail1_gr symbol to the Stage, then place it by changing the X value to **49.8** and Y value to **84.5**.

g. Create a new layer named **rail2**, move it beneath the rail1 layer in the Timeline, drag an instance of the rail2_gr symbol to the Stage, then place it by changing the X value to **61.6** and Y value to **79.3**.

h. Create a new layer named **rail3**, move it beneath the rail2 layer in the Timeline, drag an instance of the rail3_gr symbol to the Stage, then place it by changing the X value to **120.3** and Y value to **93.2**.

i. Create a new layer named **rail4**, move it beneath the rail3 layer in the Timeline, drag an instance of the rail4_gr symbol to the Stage, then place it by changing the X value to **105.8** and Y value to **70.4**.

j. Select the foliage_Front_gr instance on the Stage, then use the Tint style in the Color Effect section of the Properties panel to change the color of the instance to **#3DAC4F**. (*Hint*: Click the Tint color swatch.)

k. Edit the foliageBack_gr symbol, changing the fill color of the symbol to **#328340**, then return to Scene 1. (*Hint*: Use the Library.)

l. Click the Pasteboard, compare your screen to Figure C-23, save and close the document, then exit Flash.

FIGURE C-23

Independent Challenge 2

As the new Program Director at Lingoroots, an educational Web site specializing in linguistics, you're constantly looking for exciting ways to engage new visitors. For the next Web site feature, you'll compare the evolution of written Chinese across its 4,000-year history. The earliest written Chinese characters were pictures and evolved to a more stylized and artistic writing form. You want to show how Chinese calligraphy has changed over time, and begin constructing an animation using three characters.

a. Start Flash, open the file FL C-4.fla from the location where you store your Data Files, then save it as **lingoroots_symbols.fla**. Make sure guides are visible in the document. (*Hint*: Substitute a font available on your computer if prompted.)

b. Create a new layer named **moon-ancient text**, drag an instance of the moonAncientTxt_gr symbol to the Stage, then use the green guides to align it under the original moon character on the left. (*Hint*: Make sure Snap to Guides is selected as a snapping option and refer to Figure C-24.)

c. Create a new layer named **moon-current text**, drag an instance of the moonCurrentTxt_gr symbol to the Stage, then use the green guides to align it under the current moon character on the right.

d. Create a new layer named **sun-ancient text**, select the Text tool, select Classic Text as the Text engine, set the font to Adobe Garamond Pro, 14 pt, italic, color **#666666**, click under the original sun symbol, then type **Sun-Ancient**.

e. Use the guides to align the text object under the original sun character. (*Hint*: Use the Selection tool.)

f. Convert the text object to a graphic symbol named **sunAncientTxt_gr**.

g. Create a new layer named **sun-current text**, select the Text tool if necessary, click under the current sun symbol, then type **Sun-Current**.

h. Use the guides to align the text object under the current sun character.

i. Convert the text object to a graphic symbol named **sunCurrentTxt_gr**.

j. Create a new folder on the Library panel named **mountain**, then move the mountain symbols into that folder.

FIGURE C-24

k. Click a blank part of the Library panel, create a new folder named **moon**, then move the moon symbols into that folder.

l. Click a blank part of the Library panel, create a new folder named **sun**, then move the sun symbols into that folder.

m. Hide the guides, save the document, then compare your screen to Figure C-24.

Independent Challenge 2 (continued)

Advanced Challenge Exercise

- Select the text instances in the ancient column on the Stage, click Modify on the Application bar, point to Align, make sure Align to Stage is not selected, click Right, then compare the command alignment to your manual alignment.
- Select the text instances in the current column on the Stage, right-align them, then compare the command alignment to your manual alignment.
- Break apart the instance of the calligraphyTxt_gr symbol, then delete it from the Library panel. (*Hint*: Use a command on the Modify menu or right-click (Win) or [control]-click (Mac) the instance.)

n. Save and close the document, then exit Flash.

Independent Challenge 3

You work for ibRobotz, an online entertainment site. Users can download ibRobotz characters or create their own to insert in stories. You've been assigned to develop a character for younger users, so you begin building one using various Flash drawing tools.

a. Start Flash, open the file FL C-5.fla from the location where you store your Data Files, then save it as **ibrobotz_ symbols.fla**. (*Hint*: Substitute a font available on your computer if prompted.)

b. Select the entire pink square and black stroke that currently make up the robot's hand, convert it to a graphic symbol named **smPinkSquare_gr**, then add instances of the symbol as feet, the other hand, and the top of the antenna. Modify instances in minor ways as desired. (*Hint*: You can copy the instance on the Stage instead of dragging it from the Library.)

c. Add an instance of the greenRectangle_gr symbol to the Stage, then place it on the robot as the mouth. Add another instance as part of the antenna, then modify that instance by adjusting the Selection width on the Properties panel. (*Hint*: The antenna should be about as wide as the robot body; refer to Figure C-25.)

d. Rename Layer 1 **ibROBOTZ**.

e. Create a new layer named **itzyBOTZ**, drag an instance of the itzyBotz_gr symbol to the Stage, then place it by changing the X value to **304** and the Y value to **205.8**. (*Hint*: Open the Info panel or show the Properties panel.)

f. Edit the itzyBotz_gr symbol, then drag an instance of the smPinkSquare_gr symbol to the Stage. Resize the instance to W: **11.3** and H: **11.3**, then using Figure C-25 as a guide, copy the instance to create the hands, feet, and antenna. Return to Scene 1. (*Hint*: To rotate the instance 45° for the hands, press and hold [Shift], then rotate an instance clockwise or counterclockwise.)

g. Create a new layer named **furnishings**, then drag an instance of the picture_gr symbol to the Stage, then place it by changing the X value to **375.4** and the Y value to **38.5**.

h. Edit the picture_gr symbol by changing the frame color to **#FF9865**.

i. Create a new layer named **wall & floor**, then drag an instance of the wallPaper_gr symbol to the Stage, then place it by changing the X value to **–9.1** and the Y value to **–4.1**.

j. On the wall & floor layer, drag an instance of the floor_gr symbol to the Stage, and place it by aligning the squares to the instance of the wallPaper_gr symbol. (*Hint*: Change the X value to **–25.1** and the Y value to **293.9**.)

Independent Challenge 3 (continued)

k. Move the wall & floor layer to the bottom of the Timeline.

l. On the Library panel, create a new folder named **wall & floor**, then move the wallPaper_gr and floor_gr symbols to it.

m. Save the document, test the movie using a keyboard command, then close the Flash Player.

n. Compare your screen to Figure C-25.

Advanced Challenge Exercise

- Change the color of the botPod_gr symbol to a color of your choice. (*Hint*: Zoom in and change just the selected botpod box.)
- Change the color of the instance of the floor_gr symbol to a color of your choice.
- Add another instance of the picture_gr symbol, transform or reshape it, then modify it using two style settings in the Color Effect section of the Properties panel.

o. Close the document, then exit Flash.

FIGURE C-25

Real Life Independent Challenge

This Independent Challenge will continue to build on the personal Web site that you created in Unit B. Here, you create symbols and prepare elements to be animated.

a. Start Flash, open the file myproject.fla, then save it as **myproject_symbols.fla**.

b. Create symbols to represent the objects that you plan to animate, adding layers as needed.

c. Add instances to the Stage and reshape, modify, and transform them however you like.

d. Create folders on the Library panel for related items if necessary.

e. Check your document for proper alignment and design consistency.

f. Save and close the document myproject_symbols.fla, then exit Flash.

Visual Workshop

Visiting Web sites and watching Flash movies are great ways to get inspired for your own projects. Figure C-26 shows a frame from the Flash movie *The Corruptibles* produced by the Electronic Frontier Foundation. Open your browser, go to http://w2.eff.org/corrupt/, watch the movie, and then answer the following questions. For each question, include why or how you reached a conclusion. You can open a word processor or use the Text tool in Flash to complete this exercise. When you are finished, press [Print Screen] (Win) or [⌘][Shift][4] to select the window using the mouse (Mac), paste the image into a word-processing program, add your name at the top of the document, then print or post the document. Please check with your instructor for assignment submission instructions.

a. What is the Web site's purpose and goal? What is the movie's purpose?

b. Who is the target audience? How does the design (look and feel) of the Web site fit the target audience?

c. Looking at the animation:

- How are vector and bitmap shapes used?
- How many instances of symbols do you see?
- How do objects appear to have been modified or transformed?
- How is text used on this page? How many fonts are there?

d. How is animation used?

e. What is your overall opinion of the design, organization, and function of this movie? How would you improve it?

f. Close your browser.

FIGURE C-26

Electronic Frontier Foundation: www.eff.org

This work is licensed under a Creative Commons Attribution-NonCommercial-ShareAlike 2.5 license

Creating Animation

Animation plays a huge role in the computer, advertising, marketing, and entertainment industries. It has become one of the Web's most distinctive—and notorious—features. Animation can easily annoy or overwhelm your audience if you overuse it or do not build in good design. Adding Flash animation to a Web site makes it easy to take a Web page to the next level. Flash offers a few different ways to animate your projects, and, with a little practice, you can create effective animations that help communicate any online message.  Vanessa has reviewed the document for GreenWinds Eco-Cruise and has begun animating various elements. She's given you the go-ahead to finish the document using Flash animation methods.

OBJECTIVES

Understand animation

Use frames

Create a motion tween

Create and copy a motion path

Use easing

Add nested symbols to a movie clip

Animate nested symbols

Create frame-by-frame animation

Create a shape tween

Use shape hints

Plan and specialize animation

Understanding Animation

Creating animation in Flash involves object-based animation: creating and adjusting frames and the artwork that appears in them, determining the length of the animation, and setting a frame rate to control the animation's speed. You can animate many attributes or aspects of an object, such as its shape, size, color, and position. When working with frames, it is useful to refer to a group of frames as a **frame span**. Before animating objects in the GreenWinds Eco-Cruise project, you review the different types of animation.

DETAILS

To create an animation, you do the following:

- ### Specify frames

  Animation shows change over time, which, in Flash, is represented by frames in the Timeline. As the creator, you use frames to define when artwork appears and how it changes in a movie. When you open a new document, the Timeline contains a single frame, known as a **blank keyframe**, indicating that there is currently no artwork on the Stage in that frame. When you add content, such as an instance, to a blank keyframe, it becomes a keyframe. A keyframe is a special frame that signals a change in a movie, such as adding or creating artwork on the Stage, or in an animation, such as a change in an object's appearance, location, or behavior.

QUICK TIP

In traditional hand-drawn film animation, senior artists drew the animation's major action points (which they named keyframes), and junior artists, having the monotonous job of drawing the frames in between, were known as *tweeners*.

- ### Select animation methods

  In Flash, you can create animation literally frame by frame or have Flash do some—or all—of the work for you. It's up to you to decide how much specific control you need to create the final result. Regardless of how you create an animation, you can always edit it.

  In **frame-by-frame animation**, Flash animates an object gradually over several consecutive frames. You can control the action in every frame, which may be necessary in a complex animation. Be aware, however, that the more keyframes a movie contains, the larger the file size and the longer it will take users to view it on a Web page. And, because you're creating each frame as you go along, frame-by-frame animation can be time consuming. Figure D-1 shows a sample of frame-by-frame animation with an outline view of the previous frames.

  With **tweened animation**, Flash automatically creates animation between two keyframes. You define the starting and ending keyframes, and then modify the object or symbol. "Tween," the term for this automatically created animation, comes from the phrase "in between," because Flash creates the animation between the two keyframes. The most common types of tweens in Flash are motion tweens and shape tweens.

  - **Motion tweens** show movement on the Stage as an instance moves from one position to another or changes properties such as color, size, or rotation. Because a motion tween uses symbols, it is an efficient way to animate objects. Figure D-2 shows a sample motion tween with a curved motion path.
  - **Shape tweens** change one shape to another, in a process known as morphing. You can control how the shape changes by adding and positioning small lettered circles around the area of the shape that you want to preserve. Figure D-3 shows a shape tween morphing one shape into another.

QUICK TIP

To access options for viewing, selecting, or removing keyframes, right-click (Win) or [control]-click (Mac) a keyframe in a layer, then select an option in the list.

- ### Understand tweens in the Timeline

  When you create a tweened animation, Flash creates a frame span, called a **tween span**, on its Timeline layer in between two keyframes. Motion tween spans are blue, and shape tween spans are green. In a motion tween animation, Flash creates **property keyframes**, which contain the specific property values that change in that frame: position, scale, skew, rotation, color, or filter.

FIGURE D-1: Sample frame-by-frame animation

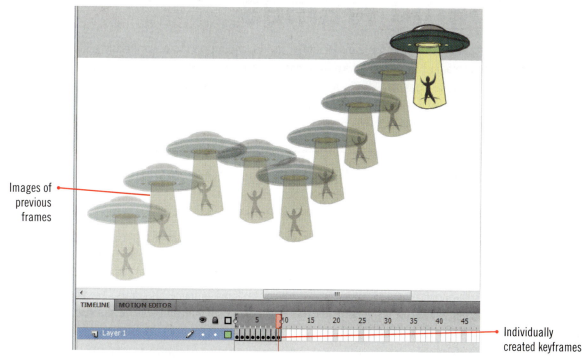

Images of previous frames

Individually created keyframes

FIGURE D-2: Sample motion tween

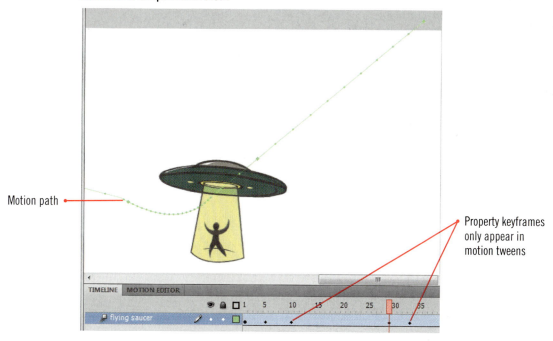

Motion path

Property keyframes only appear in motion tweens

FIGURE D-3: Sample shape tween

Using Frames

You can insert keyframes in a document, or depending on the action, Flash will create keyframes for you. You can adjust the length of a frame span or move selected frames in the Timeline. Table D-1 describes different frame types. You and Vanessa go over the different elements that will appear in the GreenWinds movie. Since you'll be working with objects on various points in the Timeline, you learn more about frames and frame spans in a simple movie.

STEPS

1. **Start Flash, open the file FL D-1.fla from the location where you store your Data Files, then save it as GreenWinds_frames.fla**

   The document does not have any content, so a blank keyframe ▣ appears in frame 1.

   > **QUICK TIP**
   > You can also press [F5] to insert a frame.

2. **Show the Library panel, drag an instance of the cruiseShip_gr symbol to the middle of the Stage, click frame 15, click Insert on the Application bar, point to Timeline, then click Frame**

   The movie is now 15 frames long. The blank keyframe in frame 1 becomes a keyframe ▣, and the last frame ▣ indicates that it is the last frame in a frame span containing artwork, as shown in Figure D-4. You want to extend the length of the frame span by adding another frame in the Timeline.

   > **TROUBLE**
   > It's important to distinguish between frames not used in a movie, which could at first glance be considered blank or empty, and blank frames, which are part of a movie and intentionally do not contain artwork.

3. **Click frame 24, click Insert on the Application bar, point to Timeline, then click Frame**

   Clicking a frame in the Timeline selects it so you can then add, remove, or modify that frame. Flash inserts a new frame, which extends the frame span to 24 frames. You can also click and drag the last frame to extend the ending frame.

4. **Press and hold [Ctrl] (Win) or [⌘] (Mac), position the pointer ↔ over the last frame, as shown in Figure D-5, then drag the frame to frame 35**

   The frame span now consists of 35 frames. You want to move the frame span to a new location in the Timeline.

   > **QUICK TIP**
   > If you need to undo an action, press [Ctrl][Z] (Win) or [⌘][Z] (Mac).

5. **Press and hold [Shift], click frame 1 to select all 35 frames, release [Shift], drag the frame span until the first frame aligns with frame 10, then release the mouse button**

   Blank frames appear in frames 1 to 9. The ship will not appear in the movie until frame 10; it then exits after frame 44, as shown in Figure D-6.

6. **Save and close the document**

TABLE D-1: Frame types

icon	type	description
▣	Blank keyframe	Determined by user to not contain artwork
▣	Keyframe	Determined by user; contains artwork, signifies change
▣	Frame	Determined by last keyframe or by Flash creating frames; contains artwork that doesn't change
▣	Last blank frame before keyframe	Determined by last keyframe
▣	Last frame before keyframe	Determined by last keyframe or by Flash creating frames; contains artwork that doesn't change
▢	Blank frame	Determined by last keyframe
▣	Property keyframe	Determined by a change to an object's property in a motion tween

FIGURE D-4: Viewing a frame span

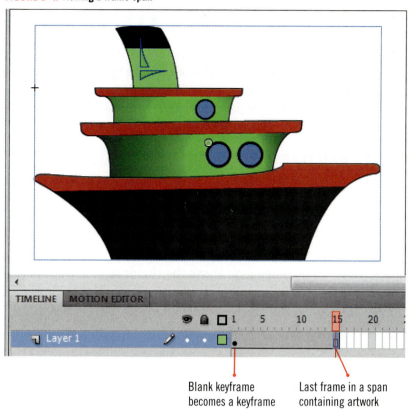

Blank keyframe
becomes a keyframe

Last frame in a span
containing artwork

FIGURE D-5: Extending a frame span by dragging

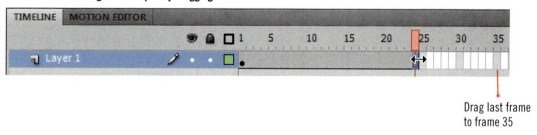

Drag last frame
to frame 35

FIGURE D-6: Moving a frame span

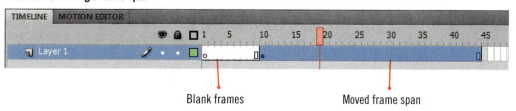

Blank frames

Moved frame span

Flash CS5

Creating a Motion Tween

You apply a motion tween to a symbol by placing an instance in the starting keyframe, and then modifying the position or transformation properties of the instance in the last keyframe of the animation. Vanessa tells you that she'd like to add a lot of action to the GreenWinds movie. You begin by creating a simple motion tween that shows the logo fading in partway through the movie.

STEPS

1. **Open the file FL D-2.fla from the location where you store your Data Files, save it as GreenWinds_animation.fla, then press [Enter] (Win) or [return] (Mac) to view the animation**

   The wave and ship objects are animated with a motion tween in frames 1–147, indicated by the light blue tween span between the keyframes. All document objects are on locked layers. You want to insert the logo in the movie, but you want to delay the logo's appearance for a few seconds. You do this by creating a new layer and then inserting a keyframe in a later frame of the movie.

   > **QUICK TIP**
   > You can also press [F6] to insert a keyframe.

2. **Insert a new layer named logo above the clouds layer in the Timeline, click frame 80 in the logo layer, click Insert on the Application bar, point to Timeline, then click Keyframe**

   The keyframe indicates that a change to an object will take place in frame 80. Because the layer does not yet have artwork, frame 80 contains a blank keyframe, as shown in Figure D-7. Next, you need to choose and position the symbol you want to animate.

   > **QUICK TIP**
   > Open or undock the Transform, Info, Library, and Properties panels as needed or switch to another workspace to make your work easier throughout this unit.

3. **Show the Library panel, drag an instance of the greenWindsLogo_gr symbol from the Library panel to the Stage with an X value of 19, a Y value of 50.5, a Selection width value of 355.6, and a Selection height value of 109.4**

   The logo appears in the movie starting in frame 80, and the blank keyframe ○ changes to a keyframe ●, indicating that it now contains a symbol instance. Next, you instruct Flash to create a motion tween.

4. **Click Insert on the Application bar, then click Motion Tween**

   The frame span to the right of frame 80 turns blue, indicating that it is a motion tween span. Next, you adjust the alpha setting for the logo at the beginning and end of the tween to achieve the fade-in effect.

5. **Click the Selection tool ▶ on the Tools panel if necessary, click the logo instance on the Stage to select it, show the Properties panel, click the Color styles list arrow in the Color Effect section, click Alpha, then drag the Alpha slider △ to 0**

   The logo is still selected but is no longer visible on the Stage because you've set its alpha (transparency) to 0, as shown in Figure D-8. To complete the motion tween, you add a property keyframe in the frame where you want the logo to be fully visible and adjust the alpha back to 100%.

   > **TROUBLE**
   > You must select an instance on the Stage to access properties for the instance; otherwise, properties for the animation appear on the Properties panel.

6. **Click frame 100 in the logo layer, click Insert on the Application bar, point to Timeline, click Keyframe, click the logo instance on the Stage to select it if necessary, then drag the Alpha slider △ to 100 on the Properties panel**

   The logo is visible on the Stage, and a new property keyframe ◆ appears in the Timeline. You check to see that the logo fades in from frames 80 to 100, then remains visible for the rest of the movie.

7. **Scrub the playhead from frames 80 to 100 to view the animation, drag the playhead to frame 87, compare your screen to Figure D-9, then lock the logo layer**

   Scrubbing the Timeline is a great way to quickly view an animation. To preview the final result, you test the movie.

8. **Test the movie, close the Flash Player, then save the document**

   The movie plays, then after a few seconds, the logo fades in. In future lessons in this book, the instruction "Test the movie" will assume that you open the Flash Player, view the movie, then close the Flash Player.

FIGURE D-7: Adding a keyframe to a layer

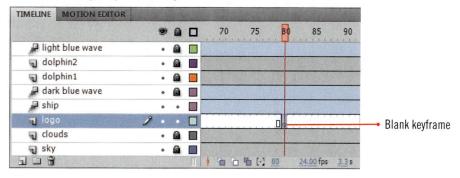

Blank keyframe

FIGURE D-8: Adjusting the value of a property keyframe

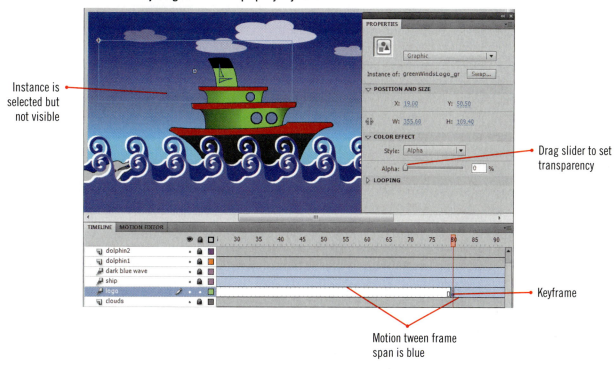

Instance is selected but not visible

Drag slider to set transparency

Keyframe

Motion tween frame span is blue

FIGURE D-9: Viewing a motion tween

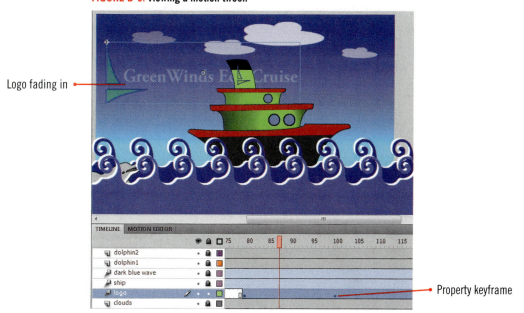

Logo fading in

Property keyframe

Creating Animation

Creating and Copying a Motion Path

After you create a motion tween and move an instance on the Stage, you create a motion path. You can copy and paste a motion tween on other layers to keep your animations consistent and save time. Vanessa wants the dolphins to look like they're jumping out of the water. You create a motion path in the dolphin1 layer, edit the path, then paste the completed motion path into the dolphin2 layer.

STEPS

1. **Hide the light blue wave layer, unlock the dolphin1 layer, click anywhere in its frame span, click Insert on the Application bar, then click Motion Tween**

   A motion tween is created in frames 1–147. You create a motion path by moving the dolphin instance to the other side of the Stage, which you will do using keyboard keys.

2. **Click frame 147 (the last frame), select the dolphin1 instance on the Stage, press and hold [Shift], press the right arrow key until the dolphin appears in the location shown in Figure D-11 (the X value is approximately 380), release [Shift], show the Transform panel, then set the Rotate value to 64.7°**

   As soon as you move the dolphin instance, Flash inserts a keyframe in frame 147. You have set the dolphin instance to move straight across the Stage and rotate, as if diving back in the water.

3. **Scrub the playhead across the Timeline from frames 80 to 147 to view the animation**

   The dolphin instance moves across the Stage and gradually rotates. Next, you modify the motion path to curve into an arc to create a more natural motion.

4. **Make sure the Selection tool is selected, position the curve pointer on the motion path, drag the path up to the location shown in Figure D-12, then test the movie**

   The dolphin flies in a gentle arc. You want to apply the same animation to the other dolphin instance, so you copy the tween span in the dolphin1 layer to the dolphin2 layer.

5. **Click frame 1 in the dolphin1 layer, click Edit on the Application bar, point to Timeline, then click Copy Motion**

6. **Unlock the dolphin2 layer, click anywhere in its frame span, click Edit on the Application bar, point to Timeline, then click Paste Motion**

   The dolphin2 layer frame span turns blue, indicating that you have pasted the copied motion tween span there.

7. **Test the movie, then compare your screen of flying dolphins to Figure D-13**

8. **Lock the dolphin1 layer, show the light blue wave layer, then save the document**

Using the Motion Presets panel

Flash provides several predesigned motion tweens you can apply to symbol instances. Open the Motion Presets panel from the Window menu, open the Default Presets folder, then select a preset. Flash previews the preset at the top of the panel. To apply a preset, select the instance on the Stage, select a preset, then click Apply at the bottom of the panel. Figure D-10 shows a sample preset. To save any motion tween as a custom preset, right-click (Win) or [control]-click (Mac) a motion tween span in the Timeline, click Save as Motion Preset, type a name in the Preset name text box, then click OK to close the Save Preset As text box. The preset appears in the Custom Presets folder on the Motion Presets panel.

FIGURE D-10: Motion Presets panel

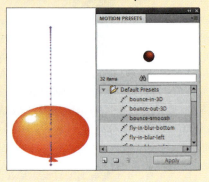

FIGURE D-11: Creating a motion path

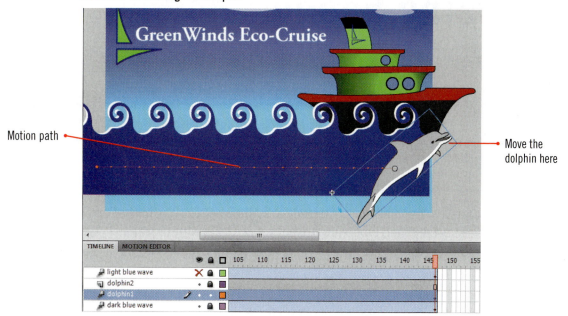

Motion path

Move the dolphin here

FIGURE D-12: Modifying a motion path

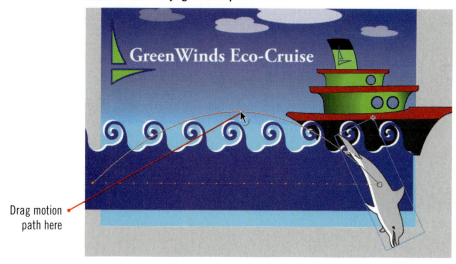

Drag motion path here

FIGURE D-13: Viewing motion tweens

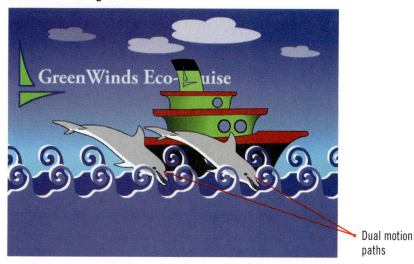

Dual motion paths

Using Easing

When you play a motion tween, the animation moves at one speed from beginning to end; this may not always provide realistic or organic movement. You can speed up or slow down the start or end of an animation by adjusting its **easing** on the Properties panel. When an object eases in, it starts out slow and then speeds up at the end. When it eases out, the opposite happens: it starts out fast, then slows down. When you use easing, you may have to experiment with different values to get the effect you want. Currently, the dolphins look and move at the same speed throughout the movie. You use the easing setting to change the speed for one of the dolphins.

STEPS

1. **With the dolphin2 layer selected, click the Ease text box in the Ease section of the Properties panel, type –100, then press [Enter] (Win) or [return] (Mac)**

   To ease an object in, you enter a negative value. The word "in" appears after the value.

2. **Test the movie**

   The dolphin in the dolphin2 layer lags significantly behind the first dolphin, as shown in Figure D-15. This is not the effect you wanted, so you ease out the motion tween.

3. **Click the Ease text box on the Properties panel, type 100, press [Enter] (Win) or [return] (Mac), then test the movie**

   The word "out" appears after the value. Now the dolphin enters the movie so quickly that its path crosses the dolphin1 path, as shown in Figure D-16. This effect detracts from the overall look of the movie, so you decrease the amount of easing out.

4. **Click the Ease text box on the Properties panel, type 20, press [Enter] (Win) or [return] (Mac), then test the movie**

   This setting adds enough of an effect without being distracting, as shown in Figure D-17.

5. **Lock the dolphin2 layer, then save the document**

Using the Motion Editor

Using the **Motion Editor**, you can control every property of object-based animation independently, including timing, motion paths, rotation, and color. To use the Motion Editor, select a motion tween span, then open the Motion Editor from the Window menu or click the tab behind the Timeline. The values are shown both as numbers and as curves. To expand a property and see your animation frame by frame, click a blank part of the property section. Use controls on the bottom of the panel to adjust the size of the layers and Timeline. The Motion Editor is divided into property sections: Basic Motion, Transformation, Color Effect, Filters, and Eases.

Each property has its own Timeline where you can adjust X and Y values, add keyframes, create custom easing, or apply a preset easing option. When you select custom easing for an animation, you can control the timing in your animation by adjusting the animation line for that object. If you drag a keyframe, you create a Bezier curve and can then easily adjust the Bezier handles to create very smooth and realistic animation. The steeper the curve, the faster the animation

plays in those frames. Figure D-14 shows custom easing applied to an object in the Motion Editor.

FIGURE D-14: The Motion Editor

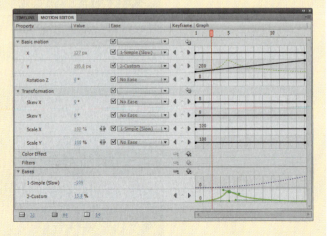

FIGURE D-15: Viewing animation at maximum easing in

Dolphins' paths are out of synch

Negative value eases an object in

FIGURE D-16: Viewing animation at maximum easing out

Dolphins' paths cross

Positive value eases an object out

FIGURE D-17: Corrected easing

Creating Animation

Adding Nested Symbols to a Movie Clip

A movie clip lets you play an animation within your movie. You can animate a single graphic or button symbol, or animate multiple symbols on several layers. Placing a symbol inside another symbol creates a **nested symbol** and is a great way to create a unique new symbol while preserving the individuality of the original symbols. Each movie clip has its own timeline. Common timeline commands are shown in Table D-2.  Vanessa wants you to add flashing lights to the bow of the ship. First you convert the ship graphic symbol to a movie symbol, then add (nest) instances of a light symbol to it.

STEPS

1. **Unlock the ship layer, click frame 1, select the ship instance on the Stage, click Modify on the Application bar, then click Convert to Symbol**

   The Convert to Symbol dialog box opens.

TROUBLE

If the ship graphic shrinks in size, click the Reset button on the Transform panel.

2. **Type shipWithLights_mc in the Name text box, click the Type list arrow, click Movie Clip, compare your dialog box to Figure D-18, then click OK**

   Flash converts the graphic symbol into a new movie clip symbol, which appears on the Library panel. The "_mc" extension in the symbol name easily identifies it as a movie clip symbol.

3. **Double-click the ship instance on the Stage to open the movie clip Timeline, rename Layer 1 ship in the Timeline, then create a new layer named lights**

   The symbol opens in an edit window. Changes you make in a movie clip symbol will play continuously in the main movie. First, you extend the frame span in the movie clip.

QUICK TIP

Adjust the zoom as needed.

4. **Press and hold [Shift], click frame 24 in the lights layer and the ship layer, release [Shift], click Insert on the Application bar, point to Timeline, then click Frame**

   The new frame is added to both layers and indicates that the flashing lights animation will start in frame 1 and continue to frame 24. Because the default frame rate is 24 fps, by adding 24 frames to the movie clip, the action will be one second long in the main movie. See Figure D-19.

5. **Zoom in on the bow of the ship as needed, click frame 1 in the lights layer, show the Library panel, drag an instance of the light_gr symbol to the bow of the ship, then set the X value to 262.6 and the Y value to 115.75**

   Two yellow lights appear on the ship's bow, as shown in Figure D-20. The light_gr symbol is nested in the movie clip.

6. **Save the document**

FIGURE D-18: Creating a Movie Clip symbol

FIGURE D-19: Extending a frame span to multiple layers in a movie clip

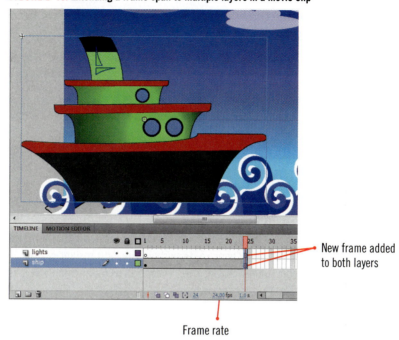

New frame added
to both layers

Frame rate

FIGURE D-20: Symbol nested in a movie clip

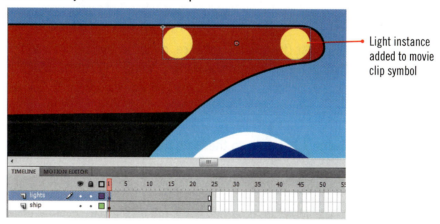

Light instance
added to movie
clip symbol

TABLE D-2: Timeline commands

command	use to
Remove Frames	Physically remove frames from the Timeline, shortening its length
Cut Frames	Keep the frames, but remove content from them and place it on the Clipboard
Copy Frames	Copy frames and content
Paste Frames	Paste frames and content
Clear Frames	Remove content from frames but not place it on the Clipboard
Select All Frames	Select all frames in all layers

Animating Nested Symbols

You can animate any part of a movie clip. Animating a nested symbol still allows you to reuse the symbol in other parts of the movie, where it can be part of another animation. You create a series of flashing lights by aligning two instances of the light_gr symbol and then changing the instances' color in a later keyframe.

1. Make sure that the edit window for the shipWithLights_mc symbol is open and the light_gr instance is selected

TROUBLE
Drag the Tint slider ◻ to 100%, if necessary.

2. Click the Color styles list arrow in the Color Effect section of the Properties panel, click Tint, click the Tint color swatch, click the hexadecimal text box, type #00FFCB, then press [Enter] (Win) or [return] (Mac)

The lights turn turquoise. You add a second instance of the lights symbol to the layer.

3. Show the Library panel, drag another instance of the light_gr symbol to the bow of the ship, set the X value to 249 and the Y value to 115.75, then compare your screen to Figure D-21

QUICK TIP
To move one frame at a time in the Timeline, press [.].

4. Click frame 12 in the lights layer, click Insert on the Application bar, point to Timeline, then click Keyframe

Currently, the movie clip shows yellow and turquoise lights that do not change. By adding a keyframe to frame 12, you can now change a property of the light instances. You change the colors of the light instances in this keyframe so they change color every half second, which will make them appear to flash in alternating colors when Flash plays the movie.

5. Click another part of the Stage to deselect both instances, click the left (yellow) instance, click the Color Styles list arrow in the Color Effect section of the Properties panel, then click Tint

Because you had selected the turquoise color in Step 3, the instance color automatically changes to this color. You change the color of the other instance to yellow.

6. Click the right (turquoise) instance, click the Tint color swatch, click the hexadecimal text box, type #FFFF00, then press [Enter] (Win) or [return] (Mac)

The colors of the lights in frames 12 to 24 are reversed from the colors in frames 1 to 11, as shown in Figure D-22. You can scrub the Timeline to quickly view the lights changing color, but you must test the movie to see the movie clip play.

7. Click Scene 1 to return to the main movie, test the movie, then compare your screen to Figure D-23

The lights flash in alternating colors as the ship moves across the Stage.

8. Lock the ship layer, then save the document

FIGURE D-21: Modified nested symbols

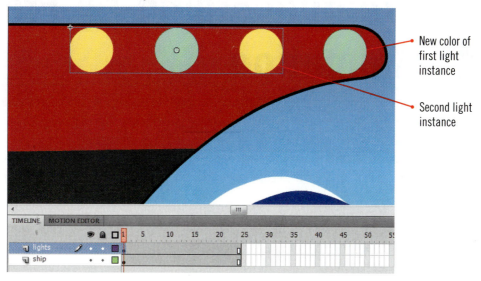

New color of
first light
instance

Second light
instance

FIGURE D-22: Modifying instances in a new keyframe

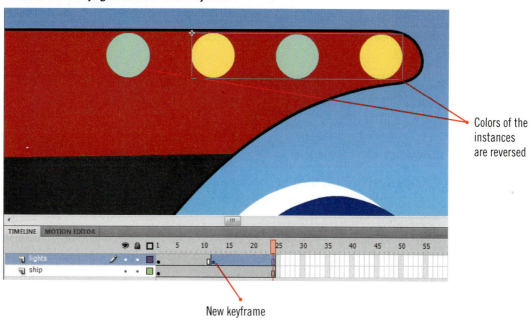

Colors of the
instances
are reversed

New keyframe

FIGURE D-23: Viewing a movie clip

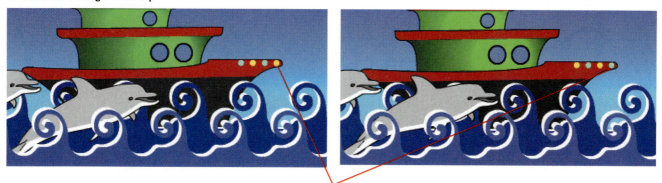

Lights flash in
alternating colors

Creating Frame-by-Frame Animation

Frame-by-frame animation in Flash comes closest to traditional animation techniques. In tweening, Flash creates all the transition frames, but with frame-by-frame animation, you create the content in every frame. Although it can be time consuming, frame-by-frame animation offers detailed control over the animation.  Vanessa wants you to reinforce the GreenWinds Eco-Cruise message with a brief skywriting animation. You use the Pencil tool to create a handwritten message using frame-by-frame animation.

STEPS

1. Create a new layer named yes above the dolphin2 layer, click View on the Application bar, point to Guides, click Show Guides, then zoom in the Stage where the guides form a rectangle

2. Click the Pencil tool ✎ on the Tools panel, then set the following properties: stroke color: #FFFFFF (white), Stroke height: 2, Stroke style: Dotted

3. Click the Edit stroke style button ✎ on the Properties panel, then in the Stroke Style dialog box, double-click the Dot spacing text box, type 1, then click OK

   You want to spell out a word that begins in the same frame as when the GreenWinds logo reaches 100% alpha visibility.

4. Click frame 100 in the yes layer, click Insert on the Application bar, point to Timeline, then click Keyframe

   The animation will start at frame 100.

5. Draw a Y in the rectangle created by the guides, as shown in Figure D-24

   You space out the content in the Timeline so the letters do not appear in the movie too fast.

6. Click frame 110 in the yes layer, insert a keyframe, draw an E, click frame 120, insert a keyframe, draw an S, deselect the letters, compare your screen to Figure D-25, then scrub the playhead over the frames

   The word "YES" is spelled out one letter at a time, with the letters appearing 10 frames apart. To better evoke the spirit of a vacation cruise, you change the movie's frame rate to slow down the animation when it plays.

7. Click the frame rate text box at the bottom of the Timeline, type 12, then press [Enter] (Win) or [return] (Mac)

8. Test the movie, then compare your screen to Figure D-26

9. Hide the guides, lock the yes layer, then save the document

FIGURE D-24: Drawing a letter in a frame

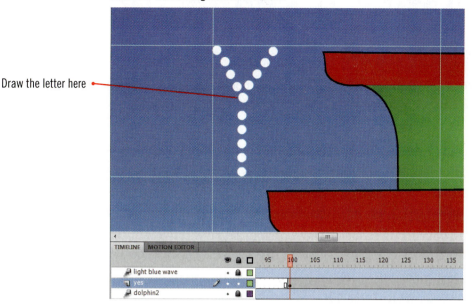

Draw the letter here

FIGURE D-25: Completed frame-by-frame animation

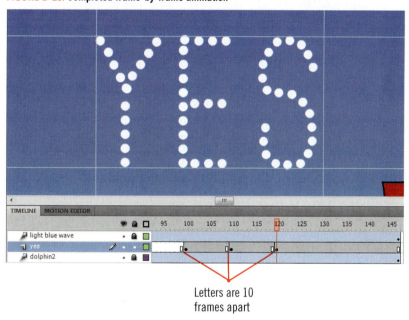

Letters are 10
frames apart

FIGURE D-26: Viewing frame-by-frame animation

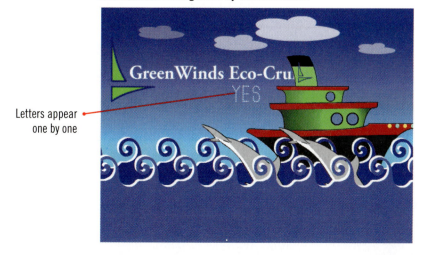

Letters appear
one by one

Creating a Shape Tween

Shape tween animation changes, or **morphs**, a starting shape into a different ending shape. So, you use shapes instead of symbols, bitmap images, or text to create a shape tween. To create a shape tween, you place the starting shape in the first frame and the ending shape in the last frame, and then create the shape tween. For the GreenWinds Eco-Cruise project, Vanessa wants to show a cloud blowing across the sky. You create a cloud that changes shape as it moves across the Stage.

STEPS

> **TROUBLE**
> Make sure the Break Link icon is active on the Properties panel.

1. Create a new layer above the clouds layer named cloud shape tween, click frame 1, click the Oval tool on the Tools panel, make sure Object Drawing mode is not selected, select the No color icon for the stroke, then select #FFFFFF (white) for the fill

2. Adjust your zoom, create an oval with a Selection width of 110 and a Selection height of 40, then place it on the Stage with an X value of 448 and a Y value of 33

> **TROUBLE**
> When you copy the oval, be sure to drag or paste it away from the original.

3. Create a copy of the oval, set its X value to 505 and its Y value to 8.5, create another copy of the oval, set its X value to 512 and its Y value to 27, then click the Pasteboard

   The composite shape resembles a fluffy cloud, as shown in Figure D-27.

4. Select and copy the cloud shape, click frame 147 in the cloud shape tween layer, click Insert on the Application bar, point to Timeline, then click Blank Keyframe

   Because a shape tween requires two separate shapes, you must insert a blank keyframe before you create the ending shape. First you paste and reposition the cloud so it will appear to move across the Stage.

5. Paste the cloud shape, select it on the Stage, then set the X to –72 and the Y to 8.5

   The cloud is now on the left side of the Stage, so the shape will move across the sky as it morphs. Next, you modify its ending appearance.

> **QUICK TIP**
> You can use a shape created by the Shape tools in Merge Drawing or Object Drawing, or you can use other vector objects in a shape tween.

6. Show the Transform panel, set the Scale Height to 78%, click the Skew option button, set the Skew Horizontal to –68, then compare your screen to Figure D-28

   The cloud's ending shape looks flattened. Now you're ready to tell Flash to create the shape tween.

7. Click in the frame span on the cloud shape tween layer, click Insert on the Application bar, then click Shape Tween

   The tween span turns green, indicating a shape tween. When you test the movie, you will see the cloud morph from fluffy to flattened as it moves from right to left across the Stage.

8. Test the movie, compare your screen to Figure D-29, lock the cloud shape tween layer, then save and close the document

---

Understanding and fixing tweening errors

You may discover that an animation it is not working properly or at all because you have not followed the rules for creating that particular animation. In some cases, Flash will prompt you for the fix, such as to convert an object to a symbol if you are trying to apply a motion tween to a shape. When created properly, a successful motion tween layer is blue and has diamond-shaped property keyframes, a shape tween layer is green and has a solid arrow, and a classic tween layer is purple with a solid arrow. If you break a rule, the tween will show as a dotted or dashed line instead, or the property keyframe in a motion tween will be a circle, indicating that the tween is broken. To fix a broken shape tween or classic tween, check that you have added an ending keyframe. For a shape tween, also make sure that the ending object is a drawing object. If you added a symbol instead, you can apply the shape tween, but it will be broken and the top of the Properties panel will display a Mixed type icon. The easiest way to fix the tween is to click the symbol in the ending keyframe and then click the Break Apart command on the Modify menu. When you fix a broken tween, the line changes to a solid arrow.

FIGURE D-27: Creating a cloud shape

Shape composed of three ovals

FIGURE D-28: Reshaping an object in a shape tween

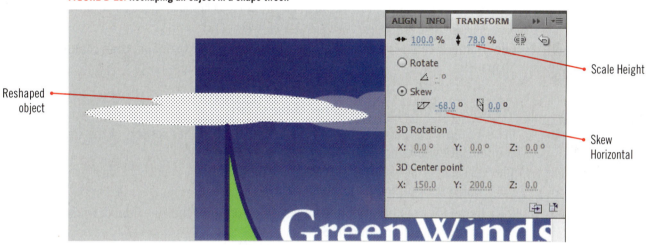

Reshaped object

Scale Height

Skew Horizontal

FIGURE D-29: Viewing a shape tween

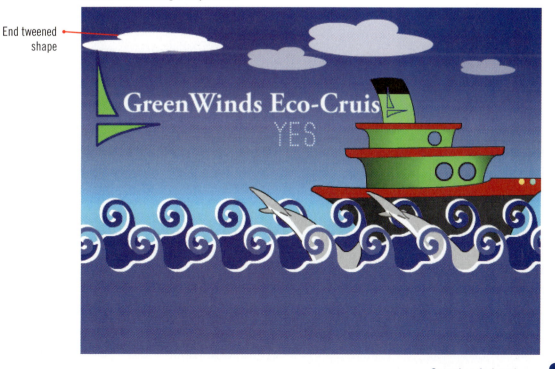

End tweened shape

Using Shape Hints

Sometimes the way Flash morphs a shape looks awkward or unrealistic. You can correct the appearance of a shape tween using shape hints. **Shape hints** mark specific points on the beginning and ending shapes that Flash uses to transition one area into another. The more complex or asymmetrical the shape, the more shape hints you'll need. Vanessa wants to show the GreenWinds client how effective a shape tween can be. You show her how using shape hints can improve a shape tween she created.

STEPS

1. **Open the file FL D-3.fla from the location where you store your Data Files, save it as GreenWinds_shapehints.fla, then test the movie**

    The animation shows a square turning into an "E", but the transition is rough and not particularly attractive. You add shape hints to control how the square morphs into the "E". To use shape hints, you place them on the shape in the first frame, then place them on the corresponding areas in the last frame. You can add new shape hints only in the first frame of the shape tween span.

QUICK TIP

You can also press [Ctrl][Shift][H] (Win) or [⌘][Shift][H] (Mac) to insert a shape hint.

2. **Click frame 1, click Modify on the Application bar, point to Shape, then click Add Shape Hint**

    A shape hint lettered "a" appears in the middle of the square.

3. **Drag hint a to the upper-left corner of the square**

QUICK TIP

Shape hints work most effectively when arranged in a clockwise or counterclockwise pattern.

4. **Repeat Step 2 three times, then drag the hints to the other corners of the square in a counterclockwise direction, as shown in Figure D-30**

    The hints are set in the beginning shape in the first frame. Next, you position the hints in the same location on the ending shape in the ending frame.

TROUBLE

If the shape hints are not visible on the Stage, click View on the Application bar, then click Show Shape Hints.

5. **Click frame 62, drag hint d to the upper-right corner of the "E", then drag the remaining hints so they resemble Figure D-31**

    At first, the hints in frame 62 are stacked on top of each other in the middle of the object in the order in which they were created. When you move them close to their corresponding location in the starting shape, they snap into position and turn green, indicating that they are placed properly.

6. **Test the movie, then compare your screen to Figure D-32**

    The shape tween is much cleaner because you placed the shape hints on the areas you want Flash to preserve.

7. **Save the document, then exit Flash**

FIGURE D-30: Positioning shape hints on the starting shape

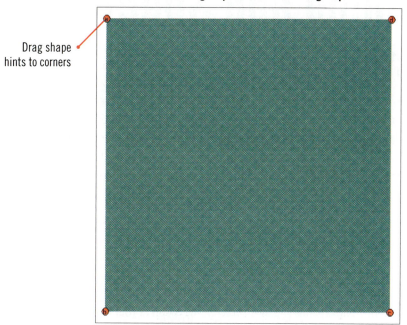

Drag shape
hints to corners

FIGURE D-31: Positioned shape hints on the ending shape

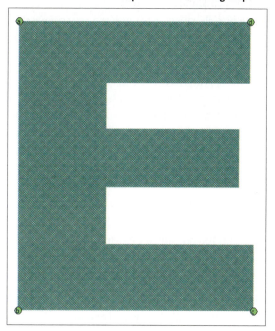

FIGURE D-32: Improved shape tween

Planning and Specializing Animation

Many features in Flash help you organize your graphic and other media elements so you can work as efficiently as possible. Your most important tool, however, is a storyboard, your main planning document for any project. Flash provides increasingly sophisticated special effects and animation techniques. Masking allows you to hide all or part of an object or text, and you can use the Bone tool to create organic motion using hinged movement. 🎨 To ensure the current GreenWinds Eco-Cruise project is well-prepared for future enhancements, you review storyboarding and additional types of effects and animation.

Planning and sophisticated effects include the following:

QUICK TIP

A quick way to determine if you need to remove or redo a scene on your storyboard is if you cannot determine what is going on in the scene without reading the storyboard panel's caption.

• ### Planning movies with storyboards

A successful animation is planned, and using a storyboard can be a great planning tool. A **storyboard** is a visual script containing captions you use to describe the action in your movie. Basic storyboards should provide an organizational and page-level view. A good storyboard uses panels to map out the sequence and major action points and events of the animation. Often, each panel in a storyboard correlates to a keyframe in the animation, although it is also important to note transitions, sequencing and timing, navigation, images, text, audio, placement of Stage elements, and interactivity.

A storyboard can be elaborately drawn or just a very simple sketch, as shown in Figure D-33. One benefit of creating a storyboard for any length of animation is that you and your clients can clearly see the beginning, middle, and end of the sequence, so you can correct or tweak it ahead of time.

QUICK TIP

To unmask layers, right-click (Win) or [control]-click (Mac) the mask layer, then click Mask to deselect it, or in the Layer Properties dialog box, click Normal.

• ### Creating a mask

For a special transition or special effect that uses the shape of one object to reveal content in another shape, you can create a **mask**, where you use the shape of an object on one layer to expose the content of the layer directly beneath it. To do so, you first add content to the layer that will be revealed by the mask—the masked layer. Next, create a shape on a new layer through which content will be viewed—the mask layer. Select a shape tool without a stroke, create the shape, right-click (Win) or [control]-click (Mac) the layer name, then click Mask. Figure D-34 shows a layer being masked and the result of the mask. Flash automatically creates the mask and locks the mask layer 🔲 and the masked layer 🔳.

You can also select layers as the mask or masked layers by opening the Layer Properties dialog box from the Modify, Timeline menu. You can animate either the mask or masked layers. Animating the mask layer has the effect of a shape moving over and exposing different areas of the masked layer. Animating the masked layer changes the content visible within the mask layer shape.

QUICK TIP

In the Spring section of the Properties panel, you increase the Strength to increase rigidity and increase the Damping to increase the speed at the end of the movement.

• ### Animating using the Bone tool

The Bone tool allows you to create **inverse kinematics (IK)**, a way to create animated poses by attaching bone segments that have natural movement. You first draw or import one or more objects, convert the objects to a symbol, and then use the Bone tool to click and draw hinged segments in the object(s). Each segment acts like a joint, which you can then arrange in a motion, such as walking. As you move one joint, other segments respond. Once you create the bone segments, Flash creates a new layer, known as an Armature or pose layer, which you can then animate using a motion tween. Adjusting the configuration of the joints in each keyframe is known as creating a **pose**.

You can use controls in the Properties panel to apply organic movement effects either to the IK as a whole or to individual segments of the IK. To adjust the IK as whole, select a frame, then adjust the easing in or out using the Strength setting. You can also apply preset easing from the Type list. To adjust a segment, click a frame, then click a segment in the IK. Figure D-35 shows a simple shape as it was created with bones and then posed.

FIGURE D-33: Sample storyboard

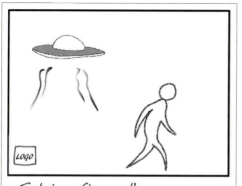 

Fade in as figure walks unaware
Saucer glides in fast from left

Saucer hovers briefly, then flies off in
a fast blur to top-right corner

FIGURE D-34: Creating a mask

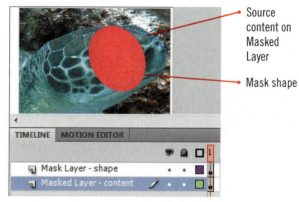

Source content on Masked Layer

Mask shape

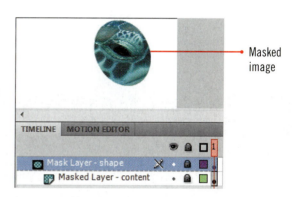

Masked image

FIGURE D-35: Viewing Inverse Kinematics animated objects

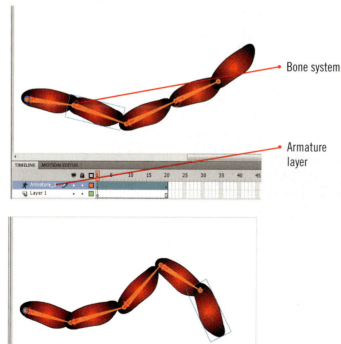

Bone system

Armature layer

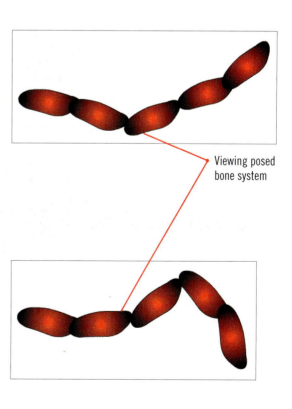

Viewing posed bone system

Practice

Concepts Review

For current SAM information, including versions and content details, visit SAM Central (http://www.cengage.com/samcentral). If you have a SAM user profile, you may have access to hands-on instruction, practice, and assessment of the skills covered in this unit. Since various versions of SAM are supported throughout the life of this text, check with your instructor for the correct instructions and URL/Web site for accessing assignments.

Label the elements of the Flash screen shown in Figure D-36.

FIGURE D-36

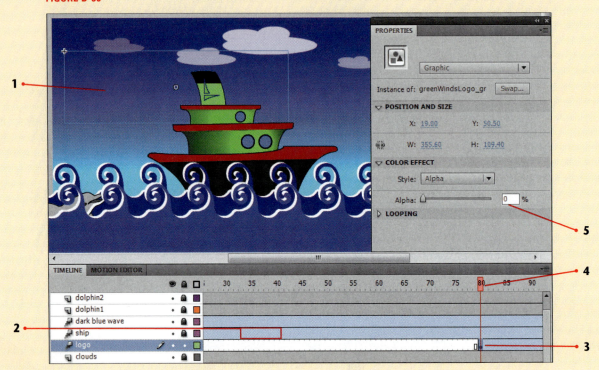

1. _____
2. _____
3. _____
4. _____
5. _____

Match each term with the statement that best describes it.

6. Shape hint
7. Storyboard
8. Nested symbol
9. Frame-by-frame animation
10. Motion tween
11. Property keyframe

a. Offers the most control when creating every frame in an animation
b. A marker used to tell Flash how to morph one shape into another
c. A symbol placed in another symbol
d. Shows a change in color, position, or size
e. Sketches used to show major action frames in a movie
f. Shows movement or transformation changes in an animation

Select the best answer from the list of choices.

12. Which animation method does not use symbols?

    a. Motion tween   **c.** Frame-by-frame

    b. Shape tween   **d.** Classic tween

13. What is the main difference between a keyframe and a blank keyframe?

    a. Whether the frame contains artwork   **c.** Whether the frame contains animation

    b. The color of the tween span   **d.** Whether the object is a symbol or a shape

14. Which of the following is *not* associated with changes in a motion tween?

    a. Transparency   **c.** Shape hints

    b. Tint   **d.** Location

15. Which easing value shows an object starting fast and ending slowly?

    a. 0   **c.** No value

    b. –100   **d.** 100

16. Which of the following is probably true if an object fades out in a movie?

    a. The alpha setting is 0 in the last blank keyframe.   **c.** The alpha setting is 0 in the last keyframe.

    b. The alpha setting is 100 in the last blank keyframe.   **d.** The alpha setting is 100 in the last keyframe.

Skills Review

1. Understand animation.

    a. Describe the role keyframes play in an animation.

    b. Explain the difference between frame-by-frame animation and tweened animation.

    c. Describe the difference between a motion tween and a shape tween.

2. Use frames.

    a. Start Flash, open the file FL D-4.fla from the location where you store your Data Files, then save it as **LightFootRecycling_animation.fla**.

    b. Unlock the newspaper layer, then extend the frame span of the newspaper layer, using a keyboard key, to frame 120.

    c. Reduce the frame span of the newspaper layer back to frame 100, then lock the layer.

3. Create a motion tween and a motion path.

    a. Unlock the title layer, click frame 1 in the title layer, drag an instance of the title_gr symbol to the Stage, then set the X value to **–372** and the Y value to **38**. (*Hint*: The symbol will be on the Pasteboard.)

    b. Click the title layer's frame span, verify that the title object is selected, create a motion tween, click frame 1, select the instance, then set the alpha setting to **0**.

    c. Insert a keyframe in frame 24 of the title layer, select the instance, set the alpha to **100**, then set the X value to **153**.

    d. Scrub the playhead over the frames.

    e. Test the movie, lock the title layer, then save the document.

4. Copy a motion path.

    a. Unlock the plastic bottle 1 layer and the plastic bottle 2 layer.

    b. Click the frame span in the plastic bottle 2 layer, then copy the motion.

FIGURE D-37

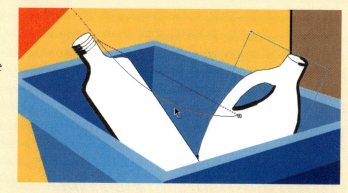

    c. Click the frame span in the plastic bottle 1 layer, then paste the motion.

    d. Click frame 100 in the plastic bottle 1 layer, click the plastic bottle object, set the Rotate value to **25°**, set the X value to **353**, then set the Y value to **240**.

    e. Using Figure D-37 as a guide, use the Selection tool to adjust the motion path so it dips down slightly.

    f. Test the movie, lock the plastic bottle 2 layer, then save the document.

Skills Review (continued)

5. Use easing.

a. Click the tween span in the plastic bottle 1 layer, set the Ease in value to **–50**, then test the movie.

b. Set the Ease out value to **50**, then test the movie.

c. Set the Ease out value to **10**, then test the movie.

d. Lock the plastic bottle 1 layer, then save the document.

6. Create a movie clip and animate nested symbols.

a. Create a new layer named **arrow movie clip** above the background layer.

b. Create a new movie clip symbol named **symbolArrows_mc**. (*Hint*: Use a command on the Insert menu.)

c. In the symbolArrows_mc editing window, drag an instance of the symbolArrows_gr symbol to the Stage, then set the X value to **0** and the Y value to **0**.

d. Insert a frame in frame 9, click the frame span, then create a motion tween.

e. Click frame 9, select the object on the Stage, then rotate the arrows **100°**. (*Hint*: You can use the Properties panel or the Transform panel.)

f. Scrub the playhead across the Timeline, then return to Scene 1.

g. Click frame 1 in the arrow movie clip layer, then drag an instance of the symbolArrows_mc symbol to the Stage.

h. Set the X value to **80**, set the Y value to **30**, then change the alpha value to **15%**.

i. Test the movie, lock the arrow movie clip layer, then save the document.

7. Create frame-by-frame animation.

a. Unlock the aluminum can layer, then insert a keyframe in frames 82, 88, 94, and 100.

b. Show the Info panel, then set the values shown in Table D-3 for the aluminum can instance.

c. Set the rotate value to **25°** in frame 100.

d. Scrub the playhead across the Timeline. (*Hint*: The motion appears jerky because the animation uses just a few frames. Smooth frame-by-frame animation requires many frames.)

e. Test the movie, lock the aluminum can layer, then save the document.

TABLE D-3: Frame values

frame	X value	Y value
82	151	232
88	181	238
94	274	248
100	320	270

8. Create a shape tween.

a. Unlock the big red arrow layer, click frame 29, then click frame 100 to view the starting and ending shapes.

b. Click the frame span after frame 30 in the big red arrow layer, then create a shape tween.

c. Test the movie, then save the document.

9. Use shape hints.

a. Click frame 30 in the big red arrow layer, then add four shape hints to each corner, starting at the upper-left corner of the rectangle and moving clockwise.

b. Click frame 100 in the same layer, then arrange the shape hints to correspond to their location in frame 30.

c. Scrub the playhead in the Timeline, then lock the big red arrow layer.

d. Save the document, test and watch the movie several times, click Control on the Application bar (Win) or application menu bar (Mac), then click Loop to deselect it, if necessary.

e. Compare your screen to Figure D-38. (*Hint*: The movie clip continues to play.)

f. Close the document, then exit Flash.

FIGURE D-38

Independent Challenge 1

You work at CoasterWoop, an online source of news by, for, and about roller coaster enthusiasts. Your boss would like you to create an animation of a roller coaster for the Web page. You create a movie clip and a frame-by-frame animation for the movie.

a. Start Flash, open the file FL D-5.fla from the location where you store your Data Files, then save it as **CoasterWoop_animation.fla**.

b. In each layer, click frame 35, then insert a frame to extend the movie.

c. Click the pinwheel instance on the Stage, convert it to a movie clip symbol named **pinWheel_mc**, then edit the symbol.

d. Rename Layer 1 **pinwheel**, create a new layer named **center**, then insert a frame in frame 15 of both layers.

e. Click the frame span in the pinwheel layer, then create a motion tween.

f. In the Rotation section of the Properties panel, set the Rotation count to **5**, set Additional Rotation to **30°**, set the Direction to **CW**, then scrub the playhead in the Timeline.

g. Click frame 1 in the center layer, drag an instance of the circle_gr symbol to the middle of the pinwheel, then return to Scene 1.

FIGURE D-39

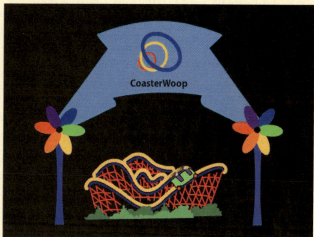

h. Create a copy of the pinWheel_mc instance on the Stage, show guides, drag it on top of the blue pedestal on the right, then hide guides.

i. Select the car instance on the Stage, click frame 1, zoom in as needed, then create frame-by-frame animation every three frames. Move the car along the bottom yellow path to the top of the rail on the right. Rotate the car when appropriate.

j. Click the frame span, then set the ease out to **100**.

k. Test the movie, compare your screen to Figure D-39, save and close the document, then exit Flash.

Independent Challenge 2

As the new program director at Lingoroots, an educational Web site specializing in linguistics, you're constantly looking for exciting ways to engage new visitors. For the next Web site feature, you'll compare the evolution of written Chinese across its 4000-year history. The earliest written Chinese characters were pictures and evolved to a more stylized and artistic writing form. You want to show how Chinese calligraphy has changed over time. You complete a movie showing just a few accomplishments of Chinese culture as it relates to Chinese calligraphy.

a. Start Flash, open the file FL D-6.fla from the location where you store your Data Files, then save it as **lingoroots_animation.fla**.

b. Unlock the calligraphy title text layer, click the title instance on the Pasteboard (above the Stage), open the Motion Presets panel, open the Default Presets folder, scroll down, click fly-in-top, then click Apply at the bottom of the panel. (*Hint*: Open the Motion Presets panel from the Window menu. The Apply button may not change color.)

c. Click frame 24 in the calligraphy title text layer, click the title instance on the Stage, then set the Y value to **53**.

d. Click frame 105 in the calligraphy title text layer, insert a frame, lock the layer, then test the movie.

e. Unlock the 510 Block Txt layer, click its frame span between frames 55 and 68, then create a motion tween.

f. Click frame 55, click the Block-book printing instance on the Stage, then set the alpha to **0**.

g. Click frame 67, use the Transform panel to set the scale to **130**, click the instance on the Stage, set the alpha to **100**, set the X value to **170**, set the Y value to **288**, then lock the layer. (*Hint*: Make sure the Constrain icon is locked on the Transform panel.)

h. Unlock the 510 layer, create a motion tween in frames 50 to 60, click frame 59, set the scale to **218**, set the X value to **236**, set the Y value to **299**, lock the layer, then test the movie.

Independent Challenge 2 (continued)

i. Unlock the moon characters layer, zoom in the Stage, create a shape tween in frames 81 to 96, scrub the playhead over the frames, then lock the layer.

j. Unlock the mountain characters layer, create a shape tween in frames 76 to 90, scrub the playhead over the frames, then test the movie.

k. Click frame 76 in the mountain characters layer, use Figure D-40 as a guide, add three shape hints, then position them as shown in the figure.

l. Click frame 90, move the shape hints to their corresponding positions in the current character, then scrub the playhead over the frames. (*Hint*: The shape hints will turn green as they snap into position.)

m. Test the movie, compare your screen to Figure D-41, then lock all layers.

Advanced Challenge Exercise

■ Create a new layer named **frame-by-frame animation** above the background layer, then create the frame-by-frame animation of your choice in the movie. Adjust the animation as needed.

n. Save and close the document.

o. Exit Flash.

FIGURE D-40

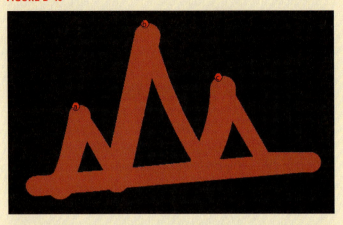

FIGURE D-41

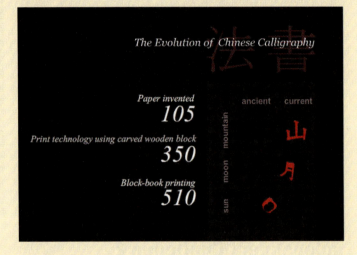

Independent Challenge 3

You work for ibRobotz, an online entertainment site. Users can download ibRobotz characters or create their own to insert in stories. You've been assigned to develop a character for younger users, which you have built using Flash drawing tools. Now you apply animations to the characters.

a. Start Flash, open the file FL D-7.fla from the location where you store your Data Files, then save it as **ibrobotz_animation.fla**.

b. Click the frame span for the itzyBOTZ layer, open the Motion Presets panel, scroll down, click wave, click Apply at the bottom of the panel, then scrub the playhead over the frames.

c. Place the pointer over frame 70 in the itzyBOTZ layer, drag the ending frame to frame 60, then test the movie.

d. Click the ibROBOTZ leg layer, create a shape tween in frames 1 to 30, then test the movie.

e. Create the motion tween or frame-by-frame animation of your choice for the itzaBug_gr instance. Adjust the motion tween as needed.

f. Select the picture_gr instance on the Stage, convert it to a movie clip symbol (give it a unique name), then open the edit symbol Document window.

g. Create a new layer named **shape**, then insert a frame in frame 20 of both layers.

h. Click frame 1 in the shape layer, create one or more shapes of your choice in the artwork, insert a keyframe in the last frame, modify the shapes, then create a shape tween. Add another keyframe in the shape tween span, modify the shapes, then test the movie. (*Hint*: If you use two or more shapes, you must transform them as a group.)

Independent Challenge 3 (continued)

i. Test the movie, compare your screen to Figure D-42 (your shapes will differ), then lock all layers.

Advanced Challenge Exercise

■ Add at least two additional shape tween, motion tween, or frame-by-frame animations to the movie. Copy or create shapes or symbols on new layers as needed. Adjust the animations as needed.

j. Save and close the document, then exit Flash.

Real Life Independent Challenge

This Independent Challenge will continue to build on the personal Web site that you created in Unit C. Here, you animate shapes and symbols.

a. Start Flash, open the file myproject.fla, then save it as **myproject_animation.fla**.

b. Create at least two shape tweens out of shapes or text. (*Hint*: If you use text, you must break it apart twice.)

c. Create at least one motion tween and one frame-by-frame animation. Adjust the animations as needed.

d. Check your document for proper alignment and design consistency.

e. Save and close the document myproject_animation.fla, then exit Flash.

Visual Workshop

Visiting Web sites is a great way to get inspired for your own projects. Figure D-43 shows a scene from an early animation, *Gertie on tour*. View the animation at the Library of Congress, http://memory.loc.gov/ammem/oahtml/animatTitles01.html. Click the [Gertie on tour - excerpts] link, click the viewing format best suited to your Internet connection speed, then answer the following questions. For each question, include why or how you reached a conclusion. You can open a word processor or use the Text tool in Flash to complete this exercise. When you are finished, write down the URL of the Web page you selected in Step d, add your name to the document, save it, print it, then close the word processor or exit Flash. Please check with your instructor for assignment submission instructions.

    a. Identify a few frames that appear to be keyframes.

    b. Which parts of the animation would you tweak using Flash techniques?

    c. Considering that the movie is 1 minute 22 seconds long at 24 fps, there are 1,968 hand-drawn frames in this movie. Would you have pursued a career as a tweener? What is your overall impression of the animation? How does it hold up over nearly 100 years?

    d. Go to one of the following Web sites, then answer the following questions about one of the sites you viewed. Be sure to look for sections or links dedicated to Flash sites.
- www.dopeawards.com
- www.thefwa.com
- www.coolwebawards.com/?go=Nothing_but_flash

    e. Who is the target audience? How does the design (look and feel) of the Web site and animation fit the target audience?

    f. Looking at the animation on the home page:
- What is animated on this page? Can you guess the kind of animation used?
- How many animations occur simultaneously?

    g. Close your browser.

FIGURE D-43

Optimizing and Publishing a Movie

After you finish designing your Flash movies, you can publish them in several formats. The format you choose should suit your project goals. For most Flash projects, you will want to publish the movie to the Web. Remember that no matter how informative or entertaining your movie might be, viewers won't stick around to watch it if they have to wait too long for the movie to load in their browser. Fortunately, Flash provides several ways of optimizing elements in your movie that reduce loading time while preserving quality. In addition to publishing the entire movie in different formats, you can export a single frame from a movie and save it in an image file format. Your boss, Vanessa, asks you to review concepts for making the GreenWinds movie accessible, as well as optimize images in the movie, publish it in different formats, and export an image file from a single frame.

OBJECTIVES

Make Flash content accessible

Optimize a movie

Understand publish settings

Publish a movie for the Web

Create and export a publish profile

Export a QuickTime movie

Create a projector file

Export image files

Making Flash Content Accessible

Flash movies containing rich media content are compelling because of their dynamic visual and auditory appeal. However, those same components can limit the user experience of those with physical challenges such as visual, hearing, or mobility limitations, or those with cognitive disabilities. Flash movies should be compatible with standard **assistive technologies**, which are used by individuals with disabilities that allows them to interact with the document or perform tasks they might not otherwise be able to do. Creating Flash movies that are accessible reaches more users in your target audience and complies with federal standards. Vanessa wants to make sure the ad can reach as many potential customers as possible. She asks you to familiarize yourself with the basics of creating accessible content.

DETAILS

Building in accessibility in a Flash document involves the following:

QUICK TIP

Assistive technologies provide captioning of video and audio content.

- **Incorporate principles of accessible design**
  - Flexibility—Build a user interface that users can customize based on their needs and preferences.
  - Choice of input technique—Make common tasks accessible by keyboard or simple mouse access.
  - Choice of output methods—Allow users to choose alternate outputs of sound, visuals, text, and graphics.
  - Consistency—Ensure the interaction between the Flash content and other applications is consistent and predicable.
  - Compatibility with assistive technology accessibility aids—Build content using standard and common user interface elements that are compatible with accessibility aids, such as screen readers, voice synthesizers, captioning, mouse-free navigation, keyboard commands, magnifier, large text, and so on. Figure E-1 shows the U.S. Department of Education Web page on standards and design requirements for assistive technology.

- **Use Flash features to build in accessibility**

  You can use the Accessibility panel, shown in Figure E-2, to prepare individual elements such as dynamic and input text, buttons, and movie clips, or apply accessibility features to an entire Flash application so that a screen reader responds when users navigate the interface. For example, when you label Flash elements by giving them an instance name on the Properties panel, screen readers provide blind users with a descriptive text equivalent for all nontext elements, such as audio, video, graphics, animation, buttons, and image maps. Adobe.com provides Flash designers and builders extensive support and guidelines for creating accessible content. Figure E-3 shows an overview of best practices from Adobe.com.

QUICK TIP

Some features, such as advanced antialiasing, should not be used for fonts larger than 48 points. Text equivalents replace the visual image, just as alt text provides a text equivalent describing the functionality

  - Control the reading order of labeled contents, reduce the file size, apply ActionScript to direct the reading order, or copy a version of the content and place it offstage in an easy-to-read column.
  - Include scalable graphics and magnification so users can zoom in on rich media content without losing quality. Add synchronized narrative audio for large blocks of text.
  - Apply video control skins that support closed-captioning and are easy to see and use. Allow users to control motion.
  - Create customized color swatches with high-contrast color palettes. Users should not have to rely on color alone to interact with content.
  - Make looping elements such as movie clips or movies inaccessible. Screen readers will respond to the movie playing and will start reading at the top of the page.
  - Build in keyboard controls so that users can navigate rich media content using mouse-free navigation.
  - Select text based on size requirements. Antialiased text has smoother edges, which is preferred when you need to show text at small sizes. In contrast, antialiased text that is animated is more difficult to read; the Flash Player can turn off antialiasing when text is animated.

QUICK TIP

in Web pages when the user points to or places the mouse over an image or tool.

FIGURE E-1: Assistive Technology Web page

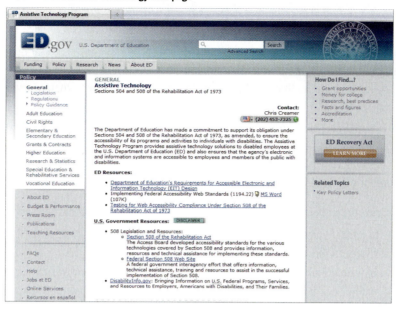

FIGURE E-2: Accessibility panel

Delivers accessibility information to a screen reader

For movie clips; ensures that nested symbol information is delivered to screen reader

Tells Flash to automatically label buttons with nearby text

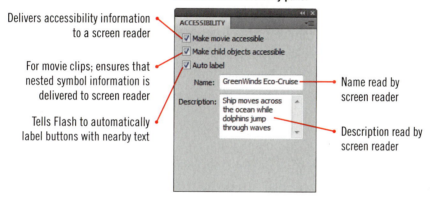

Name read by screen reader

Description read by screen reader

FIGURE E-3: Accessibility best practices Web page

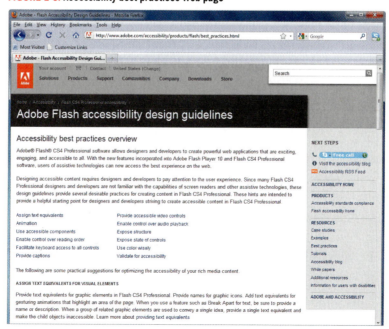

Optimizing a Movie

UNIT
E
Flash CS5

As you create and modify shapes for your movies, you add data to the file. Larger files need more processing power and slow down the time it takes for your movie to display objects correctly in a browser. Shapes with gradient fills and shapes that you have transformed and edited with many curves can take an exceptionally long time to load. So before you publish your movie for use on the Web, you should optimize your Flash movie file. When you **optimize** a file, you modify file attributes to eliminate bottlenecks in a given frame during downloading. Your goal is to ensure the movie plays well regardless of the user's Internet connection speed. 🎨 Vanessa has enhanced the fills of some objects. You replace the gradient fill for the sky and dolphin symbols with a solid color, and optimize a shape to reduce file size.

STEPS

1. **Start Flash, open the file FL E-1.fla from the location where you store your Data Files, save it as GreenWinds_publish.fla, then test the movie**

   The sky, dolphin, and ship symbols contain a gradient fill. You begin by removing the gradient from the sky symbol.

   > **TROUBLE**
   > You may need to scroll down to see the sky layer in the Timeline.

2. **Unlock the sky layer in the Timeline, click the Selection tool ▸ on the Tools panel, then double-click the sky instance on the Stage to open the edit window**

   In the edit window, you can see the various blue colors that make up the gradient, as shown in Figure E-4.

3. **Show the Properties panel if necessary, click the Fill color icon 🖉 ▬, click the hexadecimal text box, type #0033FF, press [Enter] (Win) or [return] (Mac), return to the main movie, then lock the sky layer**

   The shape color changes to a solid blue, eliminating the need for Flash to store the intermediary blue colors. You decide to keep the green gradient in the ship, so next you remove the gray gradient in the dolphins. One of the dolphin instances is hidden on the Stage, so to save time unlocking layers, you edit the dolphin symbol from the Library panel.

4. **Show the Library panel, click the dolphin_gr symbol, then double-click the thumbnail in the preview window to open the edit window**

5. **Click the gray dolphin fill, show the Properties panel, click 🖉 ▬, click the hexadecimal text box, type #999999, press [Enter] (Win) or [return] (Mac), then return to the main movie**

   The dolphins are now a solid gray color. Next, you want to optimize the cloud shape used in the shape tween. You can reduce the number of lines and points in the beginning shape by eliminating some of the curves.

6. **Unlock the cloud shape tween layer, click frame 1, select the cloud shape on the Stage if necessary, click Modify on the Application bar, point to Shape, then click Optimize**

   The Optimize Curves dialog box opens, as shown in Figure E-5. You can reduce the number of curves in the shape and view optimization results.

   > **QUICK TIP**
   > Select the Preview check box to view the changes to the shape.

7. **Drag the Optimization Strength value to 100, make sure the Show totals message check box is selected, then click OK**

   An Adobe Flash CS5 (Win) dialog box opens, as shown in Figure E-6, showing how many curves remain and the percentage reduction it achieved. Ideally, the changes do not affect the shape's appearance. It's good practice to optimize each shape in a shape tween, so you optimize the ending shape in the last frame.

8. **Click OK to close the Adobe Flash CS5 dialog box, click frame 147 in the cloud shape tween layer, select the final cloud shape on the Stage, click Modify on the Application bar, point to Shape, click Optimize, repeat Step 7, then close the Adobe Flash CS5 dialog box**

   You optimized the ending shape.

9. **Lock the cloud shape tween layer, test the movie, then save the document**

Optimizing and Publishing a Movie

FIGURE E-4: Viewing a gradient fill in a shape

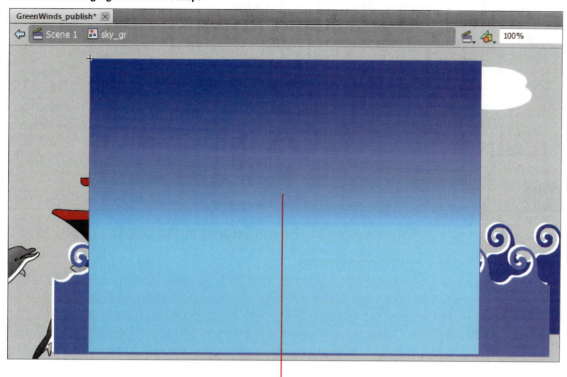

Gradient consists of many
shades of blue

FIGURE E-5: Optimize Curves dialog box

When selected, Flash will display
optimization results

Click to deselect and view
original shape

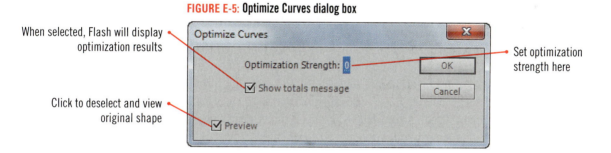

Set optimization
strength here

FIGURE E-6: Viewing shape optimization results

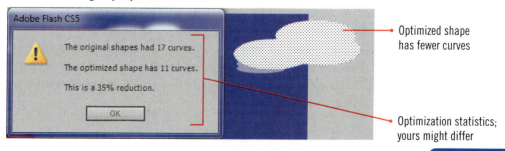

Optimized shape
has fewer curves

Optimization statistics;
yours might differ

Understanding Publish Settings

After you optimize a movie file, you are ready to publish it so users can view it on a Web page. When you **publish** your movie, you instruct Flash to create the files necessary to display it on the Web or to use it in other situations. You use the Publish Settings dialog box to choose the desired file format. ▨▨▨ Before adjusting settings for the GreenWinds Eco-Cruise project, you review the different types of publish settings and their associated file formats so you can explain them to Vanessa.

DETAILS

When you publish files using the Publish Settings dialog box, you can:

- **Choose output movie formats**

   You select file formats for your movie on the Formats tab of the Publish Settings dialog box, as shown in Figure E-7. On the left, you select the file formats you want to publish, and on the right, you specify the file name and location Flash will use to publish each file. To change the name of the file, click the text box to the right of the file format you selected, and edit the text. To change the destination for the published files, click the Select Publish Destination button to the right of the selected file format, then navigate to the location you want.

   When you first open the Publish Settings dialog box, the Flash (.swf) and HTML (.html) formats are selected by default. You learned earlier that SWF files are the output file format for Flash movies. An HTML document houses the SWF file and specifies other browser settings so you can view it on the Web.

   Each format you select has its own tab in the Publish Settings dialog box, where you can adjust settings specific to that format.

QUICK TIP
You can export an image with limited adjustable settings by clicking File on the Application bar, pointing to Export, clicking Export Image, then selecting a format. However, the Publish Settings dialog box gives you maximum control when creating still image files.

- **Choose still image file formats**

   In addition to default SWF and HTML formats, you can select additional formats described below to create a static image from a frame in a movie. You can use a static image file in other marketing pieces or when you want to go over the main points of a movie but viewing it isn't practical. When you choose a static image format, a tab with that format name appears in the Publish Settings dialog box, enabling you to refine settings for that format. Figure E-8 compares an image in GIF, JPEG, and PNG file formats, which are compressed bitmap formats.

   - **GIF (Graphics Interchange Format)** is best for creating drawings and line art. GIF files have limited image quality but can support transparency. On the GIF tab, you have the option to publish a static GIF or an animated GIF. **Animated GIFs** support simple animation, such as short sequences that repeat in clip art, and **emoticons**, symbolic facial expressions or moods, used in online chat programs, blogs, and e-mail.
   - **JPEG (Joint Photographic Experts Group)** is a versatile and popular file format for photographs and gradients. JPEGs are used extensively for optimizing images for the Web because they maintain their image quality even when they are highly compressed.
   - **PNG (Portable Network Graphics)** file format supports higher-resolution images and transparency. PNG is the native file format in Adobe Fireworks. When you publish in PNG format, the file does not include the background color.

- **Choose stand-alone file formats**

   If you want to distribute your movie to users who may not have Flash Player, you can create a projector file. A **projector** is a stand-alone application that plays a movie without using a computer's browser software or (for Flash projectors) Flash Player. You can play projector files from a desktop, CD, or DVD. Because projector files contain all the data needed to run the movie, they are significantly larger than SWF files.

FIGURE E-7: Publish Settings dialog box

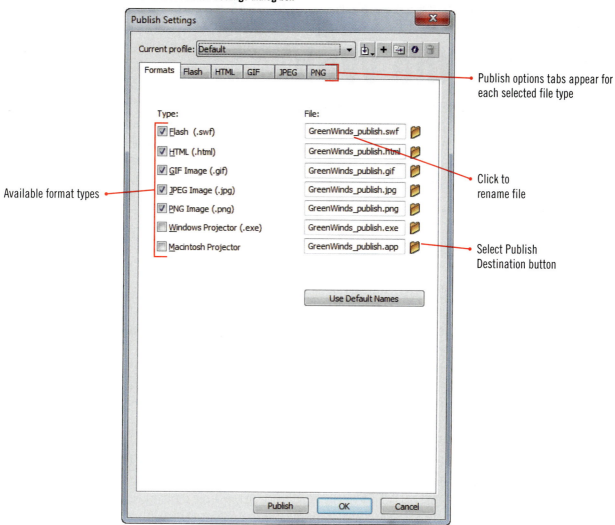

Publish options tabs appear for each selected file type

Available format types

Click to rename file

Select Publish Destination button

FIGURE E-8: Comparing image file formats

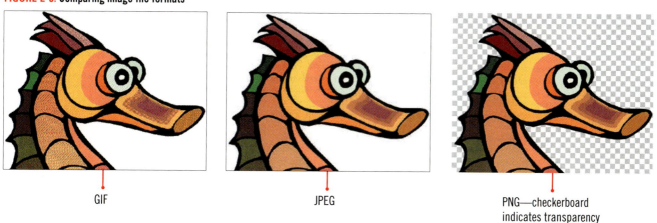

GIF

JPEG

PNG—checkerboard indicates transparency

Publishing a Movie for the Web

When you publish a movie, you prepare your Flash file in the format and with appropriate settings for use on the Web. Flash makes it easy to publish your movie. You open the Publish Settings dialog box, adjust the settings, then publish the movie. Most of the default settings in the Publish Settings dialog box make this process seamless. 🎨 Vanessa wants you to publish the GreenWinds movie for the Web, so you open the Publish Settings dialog box and adjust settings on the Flash and HTML tabs.

STEPS

QUICK TIP
You can also press [Ctrl][Shift][F12] (Win) or [option] [Shift][F12] (Mac) to open the Publish Settings dialog box.

1. **Make sure the GreenWinds_publish.fla document is open, click File on the Application bar, then click Publish Settings**

   The Publish Settings dialog box opens with the Flash and HTML format types selected by default. You can adjust settings specific to each file format on the Flash and HTML tabs. You decide to adjust the quality setting for JPEG images on the Flash tab.

2. **Click the Flash tab, drag the JPEG quality slider ⬚ until the Quality text box reads 65, then compare your dialog box to Figure E-9**

   Options on the Flash tab adjust settings in the SWF file. The JPEG quality setting affects the image quality—and size—of bitmap images in your document. In general, values between 80 and 100 create higher-quality images. For a smaller file size with often-adequate image quality, try setting the quality value between 50 and 79. You may have to experiment with different settings until you find the right balance. The default settings for the remaining options on the Flash tab are appropriate for the GreenWinds movie.

QUICK TIP
You can also select the Loop check box to have the movie play continuously.

3. **Click the HTML tab, click the Detect Flash Version check box to select it, then compare your dialog box to Figure E-10**

   Options on the HTML tab specify how the movie appears in the browser. Selecting the Detect Flash Version check box tells Flash to prompt users to update their version of Flash Player if necessary to view content in the SWF file. You can set the movie's dimensions so it matches the Stage size, is a fixed pixel width in the monitor, or is sized based on a percentage of the monitor's size. Next, you publish the movie and view the files Flash creates.

QUICK TIP
To view your movie in a browser from Flash quickly, click File on the Application bar, point to Publish Preview, then click HTML. Flash uses the last settings selected in the Publish Settings dialog box, so HTML must be selected.

4. **Click Publish, when the Publishing dialog box closes, click OK to close the Publish Settings dialog box, open the file management utility for your computer, navigate to where you store your Data Files, then compare your window to Figure E-11**

   Flash creates the files you selected: an HTML file and an SWF file. It also generates the swfobject.js file, a small JavaScript file that detects if the correct version of Flash Player is installed. **JavaScript** is a programming language used to add interactive and dynamic features in Web pages. The HTML file inserts the Flash content in the browser. Vanessa wants to see how the movie looks on the Web, so you open the HTML file.

5. **Double-click GreenWinds_publish.html, watch the movie, allow blocked content if prompted, then close your browser**

   The movie plays in the browser.

6. **Return to Flash and save the document**

Understanding publish profiles

The process of importing and exporting Flash profiles is a little different from importing and exporting files in other programs. When Flash exports a profile, it transfers the data contained in the profile, but not the profile name that appeared in the Current profile list when you created it. When you (or another user) import a profile, Flash prompts you to replace the current profile with the data in the import profile, but the name of the profile does not update to the import profile file name, which can be confusing.

FIGURE E-9: Viewing publish settings on the Flash tab

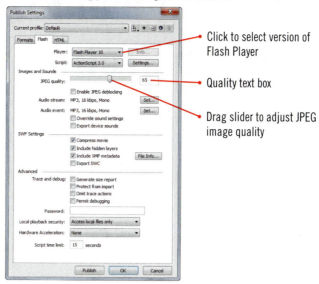

Click to select version of Flash Player

Quality text box

Drag slider to adjust JPEG image quality

FIGURE E-10: Viewing publish settings on the HTML tab

Click to prompt user to upgrade Flash Player

When selected, movie will play continuously

Click OK to save the settings and publish the movie at a later time

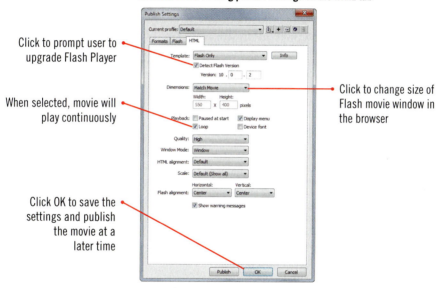

Click to change size of Flash movie window in the browser

FIGURE E-11: Viewing published files (Win)

Macintosh window will differ

Your path might differ

Your browser icon might differ

Detects current version of Flash Player

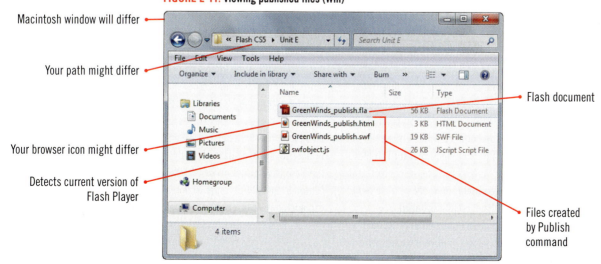

Flash document

Files created by Publish command

Optimizing and Publishing a Movie

Creating and Exporting a Publish Profile

When you adjust settings in the Publish Settings dialog box and click Publish or OK, Flash automatically saves the file setting information you specified in the document. You can make these publish settings available for use in other documents by creating a publish profile and then exporting it. A **publish profile** is a file in XML format that Flash creates and then uses when it exports data. Once you have created a publish profile, you can apply it to other movies by importing it, without having to re-create all the publish settings. This can streamline the process you use to create multiple movie files with the same settings. 🎨 You want to be able to reuse the GreenWinds project publish settings, so you create and export a publish profile.

STEPS

1. **Click File on the Application bar, then click Publish Settings**

   The Default profile appears as the Current profile at the top of the dialog box.

2. **Click the Create new profile button ⊞ at the top of the dialog box**

   The Create New Profile dialog box opens, as shown in Figure E-12. You give the current profile a unique name.

3. **Verify that the text is selected in the text box, type GreenWinds1 in the Profile name text box, then click OK**

   "GreenWinds1" appears as the current profile name in the dialog box. To be able to use the profile in other documents, you export it.

QUICK TIP
You can rename the profile in the dialog box if you wish.

4. **Click the Import/export profile button 🔁, click Export, navigate to where you store your Data Files, type GreenWinds1.xml in the Save As text box (Mac), then compare your dialog box to Figure E-13**

   The Export Profile dialog box opens, and the currently selected profile name, GreenWinds1.xml, appears in the File name text box (Win) or Save As text box (Mac). The profile has an .xml extension, indicating that it is an **XML (eXtensible Markup Language)** file, an Internet file format similar to HTML that describes information and data.

5. **Click Save to close the Export Profile dialog box, click OK to close the Publish Settings dialog box, then save the document**

   Flash exports the profile. Colleagues working on the GreenWinds project can now import it after Vanessa provides them with the file location.

6. **Navigate to where you store your Data Files, then verify that the XML file is present**

   You won't need to view the XML file contents.

Creating XML files and XMP metadata

XML files store and transport data in a format accessible by other programs. The XML format allows others to build, modify, and collaborate on projects using shared files by adding **tags** that describe the data; it is an uncompressed version of an FLA file. You can edit individual elements of a project in Flash, then save the file as an XFL file. XFL is also a default file format for FLA files that incorporates XML. Flash automatically creates a series of XML files for project elements. Advanced users can modify an element directly in the XML file—without having Flash installed.

You can embed additional data into a published SWF file, such as digital photograph, video, or audio settings, copyright status, editing history, and other descriptive content. For example, as others work in the file, their changes can be reflected in the XMP data. Adobe uses the **eXtensible Metadata Platform (XMP)** format, which is metadata able to be indexed by search engines (thus improving the file's placement in search results) and is also viewable in Adobe Bridge. To add XMP data, open the Publish Settings dialog box, click the Flash (*.swf) check box, click the Flash tab, then click the File Info button in the SWF Settings section. A dialog box opens, where you can add content in a dozen categories.

FIGURE E-12: Creating a publish profile

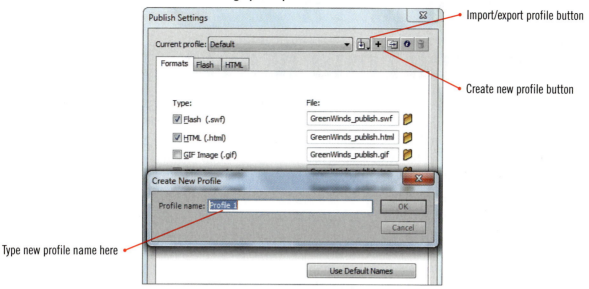

Import/export profile button

Create new profile button

Type new profile name here

FIGURE E-13: Exporting a profile

Macintosh Finder will differ

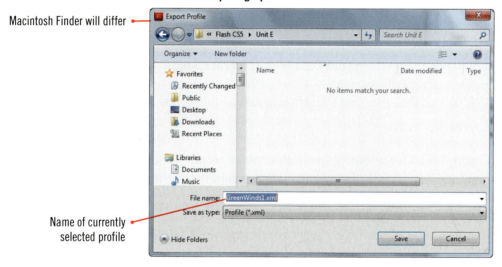

Name of currently
selected profile

Understanding Flash Player options and mobile phones

On the HTML tab in the Publish Settings dialog box, you can choose which version of Flash Player will play a movie. By default, in Flash CS5, the latest version of Flash Player, version 10, is selected as the player. Each version of Flash Player supports the features in the Flash version for which it was created. So, the Flash Player 10 supports the features of Flash CS5 and previous versions, but the Flash Player 9 (tied to Flash CS3) does not support the new features unique to Flash CS4 and higher. Be aware that if you select a previous version of the Flash Player in the Player list, features from later versions of Flash will not work properly or at all when users play the movie. Other player options are Adobe AIR, which is for desktop applications and mobile devices. You can use Adobe AIR to create applications for mobile phones. In Adobe AIR,

you can use FLV video files as source files, which allows the video to be embedded, streamed, or downloaded progressively. Video is discussed further in Unit G. Note that SWF files contain metadata, which can be as simple as a title and description. Search engines can "read" metadata, which allows your work to appear in search results. On mobile phones, SWF metadata control frame rate, size, background color, and other attributes.

To create an application for the iPhone, you can select the iPhone OS template from the Welcome Screen or New Document dialog box. You can also save an existing document for the iPhone in the Publish Settings dialog box. First, deselect the HTML check box on the Formats tab, then on the Flash tab, click the Player list arrow, then click iPhone OS.

Exporting a QuickTime Movie

Flash lets you export Flash projects to other popular movie formats so you can expand the ways users can access your movie. **QuickTime** is a popular export format because QuickTime movies play animation well, and play on both Macintosh and PC computers. QuickTime software comes standard with the Apple operating system, but Windows users who want to play movies in this format may need to download the free QuickTime plug-in from www.apple.com. In addition to creating an SWF file, Vanessa wants you to create a QuickTime movie of the GreenWinds animation. You do this by exporting the Flash document as a QuickTime movie.

STEPS

🛑 *This lesson requires that you have the latest version of the QuickTime Player installed on your computer. If you install QuickTime now, you may need to restart the Flash program and reopen the GreenWinds_publish.fla file.*

1. **Click File on the Application bar, point to Export, then click Export Movie**

   The Export Movie dialog box opens. You select QuickTime as the export format.

2. **Click the Save as type list arrow (Win) or Format list arrow (Mac), then click QuickTime (*.mov) (Win) or QuickTime (Mac)**

> **QUICK TIP**
> To customize additional QuickTime settings for the movie, click the QuickTime Settings button.

3. **Navigate to where you store your Data Files, then click Save**

   The QuickTime Export Settings dialog box opens, as shown in Figure E-14, where you can select QuickTime options. If you select the Ignore stage color (generate alpha channel) check box, the Stage color will become transparent. Other options allow you to determine when the movie stops exporting, and where to store temporary data needed to play the movie. The default settings are acceptable, so you're ready to export the movie.

4. **Click Export, wait a few moments as Flash exports, records, and compresses the movie into the QuickTime format, then when Flash has completed the export, compare your screen to Figure E-15**

   Flash alerts you that the QuickTime export is finished, and that it generated a text report listing how QuickTime captured each frame in the animation. Once you have exported a file, it's a good idea to view it.

> **TROUBLE**
> File associations can vary; if your file doesn't open in QuickTime, return to your Data File location, right-click the GreenWinds_ publish.mov file, click Open With, then click Quick-Time Player.

5. **Click OK to close the Adobe Flash CS5 dialog box, navigate to where you store your Data Files, double-click GreenWinds_publish.mov to open it in the QuickTime Player, then click the Play button ▶**

   The movie plays in the QuickTime Player, as shown in Figure E-16. Notice in your file management utility that the size of the QuickTime movie is much larger than the SWF movie.

6. **Close the QuickTime Player, then save the document**

FIGURE E-14: QuickTime Export Settings dialog box

Select to export a transparent background

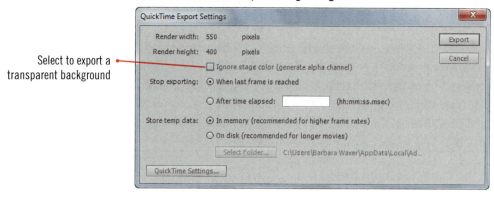

FIGURE E-15: Viewing results of QuickTime export

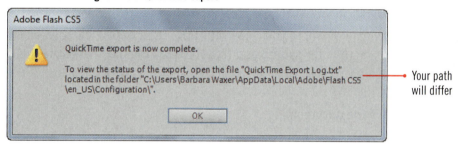

Your path will differ

FIGURE E-16: Playing a QuickTime movie (Win)

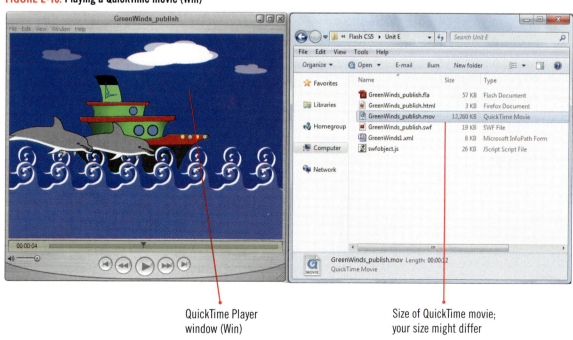

QuickTime Player window (Win)

Size of QuickTime movie; your size might differ

Optimizing and Publishing a Movie

Creating a Projector File

A projector file is a stand-alone, self-running application that lets users play a Flash movie on a computer that does not have browser software or Flash Player installed. Projector files differ by platform; you cannot run a Windows projector on a Mac, or vice versa. Table E-1 lists all the export formats you can select. 🎨 Vanessa tells you that GreenWinds wants a version of the animation that can play on both Macs and PCs, without the need for additional software. You publish a projector file for both platforms.

STEPS

QUICK TIP

If you click the Flash (.swf) check box first, Flash deselects both the Flash and HTML check boxes.

1. **Open the Publish Settings dialog box**

2. **On the Formats tab, click the Flash (.swf) and HTML (.html) check boxes to deselect them, click the Windows Projector (.exe) check box, then click the Macintosh Projector check box**

   Because the projector file generates the necessary code and files to play the SWF file in the Flash Player, you only need to select the Projector check boxes. You can publish both projector files from either a PC or a Mac, but you can only open the one associated with your computer's platform. See Figure E-17.

3. **Click Publish, then when the Publishing dialog box closes, click OK to close the Publish Settings dialog box**

TROUBLE

Mac projector files export to a folder on a PC.

4. **Navigate to where you store your Data Files, double-click GreenWinds_publish.exe (Win) or GreenWinds_publish.app (Mac) to play the file, then close the Flash Player window**

   The movie plays in Flash Player. Notice in your file management utility that the projector file is much larger than the SWF file, as shown in Figure E-18.

5. **Save the document**

TABLE E-1: Export formats

format	extension	Win and Mac	Win only	Mac only
Adobe Illustrator Sequence and Image	.ai	√		
Animated GIF, Image, and Sequence	.gif	√		
DXF Sequence and AutoCad image	.dxf	√		
Encapsulated Postscript (EPS) 3.0 w/Preview	.eps	√		
JPEG Sequence	.jpg	√		
PNG Sequence and Image	.png	√		
QuickTime	.mov	√		
SWF Movie	.swf	√		
Bitmap Sequence	.bmp		√	
EMF Sequence and Image	.emf		√	
WAV Audio	.wav		√	
WMF Sequence	.wmf		√	
Windows AVI	.avi		√	
PICT Sequence	.pct			√

FIGURE E-17: Selecting projector formats

Click to select projectors

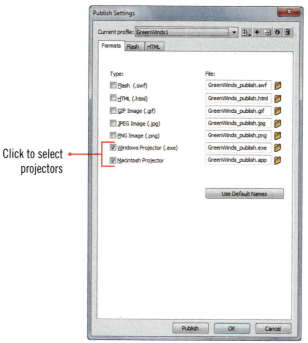

FIGURE E-18: Playing a Windows or Macintosh projector file

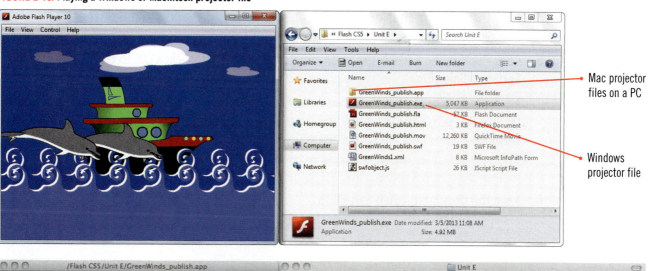

Mac projector files on a PC

Windows projector file

Mac projector file

Exporting Image Files

If you want to create a static image from your movie, you can export a scene from a single frame or simply export an object to insert in a Web page. You can select three image file formats for export: GIF, JPEG, and PNG. 🎨 Vanessa has learned that the client would like some static images from the GreenWinds animation, but you're not sure exactly how the client wants to use them. To provide the most flexibility, you export a frame in three file types.

1. **Drag the playhead to frame 100 in the Timeline to export the selected frame as an image**

2. **Open the Publish Settings dialog box, deselect the projector check boxes, then select only the GIF Image (.gif), JPEG Image (.jpg), and PNG Image (.png) check boxes**

   A tab containing options for each graphic type appears to the right of the Formats tab.

> **QUICK TIP**
>
> Generally, an animated GIF file works best with simple graphics and motion.

3. **Click the GIF tab, examine the options, then compare your dialog box to Figure E-19**

   GIF options focus on color, but they also offer the possibility of exporting an animated GIF file. You can also select whether you want areas of the image to be transparent. The default options are acceptable, so next you view the options for JPEG files.

4. **Click the JPEG tab, examine the options, then compare your dialog box to Figure E-20**

   In addition to size and quality options, you can select Progressive, which will load the JPEG image incrementally in a browser. Users will see the image gradually improve as it loads, instead of seeing nothing until the entire image appears. The default options are acceptable, so you view the options for PNG files.

> **TROUBLE**
>
> Flash publishes PNG files with a transparent background even if you select a background color in the Flash document.

5. **Click the PNG tab, then examine the options**

   Many PNG options are similar to GIF options. The default options are acceptable, so you're ready to publish.

6. **Click Publish, then when the Publishing dialog box closes, click OK to close the Publish Settings dialog box**

7. **Navigate to where you store your Data Files, right-click GreenWinds_publish.gif, point to Open with, select the program you want to preview the images with, close your viewer window, then repeat for GreenWinds_publish.jpg, and GreenWinds_publish.png**

   Notice the differences among the images, as shown in Figure E-21. Although PNG files support transparency, the blue background is visible in the PNG file because it is a shape in the Flash document.

8. **Save the document, then exit Flash**

Optimizing and testing a Flash movie

In general, the key to optimization is balancing file size and download time against image quality, but there are no set rules to follow. Optimization is more of an art than an exact formula. There are many steps you can take to reduce file size; however, which actions and how many actions you take vary depending on your movie contents. Some simple optimization steps you can take include the following:

- Reduce the frame rate.
- Use symbols.
- Optimize and resize bitmap images before importing them.
- Replace gradient fills with solid colors.
- Use alpha transparency sparingly.
- Use tween animation instead of frame-by-frame animation.

- Compress sound files.
- Use solid lines created with the Pencil tool.

   For more advanced options that perform a technical test of your movie, you can simulate the download experience users might have using the Download Settings and Simulate Download commands on the View menu in the Flash Player. To view a graphical representation of each frame's download time, open the Bandwidth Profiler from the View menu. Here you can view how much content loads in each frame. To further analyze movie data, open the Publish Settings dialog box, click the Flash tab, click the Generate size report check box, click Publish, then open the .txt report file. The report lists the size of each frame, shape, text, sound, video, and ActionScript script by frame.

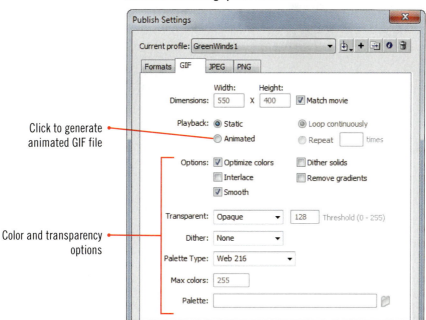

Click to generate animated GIF file

Color and transparency options

FIGURE E-20: Viewing options on the JPEG tab

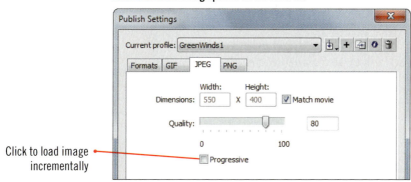

Click to load image incrementally

FIGURE E-21: Viewing GIF, JPEG, and PNG image files

GIF   JPEG   PNG

Practice

Concepts Review

For current SAM information, including versions and content details, visit SAM Central (http://www.cengage.com/samcentral). If you have a SAM user profile, you may have access to hands-on instruction, practice, and assessment of the skills covered in this unit. Since various versions of SAM are supported throughout the life of this text, check with your instructor for the correct instructions and URL/Web site for accessing assignments.

Label the elements of the Flash screen shown in Figure E-22.

FIGURE E-22

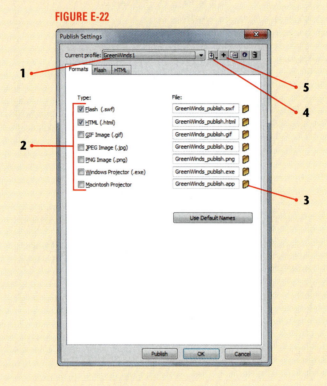

1. _____
2. _____
3. _____
4. _____
5. _____

Match each term with the statement that best describes it.

6. **Projector file**
7. **Publish profile**
8. **Gradient**
9. **QuickTime movie**
10. **Optimize**
11. **PNG**

a. Two or more colors that blend together in a pattern
b. Stand-alone application that can play a Flash movie
c. To reduce file size while maintaining quality
d. Publish settings saved in an XML file
e. Image file format that can support transparency and high quality
f. Export option that creates an animation file playable on both a Mac and PC

Select the best answer from the list of choices.

12. Which of the following is not an extension of a static image file format?

a. .xml

b. .gif

c. .png

d. .jpg

13. Which are the default file types for publishing a movie to the Web?

a. XML and MOV

b. HTML and XML

c. SWF and HTML

d. SWF and MOV

14. Which of the following is necessary to run a projector?

a. Web browser

b. Flash Player

c. Computer

d. CD or DVD

15. Where can you adjust settings for an HTML file?

a. Browser

b. Publish Settings dialog box

c. Publish destination dialog box

d. Save dialog box

16. Which of the following is *not* an available format you can publish using Flash?

a. MOV

b. EXE or APP

c. JPG

d. MP3

Skills Review

1. Make Flash content accessible.

a. Explain how assistive technologies can help you reach more users.

b. List the three items for which a screen reader can provide a text equivalent.

c. Explain one way you could achieve mouse-free navigation.

2. Optimize a movie.

a. Start Flash, open the file FL E-2.fla from the location where you store your Data Files, test the movie, then save it as **LightFootRecycling_publish.fla**.

b. Change the frame rate in the Timeline to **12 fps**.

c. Unlock the background layer, select the diamond shape behind the bags, change the alpha to **100%**, then lock the layer.

d. Unlock the arrow movie clip layer, select the arrows instance on the Stage, then change the alpha to **100%**.

e. Open the symbolArrows_mc edit window, then double-click the symbol to open the symbolArrows_gr edit window.

f. Select the three arrows, if necessary, click the Fill Color icon on the Properties panel, click the hexadecimal text box, then change the color to **#FFD300** in the color pop-up window.

g. Return to the main movie, lock the layer, then move the arrow movie clip layer to the bottom of the Timeline.

h. Test the movie, then save the document.

3. Understand publish settings.

a. Describe the relationship between an SWF file and an HTML file.

b. List the three image file formats you can use to publish an image, and describe what they publish.

c. Explain how you could use a projector file.

4. Publish a movie for the Web.

a. Use a command on the File menu to open the Publish Settings dialog box.

b. Show the Flash tab, then set the JPEG quality to **60**.

c. Show the HTML tab, select the Detect Flash Version check box, publish the movie, then close the Publish Settings dialog box.

d. Navigate to where you store your Data Files, then view the LightFootRecycling_publish.html file in a browser.

e. Close your browser, then save the document.

5. Create and export a Publish profile.

a. Open the Publish Settings dialog box.

b. Use the Create new profile button to create a new profile named **Lightfoot1**.

c. Use the Import/export profile button to export the profile to where you store your Data Files.

    d. Close the Publish Settings dialog box, then save the document.

    e. Verify that the .xml file was created and stored in your Data Files location.

6. Export a QuickTime movie.

    a. Use a command on the File menu to open the Export Movie dialog box.

    b. Select QuickTime as the export type, navigate to where you store your Data Files, then click Save.

    c. Export the QuickTime movie using the default settings, then close the Adobe Flash CS5 dialog box.

    d. Navigate to where you store your Data Files, then play the QuickTime movie.

    e. Close the QuickTime Player, then save the document.

7. Create a projector file.

    a. Open the Publish Settings dialog box.

    b. Select only the projector check boxes, publish the movie, then close the Publish Settings dialog box.

    c. Navigate to where you store your Data Files, then play the projector file applicable to your operating system.

    d. Close Flash Player, then save the document.

8. Export image files.

    a. Drag the playhead to frame 100.

    b. Open the Publish Settings dialog box.

    c. Select only the GIF, JPEG, and PNG check boxes.

    d. Change the JPEG quality to **100**.

    e. Publish the images, then close the Publish Settings dialog box.

    f. Navigate to where you store your Data Files, preview the image files, compare your screens to Figure E-23, then close the viewer windows. (*Hint*: The background will be transparent in the PNG file.)

    g. Save and close the document, then exit Flash.

FIGURE E-23

Independent Challenge 1

You work at CoasterWoop, an online source of news by, for, and about roller coaster enthusiasts. You've animated and enhanced the appearance of several objects in the movie. Now your boss asks that you optimize the movie as much as possible and export static image files from a frame in the movie.

    a. Start Flash, open the file FL E-3.fla from the location where you store your Data Files, then save it as **CoasterWoop_publish.fla**.

    b. Test the movie, then change the frame rate to **12 fps**.

    c. Unlock the entrance layer, then open the sign_gr symbol in an edit window.

    d. Select the sign shape, change the color to **#00CBFF**, return to the main movie, then lock the entrance layer.

    e. Unlock the background layer, then select the rounded shape on the lower half of the Stage.

    f. Change the color of the shape fill to **#000066**, lock the background layer, then test the movie.

    g. Open the Publish Settings dialog box, select the FLASH and HTML check boxes if necessary, show the HTML tab, click the Dimensions list arrow, click Percent, type **40** in the Width and Height text boxes, then publish the movie.

Independent Challenge 1 (continued)

h. Navigate to where you store your Data Files, then view the CoasterWoop_publish.html file in a browser.

i. Export a QuickTime movie using default settings, then play the QuickTime movie.

j. Use the Publish Settings dialog box to publish a JPEG image of frame 30 using the default settings, view the JPEG file, compare your screen to Figure E-24, then close the view window.

k. Save and close the document, then exit Flash.

FIGURE E-24

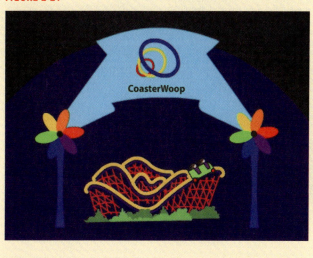

Independent Challenge 2

As the new Program Director at Lingoroots, an educational Web site specializing in linguistics, you're constantly looking for exciting ways to engage new visitors. For the next Web site feature, you'll compare the evolution of written Chinese across its 4,000-year history. The earliest written Chinese characters were pictures and evolved to a more stylized and artistic writing form. You want to show how Chinese calligraphy has changed over time. You completed a movie showing just a few accomplishments of Chinese culture and Chinese calligraphy, but now you want to optimize it so the greatest number of users can view it regardless of their computer or platform.

a. Start Flash, open the file FL E-4.fla from the location where you store your Data Files, then save it as **lingoroots_publish.fla**.

b. Unlock the calligraphy title text layer, click frame 1, click the instance in the Pasteboard above the Stage to select it, set the alpha to **100%**, then lock the layer.

c. Unlock the background layer, double-click the large Chinese characters to open the Group edit window, then select the characters. (*Hint*: Use the Selection tool to draw a selection box around the characters.)

d. Open the Fill color pop-up window, set the alpha to **100** and the color to **#660000**, then return to the main movie.

e. Select the rectangle on the Stage, open the Fill color pop-up window, set the alpha to **100** and the color to **#330000**, then lock the background layer.

f. Unlock the text layer, shift-click to select the five text boxes next to and above the Chinese characters on the rectangle on the Stage, set the font Style to Regular, open the Text (fill) color pop-up window, set the alpha to **100**, set the color to **#CCCCCC**, then lock the text layer.

g. Open the Publish Settings dialog box, select the Flash and HTML check boxes if necessary, publish the movie, then close the Publish Settings dialog box.

h. Navigate to where you store your Data Files, view the lingoroots_publish.html file in a browser, then close the browser.

i. Use the Publish Settings dialog box to publish a GIF image of frame 89, view the GIF file, compare your screen to Figure E-25, then close the view window.

j. Use the Publish Settings dialog box to publish a projector for the computer platform you use, navigate to the location where you store your Data Files, play the projector file, then close the Flash Player.

k. Save the document.

FIGURE E-25

Independent Challenge 2 (continued)

Advanced Challenge Exercise

- Publish a JPEG image of the frame of your choice, then preview the image file. Experiment with different quality settings until you find the lowest setting that generates an acceptable image. (*Hint*: Unless you save the JPEG with a unique name, Flash replaces the JPEG file each time you publish it.)
- Create a publish profile named **lingoroots_JPEG**, then export the profile to the location where you store your Data Files.

l. Close the document, then exit Flash.

Independent Challenge 3

You work for ibRobotz, an online entertainment site. Users can download ibRobotz characters or create their own to insert in stories. You've been assigned to optimize the movie, create a version that will play on a DVD, and publish image files users can download to their computers.

a. Start Flash, open the file FL E-5.fla from the location where you store your Data Files, then save it as **ibrobotz_publish.fla**.

b. Test the movie, then change the frame rate to **12 fps**.

c. Unlock the furnishings layer, double-click a stem instance to open an edit window, then select the stem. (*Hint*: Zoom in as needed.)

d. Using the Optimize command on the Modify, Shape menu, set the Optimization strength to **100** in the Optimize Curves dialog box, then click OK.

e. Note the number of fewer curves and the percentage of curve reduction, then return to the main movie.

f. Double-click the flower pot instance to open a symbol edit window, double-click the bottom of the pot to open the Drawing Object edit window, then click the bottom pot object to select it.

g. Set the color in the Fill color pop-up window to **#FF6532**, then return to the flowerpot_gr edit window.

h. Double-click the pot rim object to open a Drawing Object edit window, click the pot rim object to select it, set the color in the Fill color pop-up window to **#FEB998**, return to the main movie, then lock the furnishings layer. (*Hint*: You won't see the color change until you return to the main movie.)

i. Publish the movie to the Web using default settings, view the HTML file in a browser, then close the browser.

j. Publish a GIF image of the frame of your choice using default settings, view the image, compare your image to the sample shown Figure E-26, then close the view window.

FIGURE E-26

Independent Challenge 3 (continued)

k. Keep the same frame selected, open the Publish Settings dialog box, select JPEG as the format, on the Formats tab, change the JPEG file name to **ibrobotz_publish_JPEG60.jpg**, on the JPEG tab, set the JPEG quality to **60**, then publish the image. (*Hint*: On the Formats tab, click the file name in the text box, then type changes.)

l. Change the quality to **100**, change the JPEG file name to **ibrobotz_publish_JPEG100.jpg** on the Formats tab, then publish the image and close the Publish Settings dialog box.

m. Compare the three images, then save the document.

Advanced Challenge Exercise

- Export two publish profiles named **ibrobotz_JPEG60ACE.xml** and **ibrobotz_JPEG100ACE.xml**, respectively, to your Data File location for the JPEG images you created in Step k and Step l above. (*Hint*: Reset the quality settings as needed.)

n. Close the document, then exit Flash.

Real Life Independent Challenge

This Independent Challenge will continue to build on the personal Web site that you have been developing since Unit B. Here, you optimize the movie, and publish and export files.

a. Start Flash, open the file myproject.fla, then save it as **myproject_publish.fla**.

b. Use the skills you learned in this unit to optimize the frame rate, tweens, curves, and colors in your movie. Test the movie.

c. Publish the movie to the Web, adjusting settings as needed.

d. Publish at least one frame in the file format of your choice, adjusting settings as needed.

e. Create a projector or QuickTime movie.

f. Generate a size report of the movie. (*Hint*: Look in the Advanced section of the Flash tab in the Publish Settings dialog box.)

g. Deselect all objects, open the Accessibility panel from the Window menu, then add a name and description for the movie on the panel.

h. Open the report from the file management utility, read it, then close the file.

i. Save and close the document myproject_publish.fla, then exit Flash.

Visual Workshop

Visiting Web sites is a great way to get inspired for your own projects. Figure E-27 shows the home page for NASA's Global Climate Change Web site. View the page at http://climate.nasa.gov/. Click several items on the page, then answer the following questions. For each question, include why or how you reached a conclusion. You can open a word processor or use the Text tool in Flash to complete this exercise. When you are finished, add your name to the document, save it, print it, then close the word processor or exit Flash. Please check with your instructor for assignment submission instructions.

a. What is the Web site's purpose and goal?

b. Who is the target audience? How does the design (look and feel) of the Web site fit the target audience?

c. Did the site indicate which version of Flash Player users needed?

d. Which components of the animation would you optimize?

e. How many viewing formats were available? Could you download a movie? If so, how large was it?

f. Looking at the animation in the introduction and on the home page:
- What is animated on this page? Can you guess the kind of animation used?
- How many animations occur simultaneously?
- What is your overall opinion of the design, organization, and function of this page? How would you improve it?

g. Close your browser.

FIGURE E-27

Courtesy NASA/JPL-Caltech

Creating Buttons and Using Media

Files You Will Need:

FL F-1.fla
eel.flv
FL F-2.fla
recycle.flv
FL F-3.fla
FL F-4.fla
FL F-5.fla
robot.flv

Creating a button is an easy way to add interactivity to a Flash project. Buttons provide users with a way to navigate around your site or control a movie within it. Buttons can also act as design elements that add visual interest to your site. As you've probably noticed in your own Web surfing, a button often changes appearance based on the mouse action you've performed. For example, navigation bar buttons can change color or move when you move the mouse pointer over them, and you can use Flash to incorporate such actions into your design. Flash lets you create a button from any graphic or text. You can also enhance your users' experience by adding sound and video to your movie. Management at GreenWinds Eco-Cruise wants to make the movie interactive for users. Your boss, Vanessa, suggests you create a button that controls action in the movie. You begin by creating a button that changes appearance and plays a sound. Later, you add video to create a simple movie.

OBJECTIVES

Understand buttons and states

Create a button symbol

Edit button states

Add text to a button

Understand sound

Add sound to a button

Understand video

Add video to a movie

Understanding Buttons and States

When you create a button and convert it to a symbol, it can become a basic building block for adding interactivity to your Flash movies. **Interactivity** occurs when an element in a Web page responds to a user's mouse pointer action, such as pointing to (known as **rolling over** or **hovering**) or clicking a button. You can use buttons to let users play or stop a movie, or to move to another frame in the Timeline where something else occurs. Before adding a button to the GreenWinds movie, you verify your understanding of buttons.

Review the following important facts about buttons:

- #### Understanding button symbols and states

  Buttons start out as graphics, text, or even movie clips that you convert to button symbols. Button symbols change appearance based on the user's mouse interaction with them. In Flash, instead of numbered frames, buttons have a unique Timeline with specific frames: Up, Over, Down, and Hit. A button can change appearance in the first three frames, which correspond to user actions and are known as **states**. The last frame, Hit, is where you define the area that will react to the mouse action. The button states are described below and shown in Figure F-1.

  Up—The default state, not affected by any mouse movement.

  Over—The state after the user rolls the mouse pointer over the button.

  Down—The state after the user clicks the button with the mouse pointer.

  Hit area—The active clickable area of the button that corresponds to the button object in either the Over or the Down state.

  You can define the size of the Hit area using a shape or graphic. Although commonly referred to as a state, the Hit frame is never actually visible in the movie. You can think of the Hit state as a hotspot for a button. Figure F-2 shows the Hit area and the button Timeline.

  The Timeline in the button symbol edit window has only four frames, one for each button state. Unlike a regular Timeline, a button does not play by moving through the Timeline automatically. Rather, it jumps to a frame based on the action a user makes with the mouse.

- #### Creating buttons

  To create a button, you must first create a button symbol. When you open the button symbol edit window, Flash places the instance in the Up frame. This is how the button looks normally when the user does not interact with it. How a button changes its appearance in the other states is up to you, the designer. Usually, buttons have at least two states and undergo a transformation in color, size, skew, stroke, or filter effect. You create the button's appearance in the Over and Down states by inserting a keyframe, which copies the original button object in those frames. Then you can alter or transform the object's properties.

  Usually, the Hit area is the same size as the button shape, but this can be difficult for users. For example, if your button consists of small text or is an odd shape, users may have a hard time finding the exact spot that causes Flash to react to their mouse pointer action. To avoid this, you can use a Shape tool to create a larger area in the Hit frame so the response occurs as soon as the user's mouse pointer gets close to the button.

FIGURE F-1: Viewing button states

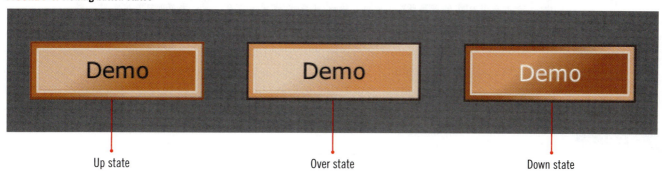

Up state   Over state   Down state

FIGURE F-2: Viewing the Hit state frame in the button Timeline

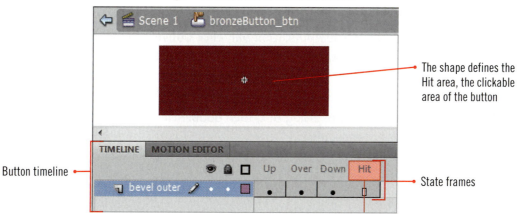

The shape defines the Hit area, the clickable area of the button

Button timeline

State frames

Using invisible buttons

Invisible buttons do not appear to be buttons when you view the movie, but are extremely useful when you want to make an area clickable. Usually, an invisible button only contains a hit area in the Hit frame, although you may add content in the Over frame. By only defining the clickable region, you can place invisible buttons over any graphics. For example, users can click an invisible button on top of a photo of food that then shows a map of local restaurants, or users could roll the mouse over areas on a food image to display callouts describing the ingredients. To create an invisible button, create a new buttons layer on the Timeline, click frame 1, select a shape tool, then create a shape. Next, convert the shape to a button symbol, then double-click the symbol on the Stage to open the button Timeline. Click the Up frame, then drag it to the Hit frame so that the Up, Over, and Down frames are blank, and the Hit frame contains the clickable area. When you test the movie, the pointer changes to an interactivity mouse pointer 🖑, which indicates to users that the object is clickable. Of course, nothing will happen until

you next add ActionScript code to it or add content to the Over frame. In Figure F-3, an invisible button appears as a translucent aqua overlay on the Stage. When you preview the movie and roll the mouse over the invisible button, the content in the Over frame is visible; in this case, a callout to an ingredient in a sushi roll.

FIGURE F-3: Invisible buttons

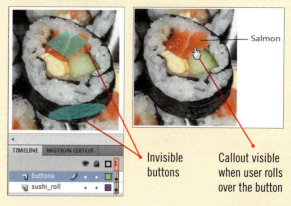

Salmon

Invisible buttons

Callout visible when user rolls over the button

Creating a Button Symbol

You can convert any object into a button symbol. When you add buttons to a movie, you should place all the buttons on a separate button layer at or near the top of the layer's stack in the Timeline. This way, you can easily find all the buttons in your movie because they'll always be in front of other objects in the movie. Vanessa wants you to add a button to the GreenWinds movie that users can click to start the animation. You begin by converting a shape to a button symbol.

1. **Start Flash, open the file FL F-1.fla from the location where you store your Data Files, then save it as GreenWinds_buttons.fla**

   A new layer, buttons, appears at the top of the Timeline. The layer contains a green splash shape in the lower-left corner, which you'll use as the button. The shape is an oval, but has a Stippled style stroke applied to it, which creates the splattered effect.

   QUICK TIP
   Zoom in the Stage as needed through-out this unit.

2. **Make sure the Selection tool is selected on the Tools panel, then drag a selection marquee around the shape to select it**

3. **Click Modify on the Application bar, click Convert to Symbol, type startButton_btn in the Name text box, click the Type list arrow, click Button, click the upper-left square of the registration icon, then compare your screen to Figure F-4**

   The suffix "btn" will help you identify this as a button symbol.

   TROUBLE
   The Stipple stroke option is dynamic; your stroke might vary from frame to frame.

4. **Click OK to close the dialog box, then double-click the button instance on the Stage**

   The button symbol edit window opens, as shown in Figure F-5. The shape is selected on the Stage and the Up frame contains a keyframe. You want to copy the shape and place it in the other frames so you can modify them later.

5. **Click the Over frame in the Timeline, click Insert on the Application bar, point to Timeline, click Keyframe, click the Down frame, click Insert on the Application bar, point to Timeline, then click Keyframe**

   The shape appears in all three frames. You want to increase the size of the clickable area of the button in the Hit frame, so you add a blank keyframe to the Hit frame before creating a shape.

6. **Click the Hit frame in the Timeline, click Insert on the Application bar, point to Timeline, then click Blank Keyframe**

   Because you inserted a blank keyframe, there is nothing on the Stage in the Hit frame. You want to create a Hit area that is not limited by the shape's configuration, so you first set properties for the Rectangle tool.

   QUICK TIP
   When drawing a shape for the Hit area, it's a good idea to select a color you haven't used in the rest of the movie so you can easily identify it.

7. **Click the Rectangle tool on the Tools panel, show the Properties panel if necessary, set the Stroke color to the No Color icon, then set the Fill color to #FFFE65**

   Not being able to see the space you need to cover makes it difficult to draw a precise Hit area. You can remedy this by turning on the onion skin feature to view a preview of the previous frame, the Down frame, where the shape is visible. **Onion skinning** displays frames before or after the current frame so you can see the content. In animation, this helps you fine-tune the action. In the button Timeline, it allows you to see exactly where to draw the Hit area.

8. **Click the Onion Skin button at the bottom of the Timeline to turn on onion skinning**

   An outline of the shape is visible in the Hit frame. Now you can draw the Hit area accurately.

   QUICK TIP
   If you do not create a Hit area, Flash will use the shape in the Up frame as the Hit area.

9. **Click and drag a rectangle that covers the shape, as shown in Figure F-6, release the mouse button, click to turn off onion skinning, then save the document**

   The yellow rectangle is the Hit area that covers the button shape. The button will respond when the user rolls the mouse over the area defined by the yellow rectangle.

FIGURE F-4: Creating a button symbol

Selected shape and stroke

Buttons layer at the top of the Timeline

In Step 3, click this square

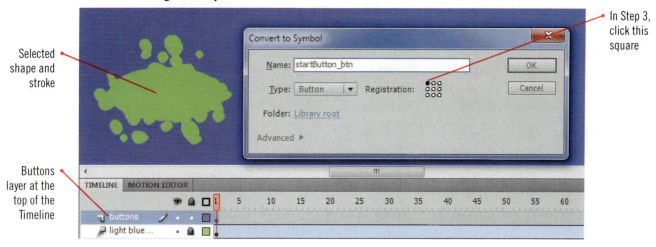

FIGURE F-5: Viewing the button symbol edit window

Shape appears in the Up frame

Frames in the button Timeline

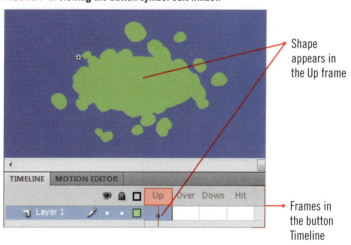

FIGURE F-6: Creating a Hit area

Onion skinning shows content from previous frames

Rectangular Hit area covers shape

Frames selected for onion skinning

Onion Skin button

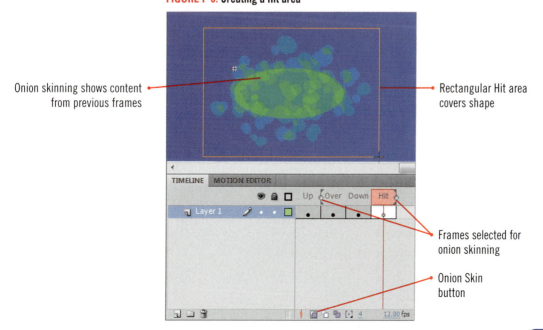

Creating Buttons and Using Media

Editing Button States

Working with button instances is different from working with other symbols because the button symbol Timeline is specific to the different button states. If you want the button to change appearance in the Over or the Down state, you modify the instance in those frames. You can test buttons in the Flash Player or on the Stage. Vanessa wants users to see the Start button change appearance when they move their mouse pointer over it, so you change the stroke color for the Over state and test the button.

1. **Make sure the button symbol's edit window is open, then drag the playhead to the Over frame**

2. **Click the Selection tool ⌘ on the Tools panel, click the stroke instance, then compare your screen to Figure F-7**

   The stroke, which appears as a broad splattered area around the shape, is selected. Next, you change the stroke color.

3. **Show the Properties panel if necessary, set the Stroke color to #00FF66, return to the main movie, then if necessary reset the zoom so you see all of the Stage**

   The button instance has not changed appearance. The button's new stroke color will not be visible until you test the movie and move the mouse over the button.

4. **Test the movie, move the mouse pointer ⌘ over the button until it changes to the interactivity mouse pointer ⌘, click and hold down the mouse button, then repeat for the Hit area near the button**

   When you move the mouse over the Hit area, the stroke color changes to bright green (the Over state). When you click and hold down the mouse button, the shape changes to the Down state, which is the same as its appearance in the Up state, shown in Figure F-8. In both cases, the pointer changes to ⌘, indicating interactivity. At this point, the button changes appearance but doesn't actually do anything in the document. By default, Flash disables button interactivity on the Stage, but you can test buttons directly in Flash, without having to open the Flash Player.

   QUICK TIP
   You can also press [Ctrl][Alt][B] (Win) or [⌘][option][B] (Mac) to turn Enable Simple Buttons on or off.

5. **Close the Flash Player window, click Control on the Application bar, click Enable Simple Buttons, move ⌘ over the button, then click the button**

   The button responds to the mouse just as it did in the Flash Player. When Enable Simple Buttons is selected, you cannot double-click the instance to open the edit window. You deselect the command so you can continue to construct the button.

6. **Click Control on the Application bar, click Enable Simple Buttons to deselect it, then double-click the button instance to open the button symbol edit window**

   The button symbol edit window opens with the Up frame selected.

7. **Save the document**

FIGURE F-7: Modifying an object in the Over state

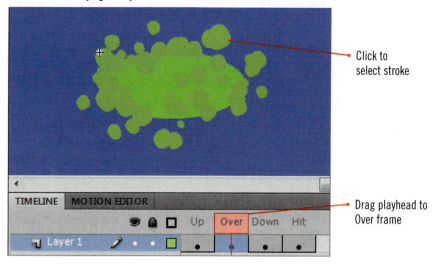

Click to select stroke

Drag playhead to Over frame

FIGURE F-8: Viewing the Up, Over, and Down states

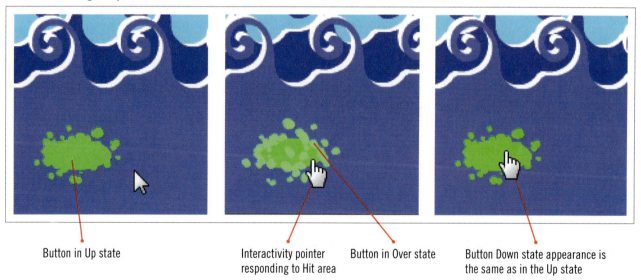

Button in Up state

Interactivity pointer responding to Hit area

Button in Over state

Button Down state appearance is the same as in the Up state

Adding Text to a Button

Text can serve a dual purpose in a button: The text itself can be the button, or you can combine text and a shape to make a button. You can first create an object and text and then convert it to a button symbol, or you can add text later to an existing button in the edit window. 🎨 You want to add text to the Start button instance, then change the text color in the Down state.

STEPS

1. Make sure the button symbol edit window is open, then create a new layer at the top of the Timeline named text

2. Click the Text tool T on the Tools panel, then set the Text engine to Classic Text, the font family to Arial, the font style to Bold, the point size to 12 pt, and the color to black (#000000)

QUICK TIP
Objects in the Hit frame are always invisible on the Stage.

3. Click the shape, type Start, click the Pasteboard, click the Selection tool ▶ on the Tools panel, click the text object, then set the X value to 9.5 and the Y value to 2 in the Position and Size section of the Properties panel

   The text appears on top of the shape, and in the Timeline, the frame range extends through all three state frames, as shown in Figure F-10. When you add a keyframe to the Up or Over frames, you can edit objects in those frames without affecting objects in other states, just like editing an instance doesn't alter the original symbol. When you edit a symbol in the Up frame, Flash updates all instances of the symbol used in the movie except those you've already modified in the Up or Over frames. You want to add a keyframe to the Down frame so you can edit the text.

4. Click the Down frame on the text layer, click Insert on the Application bar, point to Timeline, then click Keyframe

   You want to change the color of the text in its Down state.

5. Click the text on the Stage to select it, then set the text (fill) color to #006600

   The text color changes in the Down frame, as shown in Figure F-11. You need to test the movie to make sure the color changes in its Down state.

6. Test the movie, move the mouse pointer over the Start button, click and hold down the mouse button, then compare your screen to Figure F-12

   The stroke changes color in the Over state, and the text changes color in the Down state.

7. Save the document

Design Matters

Using the Buttons common library

Flash provides several preset buttons and button components in the Buttons common library. To open the library, click Window on the Application bar, point to Common Libraries, then click Buttons. Click an arrow next to a folder to display its contents, then drag a button to the Stage. Flash inserts the symbol or shape in the Library. You can modify the button by opening the button symbol edit window. Many preset buttons have effects applied to them, so the Timeline may contain multiple layers. By default, Flash locks the layers to prevent accidental editing. See Figure F-9 for samples of some Flash preset buttons.

FIGURE F-9: Sample buttons

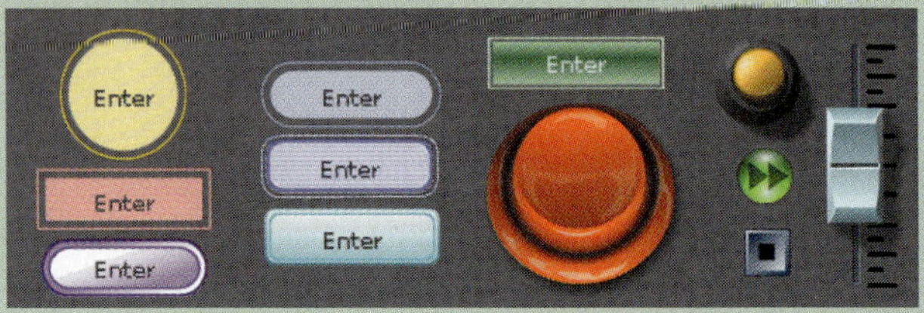

FIGURE F-10: Adding text to a button

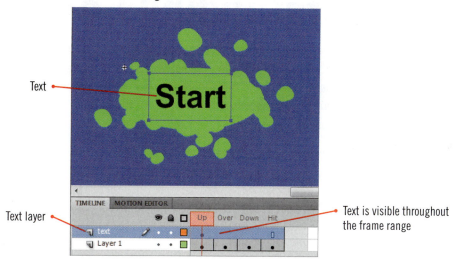

Text

Text layer

Text is visible throughout the frame range

FIGURE F-11: Modifying text in a frame

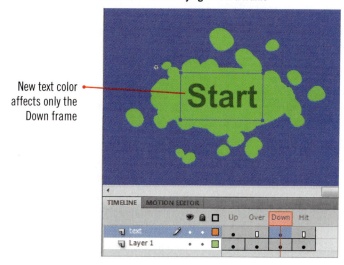

New text color affects only the Down frame

FIGURE F-12: Viewing the button in the Down state

Text in the Down state

Creating Buttons and Using Media

Understanding Sound

Adding sound to a movie can range from a musical sound track playing in the background to adding a sound effect to a button. As with any media, you need to make sure that your sounds improve and complement, rather than detract from and impair, your viewer's overall experience. Vanessa wants to talk to management about how sound can enhance the movie. You review how Flash handles sound so you can brief her before her meeting.

When you use sounds in your movies, you should:

- **Determine the sound's purpose**

  Sounds should be a planned element, just like graphics or animation. Think of how the sound will enhance your message without calling attention to itself and how it will add to the user's experience. Combining too much sound and animation in a movie can distract and even annoy users.

- **Consider the playback environment**

  You also need to think about the location of your users when they play your movie. For example, sounds or music that would be acceptable when heard privately through headphones or ear buds might be inappropriate when played through speakers in an office.

- **Understand how to add sounds**

  Flash lets you use sound in your movies in several different ways. You can have it play continuously, link it to an event or a state in a button, or synchronize it to an animation. You can use sound files in a number of different formats.

  Adding sound to a movie is just like adding any other content; you can import an audio file to the Library or Stage, and then designate the frames in which you want it to play.

  You can reuse a sound clip as often as you like in a movie. Because a sound clip is not visible on the Stage, Flash displays a graphical representation of a sound, known as a **waveform**, in the Library and the Timeline. A monophonic sound (which carries sound in one sound track) has one waveform; stereophonic sound (which carries sound on two sound tracks) has two waveforms. You can preview a sound in the Library by clicking the Play button in the Preview window, which shows the waveform. Figure F-13 shows sound files in the Library.

  It's best to create a separate layer for each sound clip before adding it to the Timeline. This way, you can easily find and edit them, and you won't be distracted by other content on the layer, such as keyframes, animation, and so on. When you add a sound to a layer, the existing frame range may or may not determine how many frames the sound occupies. For example, a short sound may take up only a few frames, whereas a sound longer than the frame range is simply cut off at the last keyframe. Figure F-14 shows sounds on layers in the Timeline (the layer height is increased to better show the waveforms).

- **Understand how to edit sound properties**

  You can add sound and adjust basic sound properties in the Sound section of the Properties panel, shown in Figure F-15. Here you can select an effect such as fading in or out, and you can synchronize the sound to the movie and choose how many times the sound will play. To customize a selected effect, click the Edit sound envelope button next to the Effect list arrow, and then adjust options in the Edit Envelope dialog box.

- **Understand sound import formats**

  You can import several sound formats into Flash movies. Be aware, however, that sound files can be large. It's best to use MP3 files, which compress data but retain sound quality. You can also compress the sound further in the Sound Properties dialog box. Common sound file types for both Windows and Mac are Soundbooth Sound Document (.asnd), MPEG Layer 3 (.mp3), Audio Interchange File Format (.aiff), Waveform (.wav), and others such as QuickTime sound (.mov) if you have QuickTime 4.0 or higher installed on your computer.

FIGURE F-13: Viewing sound waveforms in the Library

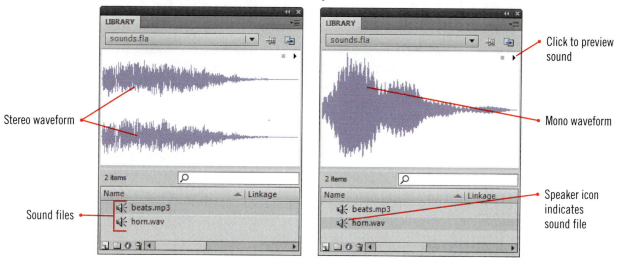

Stereo waveform

Sound files

Click to preview sound

Mono waveform

Speaker icon indicates sound file

FIGURE F-14: Viewing sounds of varying lengths in the Timeline

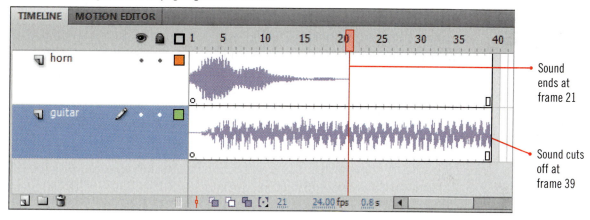

Sound ends at frame 21

Sound cuts off at frame 39

FIGURE F-15: Viewing Sound options on the Properties panel

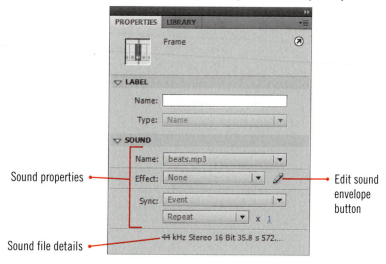

Sound properties

Edit sound envelope button

Sound file details

Adding Sound to a Button

Adding sound to a button is a great way to make it more interactive. Usually, you add sound to the Down frame to reinforce the action to users. GreenWinds may add a voice-over and music to the movie later. For now, Vanessa has imported a sound into the document, and she would like you to add it to the Start button.

STEPS

1. **Make sure the button symbol edit window is open, then create a new layer at the top of the Timeline named sound**

2. **Show the Library, click horn.wav, drag the bottom of the Preview window to expand its size if necessary, then click the Play button ▶ in the Preview window**

   A short horn sound plays. Short sounds are preferable for buttons.

3. **Click the Down frame on the sound layer, click Insert on the Application bar, point to Timeline, then click Blank Keyframe**

   Adding a blank keyframe prepares the frame for content, in this case, a sound object. When you insert sound, it plays by default in its entirety unless you direct it to stop. If a button state contains sound, it will restart and play over itself every time the user initiates the state containing the sound, which could be irritating to the user. You want to insert a short sound that will play when the user clicks the button, so you insert it using the Properties panel.

4. **Show the Properties panel, click the Down frame on the sound layer if necessary, expand the Sound section on the Properties panel if necessary, click the Name list arrow, click horn.wav, then click the Sync list arrow, and verify that Event is selected**

   The sound is inserted in the Down frame of the sound layer, the waveform appears in the Timeline, and the top of the Properties panel indicates a frame is selected, as shown in Figure F-16. The default Sync setting, Event, means that the sound will play when a user clicks the button, so you accept the default settings. Next, you view the waveform in detail by expanding the layer in the Timeline.

5. **Right-click the sound layer name in the Timeline, click Properties, click the Layer height list arrow, compare your dialog box to Figure F-17, click 300%, click OK, then click a blank part of the Stage**

   The waveform is visible in the Timeline, as shown in Figure F-18. You can see that it actually gets louder (larger) as it plays. Although you can preview the sound in the Library, the only way to check out the sound in the movie is to test it.

6. **Return to the main movie, then test the movie and the Start button**

   The horn sound plays when you click the Start button.

7. **Save and close the document**

Design Matters

Understanding MP3 audio compression

The success of MP3 audio is a combination of an excellent compression algorithm and the range and peculiarities of human hearing. The compression algorithm incorporates **psychoacoustics**, the study of how the brain interprets audio, to dramatically reduce the size of sound files. Humans can hear in a range of 20–20,000 hertz (Hz). For comparison, other mammals such as elephants can hear as low as 1 Hz and bats can hear upwards of 120,000 Hz.

Our hearing cannot adapt to hearing a soft or medium sound when a loud sound or sound with a similar frequency plays over it. The softer sound is literally drowned out of existence, like when a plane flies low overhead and you're trying to hear someone talking. The MP3 algorithm drops the sounds that we couldn't hear anyway, which reduces file size.

FIGURE F-16: Inserting sound in a button frame

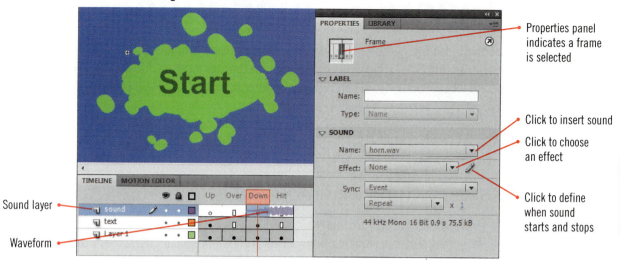

Properties panel indicates a frame is selected

Click to insert sound

Click to choose an effect

Click to define when sound starts and stops

Sound layer

Waveform

FIGURE F-17: Layer Properties dialog box

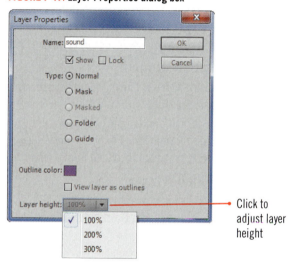

Click to adjust layer height

FIGURE F-18: Viewing the waveform in an expanded layer

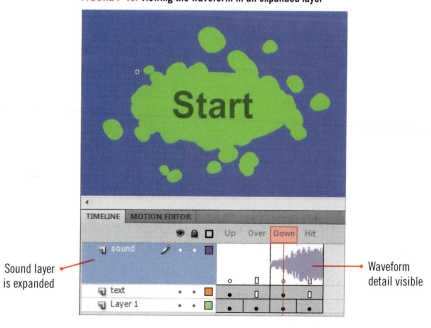

Sound layer is expanded

Waveform detail visible

Understanding Video

Inserting video into a Flash movie requires a few more steps than inserting graphic or sound files. Flash lets you import video into a Flash document, but the files must be in a proper video file format, known as Flash Video. Fortunately, Flash provides an Import Video Wizard you can use to import video step by step. Vanessa will be meeting with the head of the marketing department to discuss adding video to the movie. She asks you to research the use of video in a Flash movie and how to use the Import Video Wizard and Adobe Media Encoder to import a video.

DETAILS

To create a Flash movie with video, you need to:

QUICK TIP

Flash Video formats are .flv, .f4V, and .MP4.

- **Understand video formats**

  When you create a video with a video camera, the file format your camera uses is designed for video-editing software such as Adobe Premiere or Premiere Elements. The files are large, uncompressed, and not designed for viewing on the Internet using any device.

  When you view video posted to the Web, the files already have been converted to a format designed for rapid download or streaming. You've experienced this whenever you watch a video on sites such as YouTube or Hulu; a news site; a **vlog (video blog)**; or a live-streaming event. **Flash Video (FLV)** has become the standard for Web-based video because it compresses data efficiently.

QUICK TIP

You can also add Flash FLV video to a Dreamweaver HTML page, and decide whether to deliver it as a progressive download or streaming video.

- **Add video to a Flash document**

  The process for importing video is fairly straightforward: Obtain a video, convert it to the FLV format, and choose how to integrate the video with your Flash document.

  Depending on the format and length of the source video, even FLV videos can be large. Flash lets you embed a video, which is recommended only for short videos, download it progressively, so users can view it before it fully downloads, or stream the video from a server, which is required for live video.

QUICK TIP

Embedding a video in a Flash movie will significantly increase its file size.

- **Use the Import Video Wizard**

  Open the Import Video dialog box, shown in Figure F-19, from the File, Import, Import Video menu. If the video you want to use is already in a Flash Video format, click Browse to navigate to the location where you store the video, then click Open.

  If the video is not in one of those formats, you'll be prompted to click Launch Adobe Media Encoder at the bottom of the dialog box, then click OK in an information box if prompted. The Adobe Media Encoder sets up the video in the correct video format for Flash. Click the Add button, navigate to the location where you store the source video, click Open, then click Start Queue in the Adobe Media Encoder dialog box. The encoder codes the video, as shown in Figure F-20. Next, return to the Import Video Wizard and click Next (Win) or Continue (Mac).

  In the Skinning window, you can select the playback interface, or **skin**, for the video. Click Next (Win) or Continue (Mac) to view a summary report, then click Finish. Flash inserts the video with the selected skin on the Stage. To view the video, you test the movie. Figure F-21 shows a sample video in the Flash Player after it has been inserted in a Flash movie.

  When you embed a video, any user who has Flash Player installed can play the SWF file. You can select whether to embed the video as an embedded video that expands over frames, as a movie clip, or as a graphic.

  For progressive video, you can upload to the Web server hosting your video. For streaming video, which allows for the fastest transfer, you must upload the FLV and video skin SWF files to a Flash Media Server or Flash Video Streaming Service. You can still test a movie selected to load external video with a playback component and view it locally on your own computer. Other users, even those with Flash Player installed on their computers, cannot view the SWF files. Both progressive and streaming video require that you upload both the FLV video and the video skin SWF files to a Web server.

FIGURE F-19: Select Video window in Import Video Wizard

Click to select
video in Flash
Video format

Click to convert
video to Flash
Video format

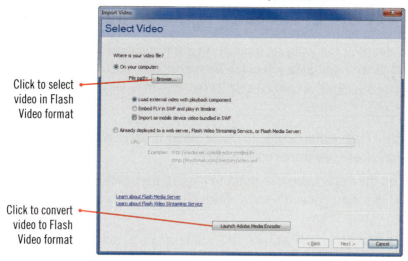

FIGURE F-20: Adobe Media Encoder

Path of video
being encoded

Video data

Encoding
progress bar

Click to add
video to queue

Preview of
video being
encoded

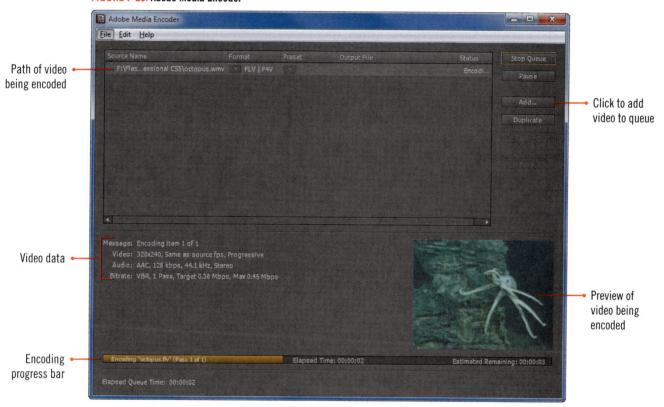

FIGURE F-21: Viewing a video

Video playing

The skin is the interface for
playback controls

Creating Buttons and Using Media

Adding Video to a Movie

By adding a video, you can illustrate products or ideas in a more exciting format to engage your viewers. Vanessa would like you to use the Import Video Wizard to insert a short ocean-themed video into a new Flash movie. To make it easy for the team to review, you embed the short video.

STEPS

1. **Create a new Flash ActionScript 3.0 movie, name it GreenWinds_video.fla, then save it in the location where you store your Data Files**

2. **Click File on the Application bar, point to Import, then click Import Video**

   The Import Video dialog box opens. You've already encoded the video for Flash, so you open the video you want to use.

3. **Click the Embed FLV in SWF and play in timeline option button, click Browse, navigate to the location where you store your Data Files, click eel.flv, click Open, compare your screen to Figure F-23, then click Next**

   The video is added to the Wizard.

4. **Click the Symbol type list arrow, click Movie clip, then compare your screen to Figure F-24**

   Selecting a movie clip reduces file size. You're ready to complete importing the video.

5. **Click Next, click Finish, then show the Library**

   The video appears on the Stage, and the eel.flv video and eel.flv movie clip symbol appear in the Library. The movie is larger than the Stage, so you resize it.

   TROUBLE
   Make sure the Lock Constrain icon 🔗 is selected.

6. **Show the Properties panel, set the W value to 500, center the playback component on the Stage, then test the movie**

   The video plays in the Flash Player, as shown in Figure F-25.

7. **Save your work, close the document, then exit Flash**

Previewing a video without importing it

You can quickly preview a video using the FLVPlayback component. To do so, click Window on the Application bar, then click Components, or click the Components icon in the iconic panels to open the Components panel. Expand the Video folder, then drag the FLVPlayback 2.5 component to the Stage, as shown in Figure F-22. The component includes a playback skin you can use inside Flash to preview a video. To insert the video, right-click the component, click Set Source, click the folder icon to navigate to the location where you store the video file, click the video, click Open in the Browse for source file dialog box, then click OK in the Content Path dialog box. To match the video to the size of the components, click the Match source dimensions check box, then click OK. To preview the video, select the Selection tool, then click the Play button on the playback skin.

FIGURE F-22: Viewing a video playback component

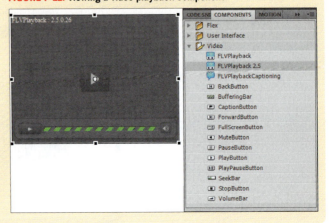

FIGURE F-23: Import Video window

Click to select video

Selected video; your
path will differ

Click to embed video

Click to move to
Embedding window

FIGURE F-24: Embedding window

Click to select
symbol type

Click to finish export

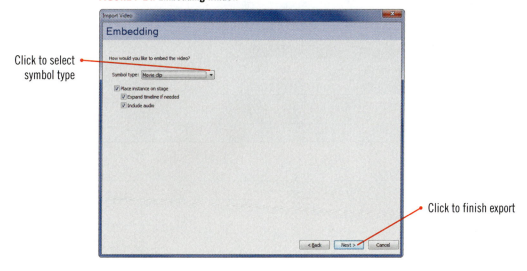

FIGURE F-25: Testing a video

Practice

Concepts Review

For current SAM information, including versions and content details, visit SAM Central (http://www.cengage.com/samcentral). If you have a SAM user profile, you may have access to hands-on instruction, practice, and assessment of the skills covered in this unit. Since various versions of SAM are supported throughout the life of this text, check with your instructor for the correct instructions and URL/Web site for accessing assignments.

Label the elements of the Flash screen shown in Figure F-26.

FIGURE F-26

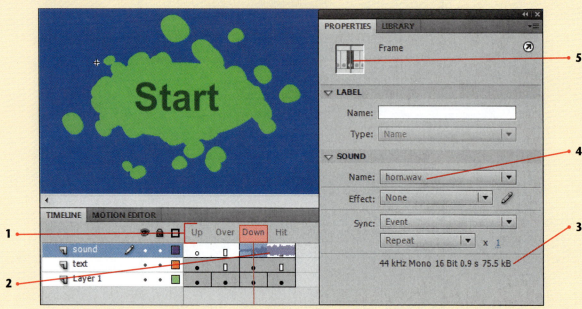

1. _____   4. _____
2. _____   5. _____
3. _____

Match each term with the statement that best describes it.

6. Flash Video   a. Button appearance based on mouse action
7. State   b. Graphical representation of audio
8. Waveform   c. Video playback controls in a movie
9. Up state   d. Clickable area of a button
10. Skin   e. Normal appearance of a button
11. Hit area   f. Format for inserting video in a Flash movie

Select the best answer from the list of choices.

12. Which button state responds to the user clicking the button and holding down the mouse button?

    a. Hit   **c.** Down

    b. Up   **d.** Over

13. Which mouse pointer indicates interactivity?

    a. 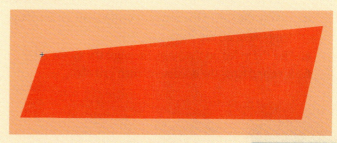   **c.**

    b.   **d.**

14. Which command enables you to test a button on the Stage?

    a. Test buttons   **c.** Button symbol edit

    b. Test movie   **d.** Enable Simple Buttons

15. Which of the following is *not* true of the Hit area?

    a. You must create one.

    b. It is invisible in the movie.

    c. The mouse pointer changes to the interactivity pointer.

    d. It can be larger or smaller than the button.

16. To which of the following frames do you usually add sound?

    a. Hit area   **c.** Over

    b. Down   **d.** Up

Skills Review

1. Understand buttons and states.

    a. List the frames in the button symbol edit window.

    b. Describe each of the button states.

    c. Describe one way to create a Hit area.

2. Create a button symbol.

    a. Start Flash, open the file FL F-2.fla from the location where you store your Data Files, then save it as **LightFootRecycling_buttons.fla**.

    b. Select the red rectangle on the Stage, then convert it to a button symbol named **startButton_btn**.

    c. Open the button symbol edit window, then add keyframes to the Over and Down frames.

    d. Add a blank keyframe to the Hit state, turn on onion skinning, then set the zoom as needed.

    e. Create a rectangle with no stroke color, a fill color of **#33FF00**, and an alpha of **75%** in the color pop-up window. On the Properties panel, set an X value of **−11**, a Y value of **−8**, a W value of **88**, and an H value of **33**. (*Hint*: Make sure the Lock width and height values together button shows the broken link icon.)

    f. Turn off onion skinning, then save the document.

3. Edit button states.

    a. Select the Over frame in the Timeline, select the Selection tool on the Tools panel, deselect the rectangle, position the pointer over the upper-right corner of the rectangle until the corner pointer is visible, then using Figure F-27 as a guide, drag the corner up and to the right. (*Hint*: To view the red rectangle more easily, click View on the Application bar, point to Preview Mode, then click Anti-Alias Text.)

    b. Position the pointer over the lower-left corner of the rectangle until the corner pointer is visible, then using Figure F-27 as a guide, drag the corner to the left.

    c. Return to the main movie, test the movie, then roll the mouse pointer over and click the button.

FIGURE F-27

    d. Enable simple buttons on the Stage, test the button, then deselect the command.

    e. Save the document.

Skills Review (continued)

4. **Add text to a button.**

   a. Open the button symbol edit window, then create a new layer above Layer 1 named **text**.

   b. Select the text layer Up frame in the Timeline, select the Text tool on the Tools panel, select Classic Text, then change the font family to Arial, the font style to Bold, the point size to 12, the color to white (**#FFFFFF**), and the alpha in the color pop-up window to **100%**, if necessary.

   c. Position the text pointer over the middle of the shape, click once, type **Start**, deselect the text, select the text object, then set the X value to **17** and the Y value to **–1**.

   d. Select the text layer Down frame, add a keyframe, select the text, then change the color to **#FFFE65**.

   e. Test the movie, click the button, then save the document.

5. **Understand sound.**

   a. Describe a good and a bad use of sound in a movie.

   b. Describe two ways you could use sound in a movie.

   c. Name two file extensions that represent sound files.

   d. Name two types of sound properties you can adjust in Flash.

6. **Add sound to a button.**

   a. Make sure the button symbol edit window is open, then create a new layer above the text layer named **sound**.

   b. Preview the little_whoosh.wav sound in the Library.

   c. Select the Down frame on the sound layer, insert a blank keyframe, then use the Properties panel to add the file little_whoosh.wav to the button.

   d. Expand the layer height of the sound layer to 200%.

   e. Return to the main movie, test the movie and the Start button, then compare your screen to Figure F-28.

   f. Save and close the document.

7. **Understand video.**

   a. Describe where you would watch video on the Web.

   b. Name a video format Flash uses to import video.

   c. Explain what a skin is.

FIGURE F-28

8. **Add video to a movie.**

   a. Create a new movie, modify the document size to **400 px** (width) by **300 px** (height), then save it as **LightFootRecycling_video.fla**.

   b. Open the Import Video dialog box, click Browse, navigate to the location where you store your Data Files, click recycle.flv, then click Open. (*Hints*: Make sure the Load external video with playback component option is selected. If necessary, copy the recycle.flv file so it appears in the same folder as LightFootRecycling_video.fla.)

   c. Click Next, select the SkinOverPlaySeekMute.swf skin, change the color to **#999999**, then finish importing the video.

   d. Modify the size of the playback component on the Properties panel to **W: 400 px** and **H: 300 px**, then align the component on the Stage.

   e. Play the video on the Stage, then test the movie.

   f. Save and close the document, then exit Flash.

Independent Challenge 1

You work at CoasterWoop, an online source of news by, for, and about roller coaster enthusiasts. You've animated and enhanced the appearance of several objects in the movie. Now your boss asks that you add a playful start button to the movie.

a. Start Flash, open the file FL F-3.fla from the location where you store your Data Files, then save it as **CoasterWoop_buttons.fla**.

b. Select all the objects on the buttons layer, then convert them to a button symbol named **startButton_btn**. (*Hint*: Use the Selection tool.)

c. Open the button symbol edit window, add keyframes to the Over and Down frames, then add a blank keyframe to the Hit frame.

d. In the Hit frame, turn on onion skinning, then create a rectangle with the following attributes: no stroke, fill color **#FF32CC**, alpha **40%**, X value **−2**, Y value **−3**, W value **47**, and H value **29**.

e. Turn off onion skinning, then zoom in the button if necessary.

f. Select the Over frame, deselect the object, select the orange segment, show the Transform panel, rotate the shape **−50°**, select the green segment, rotate the shape **−138°**, then test the movie and the button.

g. Create a layer above Layer 1 named **text**, select the Up frame, select the Text tool, then set the font attributes to Arial, Bold, 9 pt, **#FFFF00**, and alpha **100%**.

h. Type **Start**, then set the text box location X value to **.3** and the Y value to **2.3**.

i. Create a layer above the text layer named **sound**, select the Down frame, insert a blank keyframe, then use the Properties panel to insert the sound going_up.aiff.

j. Use a command on the Control menu that allows you to test the button on the Stage, test it, then deselect the command.

k. Test the movie and the button, then compare your screen to Figure F-29.

l. Save and close the document, then exit Flash.

FIGURE F-29

Independent Challenge 2

As the new program director at Lingoroots, an educational Web site specializing in linguistics, you're constantly looking for exciting ways to engage new visitors. For the next Web site feature, you'll compare the evolution of written Chinese across its 4,000-year history. The earliest written Chinese characters were pictures and evolved to a more stylized and artistic writing form. You want to show how Chinese calligraphy has changed over time. You completed a movie showing just a few accomplishments of Chinese culture and Chinese calligraphy, but now you want to add a button so users will be able to control the movie.

a. Start Flash, open the file FL F-4.fla from the location where you store your Data Files, then save it as **lingoroots_buttons.fla**.

b. Convert the shape in the buttons layer to a button symbol named **startButton_btn**.

Independent Challenge 2 (continued)

c. Open the button symbol edit window, add keyframes to the Over and Down frames, then add a blank keyframe to the Hit frame.

d. In the Hit frame, turn on onion skinning, then create a rectangle with the following attributes: no stroke, fill color **#65FF98**, alpha **75%**, X value **.3**, Y value **–3**, W value **76**, and H value **27**.

e. Turn off onion skinning, then zoom in the button if necessary.

f. Select the Over frame, select the button, open the Fill color pop-up window, then change the alpha to **100%**.

g. Create a layer above Layer 1 named **text**, select the Up frame, select the Text tool, select Classic Text, then set the font attributes to **#FFFFFF**, Arial, Regular, 12 pt.

h. Click the button, type **start**, then set the X value to **43** and the Y value to **5**.

i. Create a layer above the text layer named **sound**, select the Down frame, insert a blank keyframe, then use the Properties panel to insert the sound Gong_mf2.wav.

j. Use a command on the Control menu to test the button on the Stage, then deselect the command.

k. Test the movie and the button, then compare your screen to Figure F-30.

FIGURE F-30

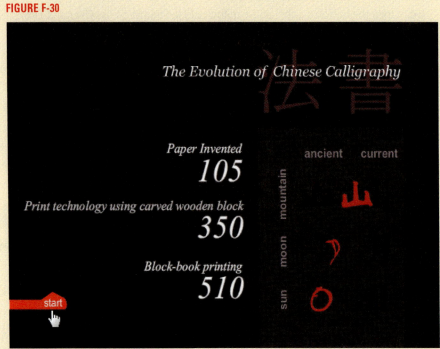

Advanced Challenge Exercise

- Edit the button, then modify one or more attributes of the shape in the Down frame of Layer 1 as desired.
- Edit the button, select the Down frame in the sound layer, then apply the effect of your choice to the sound. (*Hint*: Click an option from the Effect list on the Properties panel.)

l. Save and close the document and exit Flash.

Independent Challenge 3

You work for ibRobotz, an online entertainment site. Users can download ibRobotz characters or create their own to insert in stories. You've been asked to add a button to the movie.

a. Start Flash, open the file FL F-5.fla from the location where you store your Data Files, then save it as **ibrobotz_buttons.fla**.

b. Create a shape of your choice in the buttons layer, convert it to a button symbol named **initiateButton_btn**, then open the button symbol edit window.

c. Add keyframes to the Over and Down frames, then add a blank keyframe to the Hit frame.

d. In the Hit frame, turn on onion skinning, then create a black shape that covers the button shape.

e. Turn off onion skinning, then zoom in the button if necessary.

f. Select the Over frame, modify the shape slightly, deselect the shape, drag an instance of the flower_mc symbol on top of, next to, above, or below the button shape, then test the movie. (*Hint*: Because the flower instance is a movie clip, the shape spins when the mouse moves over it.)

g. In the initiateButton_btn edit window, create a layer above Layer 1 named **text**, select the Up frame, select the Text tool, then set the font attributes to Arial, Bold, and in an appropriate font size and color for the button you created earlier.

FIGURE F-31

h. Type **initiate**, then align the text on the button.

i. Create a layer above the text layer named **sound**, select the Down frame, insert a blank keyframe, then use the Properties panel to insert the sound boing_bounce.wav.

j. Use a command on the Control menu to test the button on the Stage, then deselect the command.

k. Test the movie and the button. Figure F-31 shows one possible solution.

Advanced Challenge Exercise

- Change an attribute of the button in another frame of Layer 1.
- In the main movie, create a new layer above the buttons layer named **sound**, add a blank keyframe in frame 4, use the Properties panel to insert the sound boing_bounce.wav, set the Sync to Stream, then test the movie.
- Add keyframes and the sound file to frames 10, 16, 22, 27, 33, 39, 45, 51, and 57, then test the movie.

l. Save and close the document.

m. Create a new document named **ibrobotz_video.fla**, then save it in the location where you store your Data Files.

n. Open the Import Video dialog box, select the Embed FLV in SWF and play in timeline option, navigate to the location where you store your Data Files, then open **robot.flv**.

o. Move to the Embedding window, change the symbol type to Movie clip, click Next, then finish the video import.

p. Adjust the size of the video on the Stage, then test the movie.

q. Save and close the document, then exit Flash.

Real Life Independent Challenge

This Independent Challenge will continue to build on the personal movie that you have been developing since Unit B. Here, you add a button to the movie.

a. Start Flash, open the file myproject.fla, then save it as **myproject_buttons.fla**.

b. Use the skills you learned in this unit to create a button symbol, modifying the states as desired.

c. Use the Sounds common library to add a sound to a layer in the main movie Timeline and to a button frame. Apply an effect or adjust the number of times it plays as desired. (*Hint*: Click Window on the Application bar, point to Common Libraries, then click Sounds.)

d. Test the movie.

e. Save and close the document myproject_buttons.fla, then exit Flash.

Visual Workshop

Visiting Web sites is a great way to get inspired for your own projects. Figure F-32 shows the home page from the International Spy Museum. Go to www.spymuseum.org, view the buttons on the site, then answer the following questions. For each question, include why or how you reached a conclusion. You can open a word processor or use the Text tool in Flash to complete this exercise. When you are finished, write down the URL of the Web page you select in Step d, add your name to the document, save it, print it, then close the word processor or exit Flash.

a. Identify the actions associated with the buttons at the International Spy Museum Web site.

b. How is sound and video used?

c. How many states do you see associated with buttons?

d. Go to one of the following Web sites, view several sites, then select one to answer the following questions. Be sure to look for sections or links dedicated to Flash sites:
   - www.thefwa.com/
   - www.coolwebawards.com/?go=Nothing_but_flash

e. For each site you visited, including the site in Step a, what is the Web site's purpose and goal?

f. Who is the target audience? How does the design (look and feel) of the Web site fit the target audience?

g. Did the site indicate which version of the Flash Player users needed?

h. Looking at the animation in the introduction and on the home page:
   - What is animated on this page? Can you guess the kind of animation used?
   - How is sound used?
   - How many animations occur simultaneously?
   - What is your overall opinion of the design, organization, and function of this page? How would you improve it?

i. Close your browser.

FIGURE F-32

Courtesy The International Spy Museum (www.spymuseum.org)

Using ActionScript 3.0

You use ActionScript 3.0 to create interactive projects in Flash, such as controlling the movie's playback and making buttons interactive in the Flash Player. You enter ActionScript in the Actions panel. In this unit, you will get a taste of ActionScript 3.0 code, but because learning extensive ActionScript is beyond the scope of this book, you will type and copy small amounts of code. These lessons are not intended to provide a complete skill set, but you will learn some simple actions.  The clients at GreenWinds Eco-Cruise have added a few more buttons to the movie. Your boss, Vanessa, wants you to add ActionScript to the movie so the buttons perform an action when users interact with them.

OBJECTIVES

Understand ActionScript 3.0

Add a stop action to a movie

Add a play action to a button

Copy and modify code

Test code

Open a Web site from a button

Add comments to code

Use code snippets

Understanding ActionScript 3.0

You have created buttons in your movies that changed their appearance when users point to and click them. However, you still need to have the buttons do what they are designed to do: perform actions. To help you add this kind of interactivity to your buttons, Flash uses a **scripting language** to interpret and execute user actions. Just as .fla files are native Flash files, ActionScript 3.0 is the native scripting language in Flash and has the .as file extension. You can use interactivity in your movies in several different ways. For example, you can have a movie open in the Flash Player but not play it until a user clicks a button. Before adding ActionScript to the GreenWinds movie, you familiarize yourself with some basics about ActionScript 3.0.

As you prepare to incorporate interactivity in your movies and Web pages, you will need to:

- ### Understand ActionScript 3.0 building blocks

  Learning to write ActionScript code resembles learning any new language: In language learning, you use vocabulary and grammar to communicate ideas. Words are the fundamental units that combine to form sentences, but they only make sense when you follow a set of rules, known as syntax. In computer languages, the **syntax** governs the order, structure, and use of words in a sentence of code. A complete sentence in ActionScript is known as a **statement**. If you make an error and create a syntax error, none of the code will work and the movie will not contain the interactivity you had intended.

  Punctuation is critical to a scripting language. Common syntax includes the following:

Curly braces	{ }	Parentheses	( )
Dot (period)	.	Quotation marks	" "
Slashes	/ or //	Semicolon	;

  Most syntax errors are the result of improper capitalization or missing punctuation. In fact, some developers find it best to first type opening and closing punctuation, such as parentheses, quotation marks, and braces, and then use the arrow keys to move back within the punctuation to type the code.

- ### Use the Actions panel

  You use the Actions panel to place ActionScript code in a movie. ActionScript must always be attached to a keyframe (or included in an external file, which is a more advanced skill). In this unit, you'll be placing ActionScript in keyframes. The Actions panel consists of the Script pane, where you type code and informational text called comments; the Actions toolbox, which contains ActionScript elements you can drag to the Script pane; and the Script navigator, which shows the Flash element associated with the code in the Script pane. A toolbar above the Script pane contains buttons for adding and checking syntax, hints, comments, debugging, adjusting the size of syntax, and other features. You can also access tools that help you insert ActionScript code for commonly used interactivity functions without having to learn ActionScript. Figure G-1 shows ActionScript code in the Script pane.

- ### Enter ActionScript code

  In this unit, you'll primarily use ActionScript to control a button's action. The basic process is to tell Flash to listen for a particular event, and then when it hears that event, perform the requested function. Figure G-2 shows code that tells a button to play a movie when the user clicks the button. Do not be concerned if all the code does not make sense to you at this point; just get an idea of how the various pieces of code work together to specify a button action.

FIGURE G-1: Viewing ActionScript 3.0 code in the Actions panel

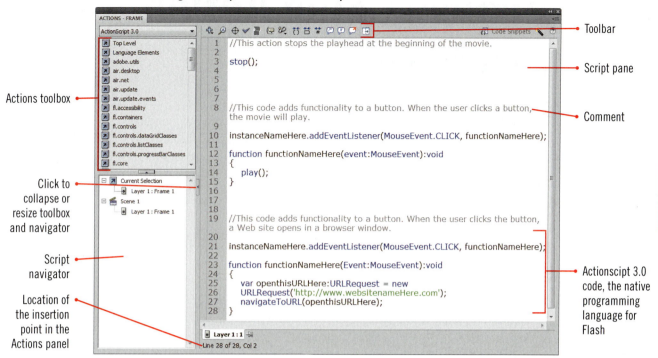

Toolbar

Script pane

Comment

Actions toolbox

Click to collapse or resize toolbox and navigator

Script navigator

Actionscript 3.0 code, the native programming language for Flash

Location of the insertion point in the Actions panel

FIGURE G-2: Viewing ActionScript that controls a button action

Name of button instance

Tells Flash you want it to listen for a particular event

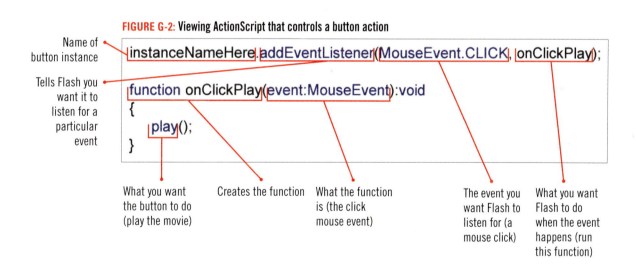

What you want the button to do (play the movie)

Creates the function

What the function is (the click mouse event)

The event you want Flash to listen for (a mouse click)

What you want Flash to do when the event happens (run this function)

Learning ActionScript 3.0

Learning a programming language like ActionScript 3.0 can take a long time. There are many books and college-level courses devoted to teaching developers how to use it. It takes a lot of practice to become proficient. Therefore, this unit provides only a brief introduction to the subject and is designed to familiarize you with a few basics. If you would like to learn more, consider taking a course, taking online training, or purchasing a book to bring your knowledge to the next level.

Adding a Stop Action to a Movie

As you've seen when you've tested your movies, the movie starts to play as soon as it opens in the Flash Player. That doesn't give users much control over the movie. You can add a stop function in the Actions panel that tells Flash to immediately stop playing the movie as soon as it opens in the Flash Player.  Vanessa wants users to be able to play the movie. So, you must first instruct Flash to stop the movie from playing when users open it. You create a layer for the ActionScript code, then add a stop action in the Actions panel.

STEPS

1. **Start Flash, open the file FL G-1.fla from the location where you store your Data Files, save it as GreenWinds_actions.fla, then create a new layer named actions at the top of the Timeline**

    Placing the layer at the top of the Timeline ensures you can keep track of it. You should place all actions on the same layer, and not add any content to the layer. The movie opens, displaying three buttons: Start, Stop, and Visit Us. Before you assign actions to them, you want to add a stop action in the first frame so the movie does not play when users first open the movie.

QUICK TIP

You can also press [F9] (Win) or [option][F9] (Mac) to open the Actions panel.

2. **Click frame 1 in the actions layer, click Window on the Application bar, then click Actions**

    The Actions panel opens and displays three panes. The main pane is the Script pane. The Actions toolbox (the upper-left pane) is useful if you already know the code you're looking for; the Script navigator (the lower-left pane) is useful when you need to navigate through extensive and complex code. You won't need either of these features right now, so you collapse them to reduce clutter.

TROUBLE

If you see a large gray area at the top of the Actions panel, this is the Script Assist pane, which is designed for users who already know ActionScript 3.0. Close it by clicking the Script Assist button at the top of the Actions panel.

3. **Click the resize pane button near the center of the panel to collapse the Actions toolbox and Script navigator**

    The Actions panel shows only the Script pane, as shown in Figure G-3. As you type ActionScript, code hints provide suggestions, which can be distracting when you're first learning syntax, so you disable the Code Hints feature in the Preferences dialog box.

4. **Click the Panel options button at the top of the panel, click Preferences, click ActionScript under Category, click the Code hints check box to deselect it, then click OK**

    Code hints will not appear in the Actions panel, and the Preferences dialog box closes.

5. **Type stop(); on line 1, then compare your Actions panel to Figure G-4**

    Flash automatically assigns colors to different types of code so you can more easily identify it. The word "stop" is in blue, indicating that it is a function. See Table G-1 for short definitions of concepts that are the building blocks of ActionScript 3.0. The parentheses are necessary to run commands in a function. A semicolon ends the statement, just as a period ends a sentence in natural language. You want to see how adding ActionScript affects frames in the actions layer.

6. **Move the Actions panel away from the Timeline if necessary, drag the playhead to frame 5 in the Timeline, then compare your screen to Figure G-5**

    The blank keyframe has a small "a" on it, indicating that it contains ActionScript. Because the movie already has content on other layers, Flash inserted a blank keyframe when you created the layer. You must use keyframes when placing ActionScript in a frame. You want to test the movie to see the effect of the stop action.

7. **Test the movie, then test a button**

    The movie shows the content in frame 1 and appears static except for the movie clip of the ship's lights. Although the buttons change appearance in the Over state and play a sound in the Down state, they don't yet do anything to control the movie.

8. **Close the Flash Player, click the Collapse to Icons arrow on the Actions panel, then save the document**

FIGURE G-3: Viewing the Actions panel

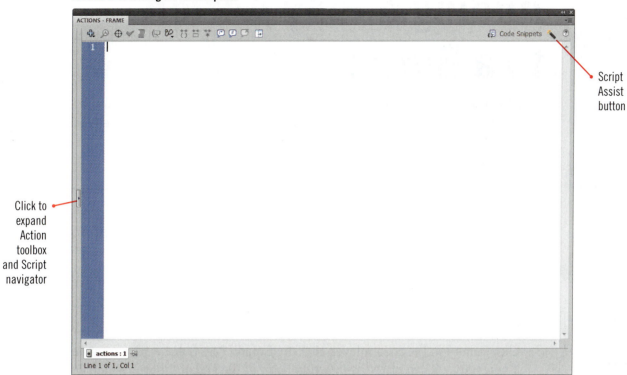

Script Assist button

Click to expand Action toolbox and Script navigator

FIGURE G-4: Viewing a stop action in the Actions panel

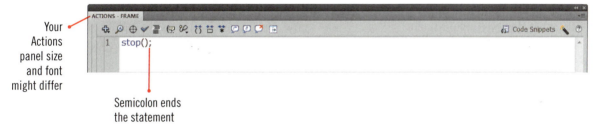

Your Actions panel size and font might differ

Semicolon ends the statement

FIGURE G-5: Viewing an ActionScript frame

Small "a" indicates ActionScript

TABLE G-1: ActionScript 3.0 programming concepts

concept	description
Event	A trigger that determines which instructions are executed and when
Function	A group of named, reusable statements that form a command
Methods	The types of actions an object performs; functions that are attached to objects
Objects	The data you want to control
Properties	The attributes of an object; variables that are connected to an object
Variable	A specific piece of information or data
Parameter	A specific value that clarifies or limits a function

Adding a Play Action to a Button

To assign an action to a button, you must first give the button an instance name in the Properties panel. In the Actions panel, you write code known as an **event handler** that tells Flash what event to listen for and then what to do once it hears the event. ▓▓▓▓ You write code to have the Start button play the movie when a user clicks the button.

1. **Click the Start button on the Stage to select it, then show the Properties panel if necessary**

   The top of the Properties panel shows a blank <Instance Name> text box. When naming instances, you must begin with a lowercase letter; however, you can have capital letters in the middle of the name.

> **QUICK TIP**
>
> If you want to name an instance with more than one word, use a capital letter in the name.

2. **Click the Instance Name text box, type startBtn, press [Enter] (Win) or [return] (Mac), then compare your screen to Figure G-6**

   In the Actions panel, Flash uses the instance name to connect to the button on the Stage. You cannot place ActionScript on a button, so you return to the actions layer before expanding the Actions panel.

3. **Click frame 1 in the actions layer, click the Expand Panels arrow ▶▶ on the Actions panel, if necessary, click to place the insertion point at the end of the stop action line, then press [Enter] (Win) or [return] (Mac) twice**

   Inserting blank lines helps you see blocks of code more easily. You want the code to always be visible regardless of the size of the Actions panel.

> **TROUBLE**
>
> After you turn on Word Wrap, depending on how you resize your Actions panel, your lines of code might not match the figures.

4. **Click the Panel options button ▤ at the top of the panel, then click Word Wrap to select it if necessary**

   The code will wrap when you resize the Actions panel. You type the first line of code on line 3.

5. **Refer to Figure G-7, type the syntax exactly as shown on line 3, then press [Enter] (Win) or [return] (Mac) twice**

   The code tells Flash critical pieces of information in a specific order: (1) the object on the Stage you want the ActionScript to work with (startBtn, the instance name that identifies the Start button); (2) that you want Flash to wait for the user (addEventListener) to do something with the mouse (MouseEvent); and (3) which action of the user's mouse (CLICK) will trigger something to happen (onClickPlay, the name of the function). You can choose any text for the button instance and function names; however, it's a good idea to use relevant words that make sense to you. At this point, Flash does not know which commands you want it to run (perform) in the onClickPlay function. You create the function in the next line of code, line 5.

6. **Refer to Figure G-8, then type the syntax exactly as shown on lines 5 through 8**

   Notice that when you pressed [Enter] (Win) or [return] (Mac) after you typed the open curly brace, Flash automatically added a close curly brace and moved the insertion point up between the two braces for you. The code defines the function (function onClickPlay) that will handle the event (event:MouseEvent), fulfills a requirement in ActionScript that you must specify that you don't need the code to return a value after running the function (void), then defines what happens when the user clicks the button ({ play(); })—that is, play the movie. You want to test the movie to see how the new functionality works with the Start button.

> **TROUBLE**
>
> If your movie starts to play as soon as it opens in the Flash Player, check your code carefully for syntax errors.

7. **Test the movie, then click the Start button**

   The movie opens to frame 1 and is static, it plays once when you click the Start button, then returns to the beginning of the movie and stops.

8. **Close the Flash Player, close the Actions panel, then save the document**

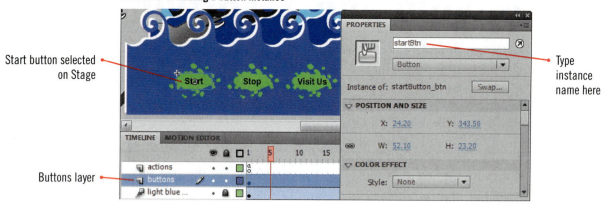

FIGURE G-6: Naming a button instance

Start button selected on Stage

Buttons layer

Type instance name here

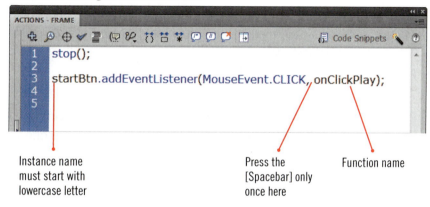

FIGURE G-7: Entering the event handler code

```
1  stop();
2
3  startBtn.addEventListener(MouseEvent.CLICK, onClickPlay);
4
5
```

Instance name must start with lowercase letter

Press the [Spacebar] only once here

Function name

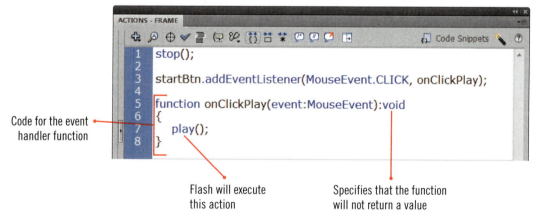

FIGURE G-8: Entering the event handler function code

```
1  stop();
2
3  startBtn.addEventListener(MouseEvent.CLICK, onClickPlay);
4
5  function onClickPlay(event:MouseEvent):void
6  {
7      play();
8  }
```

Code for the event handler function

Flash will execute this action

Specifies that the function will not return a value

Using Script Assist

If you already have a basic understanding of ActionScript 3.0 and which function, variable, and method to use, you can use Script Assist to add error-free code to your movie. Script Assist lets you build scripts by selecting items from the Actions toolbox or by clicking the blue Add menu button on the toolbar (you cannot type ActionScript when Script Assist is active). For example, to stop a movie clip from playing, click the first frame in the actions layer, open the Actions panel, then click the Script Assist button on the right side of the panel. Click the Add menu button, point to flash .display, point to MovieClip, point to Methods, then click stop. Script Assist adds a tentative stop action, but to set it you must type the name of the movie clip symbol in the Object text box.

Copying and Modifying Code

If you want to apply similar functions to different buttons, you can copy and paste code in the Actions panel, then change relevant words in the code. ActionScript is considered an **object-oriented language**, which uses a modular approach to programming, meaning you can reuse elements. Vanessa wants the Stop button to operate the same way as the Start button. You create an instance name for the Stop button, then copy and change code in the Actions panel.

STEPS

1. Make sure the Selection tool ▶ is selected, then click the Stop button on the Stage to select it

2. Show the Properties panel, click the Instance Name text box, type stopBtn, then press [Enter] (Win) or [return] (Mac)

> **QUICK TIP**
> To open the Actions panel from the Properties panel, select a symbol or frame already containing ActionScript, then click the Actionscript panel button ⬀ in the upper-right corner.

3. Click frame 1 in the actions layer, show the Actions panel, click to place the insertion point at the beginning of line 3, then drag to select the block of code on lines 3 to 8

   The code is highlighted and a vertical line appears next to the line numbers indicating the selected lines of code, as shown in Figure G-10.

4. Press [Ctrl][C] (Win) or [⌘][C] (Mac) to copy the code

   To help you visually separate blocks of code, you add blank lines in the Actions panel before pasting the code.

5. Place the insertion point at the end of line 8, press [Enter] (Win) or [return] (Mac) three times, then press [Ctrl][V] (Win) or [⌘][V] (Mac) to paste the code starting on line 11

   The code appears on lines 11 to 16, as shown in Figure G-11. Next, you replace the Start button code with text for the Stop button.

6. Select the code startBtn on line 11, type stopBtn, select the code onClickPlay on lines 11 and 13, type onClickStop, select the code play(); on line 15, then type stop();

   The script now includes the instance name for the Stop button and the function name to stop the movie, as shown in Figure G-12.

7. Save the document

Using code hints

Code hints can help streamline your workflow and avoid syntax errors when writing code in the Actions panel. Code hints are enabled by default, although you can disable them in the Preferences dialog box, along with selecting the amount of time before the code hint appears. There are two types of code hints: a pop-up options menu, shown in Figure G-9, and a code-completion feature that resembles a tooltip. Flash recognizes existing variables and functions in your code and will show you completed syntax. To use the code hint menu, begin typing code, such as a dot (period) before a variable. Flash will show you a list of hints in a pop-up window; to select one, double-click it or press [Enter] (Win) or [return] (Mac). The tooltip code hint contains a sentence of suggested syntax needed to complete the action you are typing. To manually display menu-style code hints if you have disabled them in the Preferences dialog box, click the Show code hint button 🖵 or press [Ctrl][Spacebar] (Win) or [⌘][spacebar] (Mac) on the Actions panel toolbar.

FIGURE G-9: Viewing code hints (hints window)

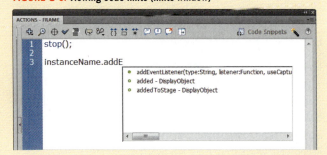

FIGURE G-10: Selecting lines of code

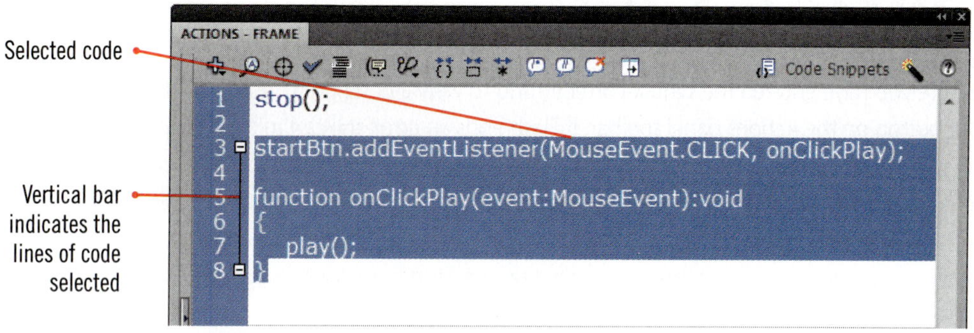

Selected code →

Vertical bar indicates the lines of code selected →

```
1  stop();
2
3  startBtn.addEventListener(MouseEvent.CLICK, onClickPlay);
4
5  function onClickPlay(event:MouseEvent):void
6  {
7      play();
8  }
```

FIGURE G-11: Viewing copied code

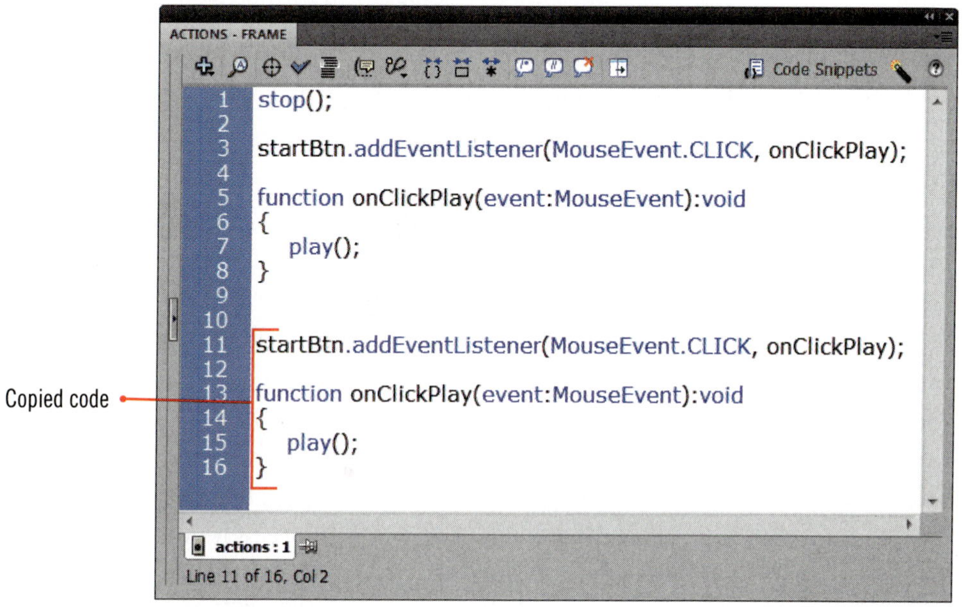

```
1  stop();
2
3  startBtn.addEventListener(MouseEvent.CLICK, onClickPlay);
4
5  function onClickPlay(event:MouseEvent):void
6  {
7      play();
8  }
9
10
11  startBtn.addEventListener(MouseEvent.CLICK, onClickPlay);
12
13  function onClickPlay(event:MouseEvent):void
14  {
15      play();
16  }
```

Copied code →

actions : 1
Line 11 of 16, Col 2

FIGURE G-12: Viewing modified code for the Stop action

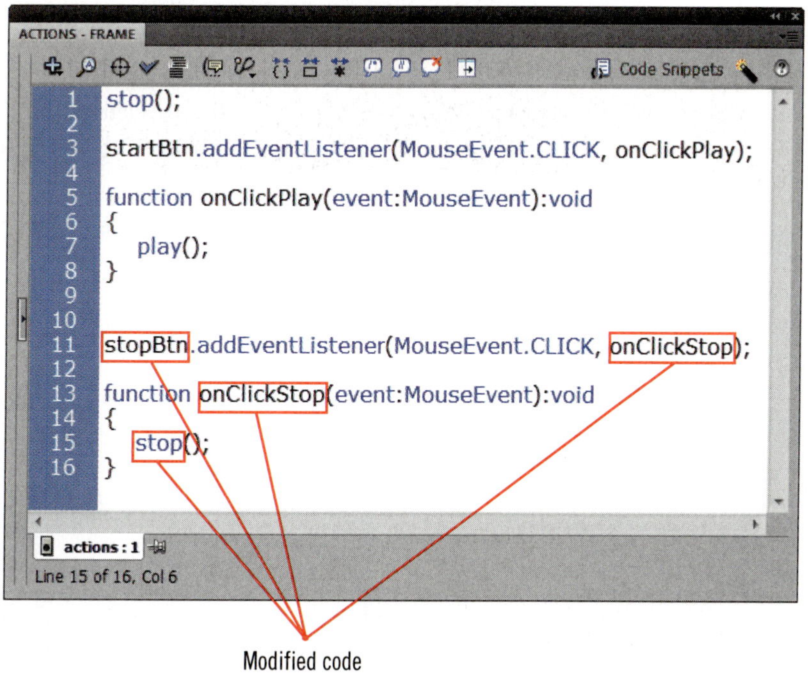

```
1  stop();
2
3  startBtn.addEventListener(MouseEvent.CLICK, onClickPlay);
4
5  function onClickPlay(event:MouseEvent):void
6  {
7      play();
8  }
9
10
11  stopBtn.addEventListener(MouseEvent.CLICK, onClickStop);
12
13  function onClickStop(event:MouseEvent):void
14  {
15      stop();
16  }
```

actions : 1
Line 15 of 16, Col 6

Modified code

Testing Code

To ensure you have entered the syntax correctly and to view a description of any errors, you can use the Check syntax button on the Actions panel toolbar. If Flash finds an error, it lists it in the Compiler Errors panel, located in the same group as the Timeline and Motion Editor. Another way to test code is to write a **trace statement**, which makes a message appear in the Output panel when you perform an action. Vanessa wants you to be familiar with how to handle error messages. She asks you to create a syntax error so you can see how to correct it, then write a trace statement to verify that the Stop button works properly before you test the movie.

STEPS

TROUBLE

Collapse or move the Actions panel if necessary throughout this unit.

1. **Make sure that frame 1 in the actions layer is selected and that the Actions panel is open**

2. **Click the Check syntax button** ☑ **on the Actions panel toolbar**

   The check does not find any errors, and the Compiler Errors panel does not appear in the Timeline group, as shown in Figure G-14. To see how Flash handles a syntax error, you make a deliberate mistake.

3. **Select the close curly brace } on line 16, press [Delete], then click** ☑ **on the toolbar**

   Flash found a syntax error, as shown in Figure G-15. The Compiler Errors panel identifies and describes the error. You want to correct the error before moving on.

4. **Click to place the insertion point at the beginning of line 16, if necessary, then type }**

   The code is corrected. You want to write a trace statement to verify that the Stop button action (but not its function) is working. You replace the code for stopping the movie with a trace statement to display text.

QUICK TIP

You can use single or double quotation marks when typing text in a trace statement.

5. **Select the code stop(); on line 15, type trace("The button clicked!");, test the movie, then click the Stop button**

   The message "The button clicked!" appears in the Output panel when you click the Stop button, as shown in Figure G-16. Next, you restore the stop action, and test the movie with the Start and Stop buttons.

TROUBLE

Trace statements can add substantial size to the code, so it's best to delete the trace statement after running it.

6. **Select trace("The button clicked!"); on line 15, type stop();, test the movie, click the Start button, then click the Stop button when both dolphins are fully visible**

   The movie opens to frame 1 and is static, it plays when you click the Start button, then stops when you click the Stop button. You can start and stop the movie as often as you wish.

7. **Close the Flash Player, then save the document**

Setting Actions panel preferences

You can modify settings for the Actions panel, such as font and colors, in the Preferences dialog box. To open the Preferences dialog box, click Edit (Win) or Flash (Professional) (Mac) on the Application bar, then click Preferences. To open it from the Actions panel, click the Panel options button, then click Preferences. Click ActionScript in the Category section, then modify settings as desired. You can decide whether to display code hints; set the font, size, and style of font; and change the colors of syntax elements such as comments, strings, and identifiers. For example, in this unit, the syntax font was set to Verdana 12 pt, as shown in Figure G-13.

FIGURE G-13: ActionScript Preferences settings

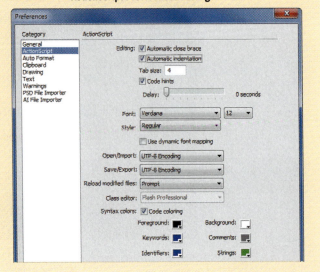

FIGURE G-14: Checking syntax

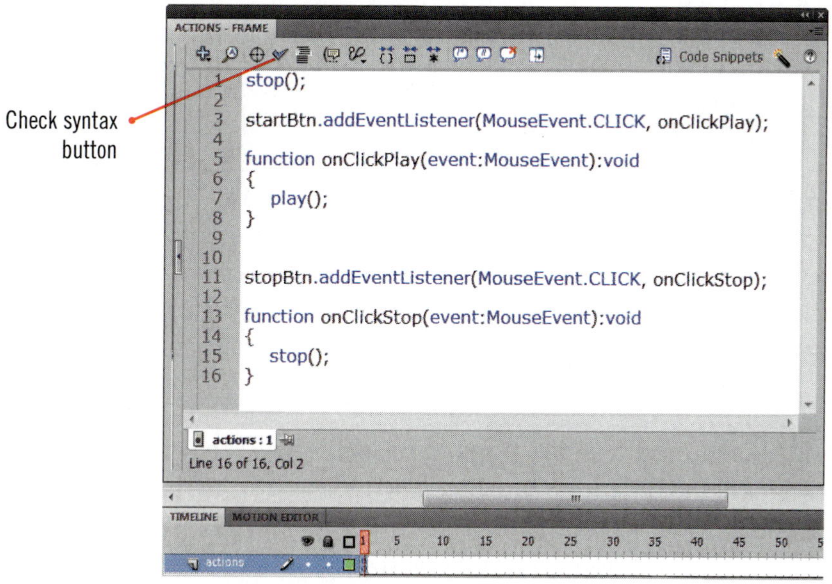

Check syntax button

```
1    stop();
2
3    startBtn.addEventListener(MouseEvent.CLICK, onClickPlay);
4
5    function onClickPlay(event:MouseEvent):void
6    {
7        play();
8    }
9
10
11   stopBtn.addEventListener(MouseEvent.CLICK, onClickStop);
12
13   function onClickStop(event:MouseEvent):void
14   {
15       stop();
16   }
```

FIGURE G-15: Viewing error in the Compiler Errors panel

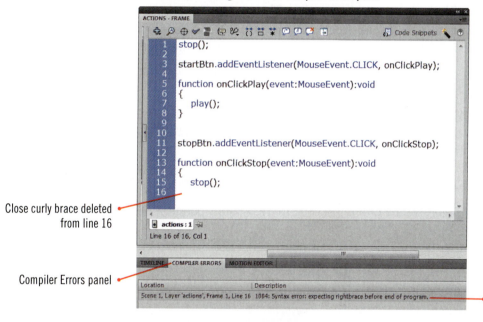

Close curly brace deleted from line 16

Compiler Errors panel

Description of error

Scene 1, Layer 'actions', Frame 1, Line 16   1084: Syntax error: expecting rightbrace before end of program.

FIGURE G-16: Viewing a trace statement

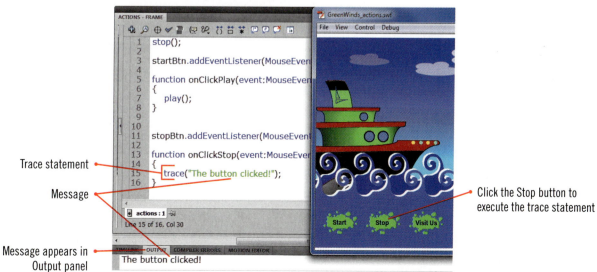

Trace statement

Message

Click the Stop button to execute the trace statement

Message appears in Output panel

The button clicked!

Opening a Web Site from a Button

Buttons often function as links to Web sites. A user clicks a button, and a Web page opens in the same or a new browser window. It takes a little bit more code than a start or stop action to tell a button to open a Web site, but once you have the basics, you can link to any Web site. Vanessa has found a code block you can use to create the code that will open a Web site when a user clicks the Visit Us button. It is in the .as file format. You will open the ActionScript file, copy and paste the code, then customize it for the GreenWinds movie.

1. **Click the Visit Us button on the Stage to select it, show the Properties panel if necessary, click the Instance Name text box, type visitUsBtn, then press [Enter] (Win) or [return] (Mac)**

   You open the ActionScript file so you can copy the code.

   > **QUICK TIP**
   > You can create a script-only file by selecting ActionScript File as the type when you create a new document.

2. **Open the file ActionScript.as from the location where you store your Data Files, then view the last block of code starting on line 21**

   Flash opens the file in its own Actions panel, next to the GreenWinds_actions.fla tab. The last block of code is shown in Figure G-17. You copy the code and paste it into the GreenWinds Actions panel.

3. **Drag to select the entire block of code on lines 21 to 28, press [Ctrl][C] (Win) or [⌘][C] (Mac), then close the file ActionScript.as**

4. **Click the Timeline tab, click frame 1 in the actions layer, show the Actions panel, click to place the insertion point at the end of line 16, press [Enter] (Win) or [return] (Mac) three times, then press [Ctrl][V] (Win) or [⌘][V] (Mac) to paste the code starting on line 19**

   The code appears on lines 19 to 26. Next, you replace the generic code containing the word "Here" with names specific to the Visit Us button.

5. **Use the table below to replace code in the Actions panel**

line(s)	select code	replace with code
19	instanceNameHere	visitUsBtn
19 and 21	functionNameHere	goToSite
23 and 25	openthisURLHere	courseURL
24	www.websitenameHere.com	www.course.com

   > **QUICK TIP**
   > You can use single or double quotation marks for the URL address.

6. **Compare your Actions panel to Figure G-18**

   The code now instructs Flash to open a specific Web site when the user clicks the Visit Us button.

   > **TROUBLE**
   > If you open and test the .swf file using the Flash Player outside of Flash, you may need to click OK or click Settings to add the location to a list of trusted sites.

7. **Test the movie, click the Start button, click the Stop button, click the Visit Us button, then display your browser if necessary**

   The home page of Course Technology (the publisher of this book) opens in your browser, as shown in Figure G-19.

8. **Close your browser, close the Flash Player, then save the document**

FIGURE G-17: Viewing ActionScript code in an .as file

```
21   instanceNameHere.addEventListener(MouseEvent.CLICK, functionNameHere);
22
23   function functionNameHere(Event:MouseEvent):void
24   {
25       var openthisURLHere:URLRequest = new
26       URLRequest('http://www.websitenameHere.com');
27       navigateToURL(openthisURLHere);
28   }
```

FIGURE G-18: Viewing the code to open a Web site from the Visit Us button

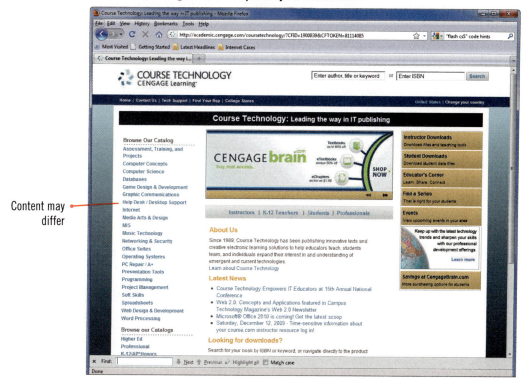

Code to open Web site when user clicks button

FIGURE G-19: Viewing the Web site opened by the Visit Us button

Content may differ

Adding Comments to Code

There will be times when you want to explain the purpose of various parts of your code, which can be useful as a memory aid and can also help others who may read or revise your code. To document your code, you can add **comments** to the Action panel, which are lines of text placed between gray asterisks or slashes within the lines of code. The slashes cause Flash to ignore the text between them when running the code. You can also use comments to temporarily deactivate code that you don't want to delete from the file. To add and remove comments, you use buttons on the Actions panel toolbar, summarized in Table G-2. 🎨 Vanessa wants you to add a comment before the Visit Us button code that identifies the Web site opened by the Visit Us button. You use the code commenting feature to add the comments.

STEPS

1. Show the Actions panel if necessary, place the insertion point in line 18, then press [Enter] (Win) or [return] (Mac) three times

QUICK TIP

Flash uses gray slashes to specify comment punctuation.

2. Press the up arrow key once to move to line 20, then click the Apply block comment button 💬 on the toolbar

   Open and close block comment codes appear on line 20, as shown in Figure G-21. Next, you add comments describing the Web site.

3. With the insertion point positioned between the asterisks, type Clicking the Visit Us button opens the Course Technology Web site, then compare your Actions panel to Figure G-22

4. Test the movie, click the Start button, click the Stop button, then click the Visit Us button

   Flash ignores the comments as it runs the ActionScript. The comments do not affect how the code works.

5. Close the browser, close the Flash Player, then close the Actions panel

6. Save and close the document

Navigating using frame labels

If you have a short movie that navigates to only a few frames, you can set ActionScript to easily navigate to a specific frame number, such as one that displays text or a graphic after a user clicks a button, as shown in the ActionScript code gotoAndStop(5);. The number "5" is the frame number.

However, always using a frame number for navigating the Timeline can be confusing. If you have several symbols that navigate to a different frame, the numbers don't immediately tell you which symbol or element they refer to. **Frame labels** increase the flexibility of your movie elements because they allow you to associate a frame with a name so when ActionScript runs the code, it references the frame name, known as the frame label.

To associate a frame number with a frame, you first create a layer to store the labels (usually named "labels"), then insert a blank

keyframe in the frame where you want to create the frame label. Next, move to the Label section of the Properties panel, then type the name you would like for the frame label (with no spaces). A small red flag appears in the frame in the Timeline, indicating that it has a frame label.

Open the Actions panel, click frame 1 of the actions layer, go to where the frame number is referenced in the function between the curly braces, then replace the frame number with a string that represents the frame label. A **string** is text that is contained in quotation marks, such as the label name "seahorses". Figure G-20 shows the frame label flag in the Timeline in frame 5; the frame number is associated with the frame label by using the green frame label string inserted in the ActionScript code; and the content associated with the frame label—in this case, a graphic—appears after a user clicks a button.

FIGURE G-20: Frame labels

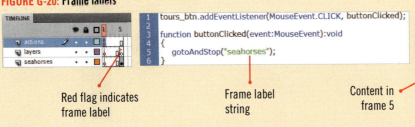
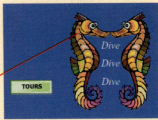

```
1  tours_btn.addEventListener(MouseEvent.CLICK, buttonClicked);
2
3  function buttonClicked(event:MouseEvent):void
4  {
5      gotoAndStop("seahorses");
6  }
```

Red flag indicates frame label

Frame label string

Content in frame 5

FIGURE G-21: Viewing the comments feature

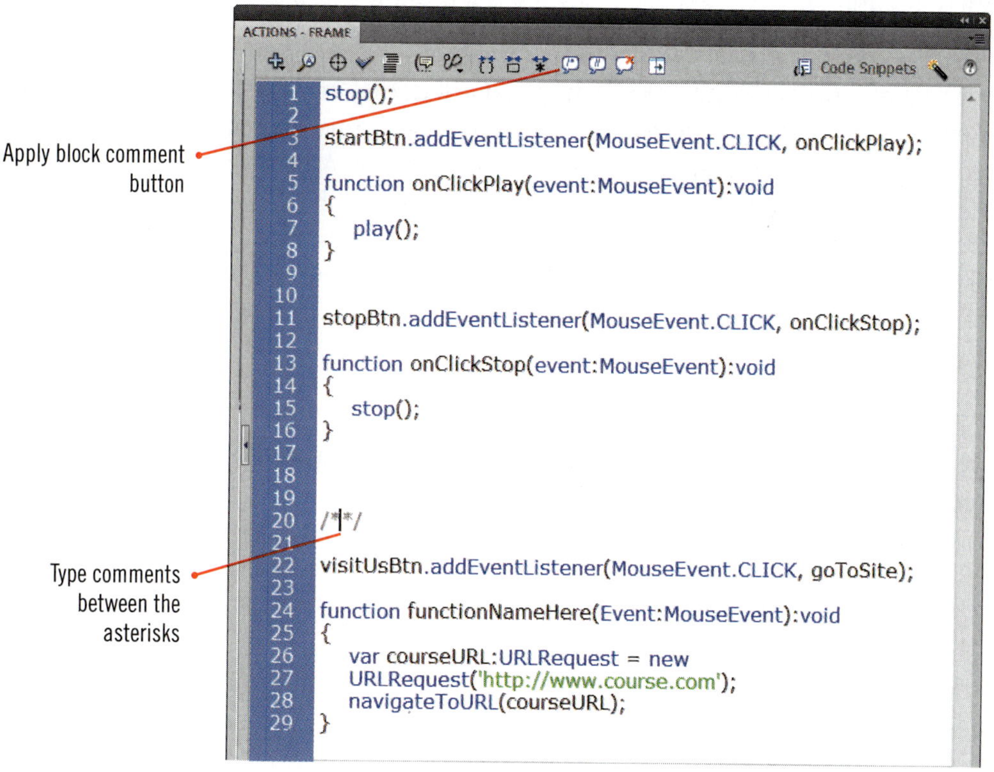

Apply block comment button →

Type comments between the asterisks →

```
1   stop();
2
3   startBtn.addEventListener(MouseEvent.CLICK, onClickPlay);
4
5   function onClickPlay(event:MouseEvent):void
6   {
7       play();
8   }
9
10
11  stopBtn.addEventListener(MouseEvent.CLICK, onClickStop);
12
13  function onClickStop(event:MouseEvent):void
14  {
15      stop();
16  }
17
18
19
20  /**/
21
22  visitUsBtn.addEventListener(MouseEvent.CLICK, goToSite);
23
24  function functionNameHere(Event:MouseEvent):void
25  {
26      var courseURL:URLRequest = new
27      URLRequest('http://www.course.com');
28      navigateToURL(courseURL);
29  }
```

ACTIONS - FRAME

Code Snippets

FIGURE G-22: Viewing comments

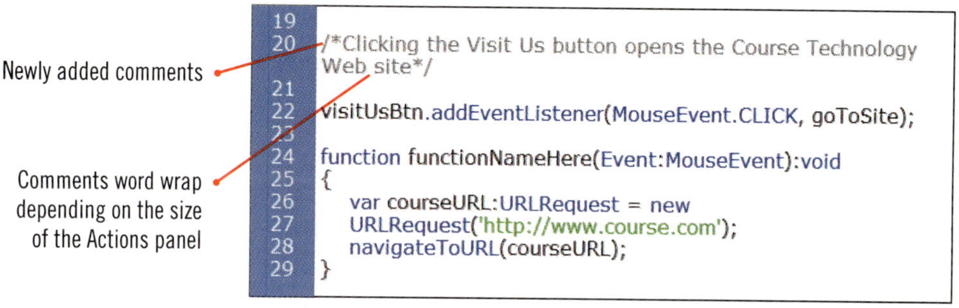

Newly added comments →

Comments word wrap depending on the size of the Actions panel →

```
19
20  /*Clicking the Visit Us button opens the Course Technology
    Web site*/
21
22  visitUsBtn.addEventListener(MouseEvent.CLICK, goToSite);
23
24  function functionNameHere(Event:MouseEvent):void
25  {
26      var courseURL:URLRequest = new
27      URLRequest('http://www.course.com');
28      navigateToURL(courseURL);
29  }
```

TABLE G-2: Comment buttons on the Actions panel toolbar

button	name	description
	Apply block comment	Use for multiline comments; comments are between forward slashes and asterisks
	Apply line comment	Use for a single-line comment; comment is after a double forward slash only
	Remove comment	Removes comment-specific punctuation from selected comments

Flash CS5

Using Code Snippets

The Code Snippets panel allows you to search for preset ActionScript code that adds common functionality to your movie. You can search in Actions, Timeline Navigation, Animation, Load and Unload, Audio and Video, and Event Handlers categories; options are listed in English, not ActionScript code, making it easier to find the functionality you want. Each option also has a tooltip that further explains what it does. Similar to using code hints, Flash identifies the variables in the project and inserts them in the code. ▨▨▨▨ Vanessa has given you a new assignment: She'd like you to create a new document for a scuba-centric trip. She'd like a graphic to appear when the user clicks a button. You're not sure how to write this in ActionScript, so you want to see how the Code Snippets panel can help.

STEPS

1. **Open the file FL G-2.fla from the location where you store your Data Files, save it as GreenWinds_codesnippet.fla, then test the movie**

   The logo is a button with an instance name already entered in the Instance Name text box on the Properties panel. The button changes shape slightly when you roll the mouse over it, and seahorses, which appear in the Timeline in frame 10, flash on and off. You want the seahorses to appear and stay visible when the user clicks the logo button.

   > **QUICK TIP**
   > To insert a code snippet in a single frame, click the frame in the Timeline.

2. **Click the logo button on the Stage to select it, show the Actions panel, then click the Code Snippets button on the toolbar**

   The Code Snippets panel opens. Because you want the playhead to move to frame 10, where the seahorses appear, you look in Timeline Navigation for code to use.

   > **TROUBLE**
   > Move the Code Snippets panel out of the way, if necessary.

3. **Click the Timeline Navigation expand arrow ▶, read the tooltip, compare your screen to Figure G-23, point to Click to Go to Frame and Stop, read the tooltip, then double-click Click to Go to Frame and Stop**

   The code is inserted in the Actions panel, as shown in Figure G-24. In the Timeline, Flash created a new Actions layer for the ActionScript. In the Actions panel, Flash inserted the instance name of the button instance in the code. Code snippets provide exact instructions in the comments, so you can see exactly how to customize the code for your movie.

4. **Click line 14, read the comments, select 5 in the parentheses, then type 10**

   Per the instructions, you typed the frame number where the seahorses appear, frame 10.

   > **QUICK TIP**
   > To create, edit, delete, import, or export code snippets, click the Options button ✱ in the Code Snippets panel, then click an option.

5. **Test the movie, then click the logo button**

   As the movie plays, the seahorses flash on and off until you click the button, which executes the code and stops the movie in frame 10, so the seahorses remain visible. To complete the movie, you add a stop action so the movie does not play until the user clicks the logo button.

6. **In the Actions panel, click to place the insertion point on line 16, press [Enter], then type stop(); on line 17**

7. **Test the movie, click the logo button, then compare your screen to Figure G-25**

   The seahorses appear when you click the logo button.

8. **Save the document, then exit Flash**

FIGURE G-23: Viewing the Code Snippets panel

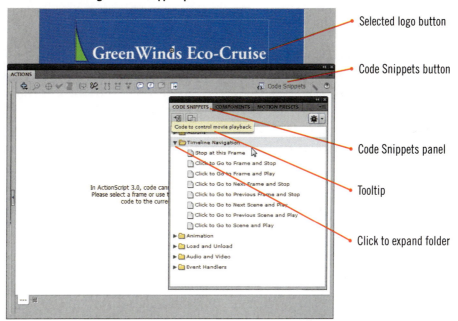

- Selected logo button
- Code Snippets button
- Code Snippets panel
- Tooltip
- Click to expand folder

FIGURE G-24: Viewing inserted code

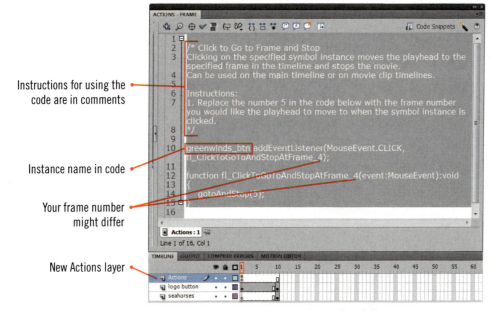

- Instructions for using the code are in comments
- Instance name in code
- Your frame number might differ
- New Actions layer

FIGURE G-25: Code snippet causes graphic to appear

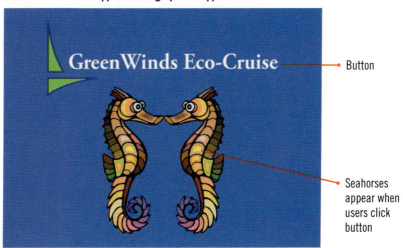

- Button
- Seahorses appear when users click button

Practice

For current SAM information, including versions and content details, visit SAM Central (http://www.cengage.com/samcentral). If you have a SAM user profile, you may have access to hands-on instruction, practice, and assessment of the skills covered in this unit. Since various versions of SAM are supported throughout the life of this text, check with your instructor for the correct instructions and URL/Web site for accessing assignments.

Concepts Review

Label the elements of the Flash screen shown in Figure G-26.

FIGURE G-26

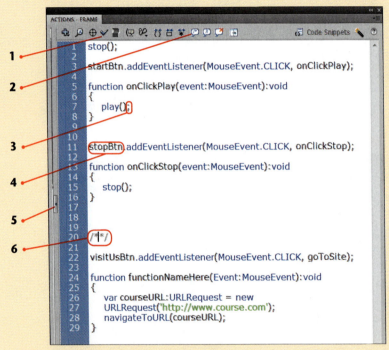

1. _____
2. _____
3. _____
4. _____
5. _____
6. _____

Match each term with the statement that best describes it.

7. **Check syntax button**
8. **Actions panel**
9. **Trace statement**
10. **Syntax**
11. **Scripting language**

a. Governs the order, structure, and use of words in code
b. Makes a statement appear in the Output panel when an action is performed
c. Determines the accuracy of punctuation in a block of code
d. A program used to execute specific commands
e. Where you create ActionScript

Select the best answer from the list of choices.

12. What is a complete sentence known as in ActionScript?

  a. Message   **c.** Instruction

  b. Statement   **d.** Command

13. What is the specific instruction that tells Flash to pay attention to an event?

  a. Mouse Listener   **c.** Event Listener

  b. Event Trigger   **d.** Event Action

14. What color are code comments?

  a. Gray   **c.** Green

  b. Black   **d.** Blue

15. On which panel can you name an instance of a button?

  a. Actions   **c.** Compiler Errors

  b. Output   **d.** Properties

16. Where can you place ActionScript?

  a. In a keyframe   **c.** On any object

  b. On a button   **d.** On any symbol

Skills Review

1. Understand ActionScript 3.0.

  a. Describe what a scripting language is.

  b. Describe how you can use ActionScript to enhance a button's functionality.

  c. Describe what happens if there is a syntax error in code.

2. Add a stop action to a movie.

  a. Start Flash, open the file FL G-3.fla from the location where you store your Data Files, then save it as **LightFootRecycling_actions.fla**.

  b. Create a new layer named **actions** above the buttons layer in the Timeline, then click frame 1.

  c. Open the Actions panel using a command on the Window menu, then adjust it so only the Script pane is visible, if necessary.

  d. Type **stop();** on line 1, press [Enter] (Win) or [return] (Mac) three times, then view the ActionScript keyframe in frame 1 of the actions layer.

  e. Test the movie, close the Flash Player, collapse the Actions panel, then save the document.

3. Add a play action to a button.

  a. Select the Start button on the Stage, show the Properties panel if necessary, then name the instance **startBtn**.

  b. Open the file ActionScript.as from the location where you store your Data Files, then copy the code on lines 10 to 15.

  c. Click frame 1 in the actions layer of the LightFootRecycling_actions.fla document, show the Actions panel, turn on Word Wrap from the panel options menu if necessary, then paste the copied code starting on line 4.

  d. Replace generic code with the following code:

line(s)	select code	replace code
4	instanceNameHere	startBtn
4, 6	functionNameHere	onClickPlay

  e. Test the movie, then click the Start button.

  f. Close the Flash Player, then save the document.

4. Copy and modify code.

  a. Select the Stop button on the Stage, show the Properties panel if necessary, then name the instance **stopBtn**.

  b. Click frame 1 in the actions layer of the LightFootRecycling_actions.fla document, show the Actions panel, then copy the code on lines 4 to 9.

  c. Position the mouse pointer at the end of line 9, press [Enter] (Win) or [return] (Mac) three times, then paste the code starting on line 12.

Skills Review (continued)

d. Replace the Start button code with the following code:

line(s)	select code	replace code
12	startBtn	stopBtn
12, 14	onClickPlay	onClickStop
16	play();	stop();

e. Save the document.

5. Test code.

a. Make sure that frame 1 in the actions layer is selected and that the Actions panel is open.

b. On line 14, delete the close parenthesis before the colon, use a button on the toolbar to check the syntax, then read the error description in the Compiler Errors panel.

c. Fix the error, then check the syntax.

d. Select the code on line 16, then type **trace("Stop the movie with the click of a button");**.

e. Test the movie, click the Stop button, read the message in the Output panel, then close the Flash Player.

f. Select the code on line 16, type **stop();**, then test the movie and the Start and Stop buttons.

g. Close the Flash Player, then save the document.

6. Open a Web site from a button.

a. Select the Visit Us button on the Stage, show the Properties panel, then name the instance **visitUsBtn**.

b. Show the ActionScript.as window, copy the code on lines 21 to 28, then close the file. (*Hint*: Collapse the Actions panel if necessary.)

c. Click the Timeline tab, click frame 1 in the actions layer of the LightFootRecycling_actions.fla document, show the Actions panel, position the mouse pointer at the end of line 17, press [Enter] (Win) or [return] (Mac) three times, then paste the copied code starting on line 20.

d. Replace generic code with the following code:

line(s)	select code	replace code
20	instanceNameHere	visitUsBtn
20, 22	functionNameHere	goToSite
24, 26	openthisURLHere	adobeURL
25	websitenameHere.com	adobe.com

e. Check the syntax, test the movie, click the Start, Stop, and Visit Us buttons, then view the Web page in your browser.

f. Close your browser and the Flash Player, then save the document.

7. Add comments to code.

a. Show the Actions panel, place the insertion point on line 19, then press [Enter] (Win) or [return] (Mac) three times.

b. Move to line 21, use the Apply line comment button on the toolbar to insert a line comment, then type **The Visit Us button opens the Adobe home page**. (*Hint*: You do not need to add any closing comment notation.)

c. Compare your Actions panel to Figure G-27.

d. Test the movie, click the Start, Stop, and Visit Us buttons, then close your browser and the Flash Player.

e. Save and close the document.

FIGURE G-27

```
1    stop();
2
3
4    startBtn.addEventListener(MouseEvent.CLICK, onClickPlay);
5
6    function onClickPlay(event:MouseEvent):void
7    {
8        play();
9    }
10
11
12   stopBtn.addEventListener(MouseEvent.CLICK, onClickStop);
13
14   function onClickStop(event:MouseEvent):void
15   {
16       stop();
17   }
18
19
20
21   //The Visit Us button opens the Adobe home page
22
23   visitUsBtn.addEventListener(MouseEvent.CLICK, goToSite);
24
25   function goToSite(Event:MouseEvent):void
26   {
27       var adobeURL:URLRequest = new
28       URLRequest('http://www.adobe.com');
29       navigateToURL(adobeURL);
30   }
```

Using ActionScript 3.0

Skills Review (continued)

8. Use code snippets.

  a. Open the file FL G-4.fla from the location where you store your Data Files, then save it as **LightFootRecycling_ codesnippet.fla**

  b. Click the bin button on the Stage, show the Actions panel, then use a button on the toolbar to show the Code Snippets panel.

  c. Expand the Timeline Navigation folder, then insert the code for Click to Go to Frame and Stop.

  d. Test the movie, then click the bin button.

  e. Place the insertion point on line 16, press **[Enter]**, then type **stop();** on line 17.

  f. Test the movie, click the bin button, then compare your screen to Figure G-28.

  g. Save and close the document, then exit Flash.

Independent Challenge 1

You work at CoasterWoop, an online source of news by, for, and about roller coaster enthusiasts. You've added buttons to the movie. Now your boss asks you to add actions to the movie and the buttons. Currently, the movie features animation of the roller coaster car rolling on the tracks and the large pinwheels spinning. Your boss wants the movie to be static when users view it, play when users click the Start button, then open a Web site when users click the Visit Us button.

  a. Start Flash, open the file FL G-5.fla from the location where you store your Data Files, then save it as **CoasterWoop_actions.fla**.

  b. Create a new layer named **actions** at the top of the Timeline.

  c. Select the Start button on the Stage, name its instance **startBtn** on the Properties panel, select the Visit Us button on the Stage, then name its instance **visitUsBtn** on the Properties panel.

  d. Unlock the Entrance layer, select the left pinwheel on the Stage, name its instance **pinWheel1Mc** on the Properties panel, select the right pinwheel on the Stage, then name its instance **pinWheel2Mc** on the Properties panel. (*Hint*: You name the instances so you can control the Timeline for the movie clips in the Actions panel.)

  e. Click frame 1 in the actions layer, show the Actions panel, write code on line 1 to stop the movie from playing when it opens, then insert three blank lines.

  f. Using Figure G-29 as a reference, type the code in the Actions panel starting on line 4.

  g. Check the syntax, then correct any errors.

  h. Test the movie, test the buttons, then view the Web page in your browser.

  i. Close your browser, then close the Flash Player.

  j. Save and close the document, then exit Flash.

FIGURE G-29

```
4    //This code stops the pinwheels from turning
5    this.pinWheel1Mc.stop();
6    this.pinWheel2Mc.stop();
7
8
9
10   startBtn.addEventListener(MouseEvent.CLICK, overPlayAll);
11
12   function overPlayAll(event:MouseEvent):void
13   {
14       play();
15   this.pinWheel1Mc.play();
16   this.pinWheel2Mc.play();
17   }
18
19
20
21   visitUsBtn.addEventListener(MouseEvent.CLICK, goToSite);
22
23   function goToSite(Event:MouseEvent):void
24   {
25       var courseURL:URLRequest = new
26       URLRequest('http://www.course.com');
27       navigateToURL(courseURL);
28   }
```

Independent Challenge 2

As the new program director at Lingoroots, an educational Web site specializing in linguistics, you're constantly looking for exciting ways to engage new visitors. For the next Web site feature, you'll compare the evolution of written Chinese across its 4,000-year history. The earliest written Chinese characters were pictures and evolved to a more stylized and artistic writing form. You want to show how Chinese calligraphy has changed over time. You decide to add actions to the movie and buttons so users will be able to control the movie. You also create a separate movie that uses code snippets to make text appear when a user clicks a button.

a. Start Flash, open the file FL G-6.fla from the location where you store your Data Files, then save it as **lingoroots_actions.fla**.

b. Create a new layer named **actions** at the top of the Timeline.

c. Select the Start button on the Stage, name its instance **startBtn**, select the Stop button on the Stage, name its instance **stopBtn**, select the Visit Us button on the Stage, then name its instance **visitUsBtn**.

d. Open the file ActionScript.as from the location where you store your Data Files, copy all the code in lines 3 to 28, then close the ActionScript.as file.

e. Make sure that frame 1 in the actions layer is selected in the lingoroots_actions.fla file, paste the copied code in the Actions panel, then using Figure G-30 as a guide, change the generic code so that the movie opens in a static state in frame 1, the Start button starts the movie when the user clicks it, the Stop button stops the movie when the user clicks it, and the Visit Us button opens a Web page at Wikipedia.org on Chinese language when the user clicks it.

FIGURE G-30

```
1   stop();
2
3
4   //When the user clicks the Start button, the movie will play.
5
6   startBtn.addEventListener(MouseEvent.CLICK, clickPlay);
7
8   function clickPlay(event:MouseEvent):void
9   {
10      play();
11  }
12
13  //When the user clicks the Stop button, the movie will stop.
14
15  stopBtn.addEventListener(MouseEvent.CLICK, clickStop);
16
17  function clickStop(event:MouseEvent):void
18
19  {
20      stop();
21  }
22
23  //When the user clicks the Visit Us button, a Web site about the Chinese language
    opens in a browser.
24
25  visitUsBtn.addEventListener(MouseEvent.CLICK, goToSite);
26
27  function goToSite(Event:MouseEvent):void
28  {
29      var chineseLangURL:URLRequest = new
30      URLRequest('http://en.wikipedia.org/wiki/Chinese_language');
31      navigateToURL(chineseLangURL);
32  }
```

f. Add comments of your choice above each button's code in the Actions panel, then remove blank lines if desired.

g. Test the movie, test the buttons, then view the Web page in your browser.

h. Close your browser, then close the Flash Player.

i. Save the document.

Advanced Challenge Exercise

▪ Place the mouse pointer at the end of the stop(); line of code on line 20, add a new line, create the trace statement of your choice, test the movie, click the stop button, then view the message in the Output panel.

j. Close the document, navigate to the location where you store your Data Files, open FL G-7.fla, then save it as **lingoroots_codesnippet.fla**.

k. Click the dragon button on the Stage, show the Actions panel, show the Code Snippets panel, then insert a code snippet that will go to a frame and stop the movie.

l. Follow the comment instructions to customize the code. (*Hint*: Have the playhead stop at frame 10.)

m. Insert code at the bottom of the Actions panel to make sure the movie does not play until the user clicks the button.

n. Test the movie, save and close the document, then exit Flash.

Independent Challenge 3

You work for ibRobotz, an online entertainment site. Users can download ibRobotz characters or create their own to insert in stories. Your boss wants the buttons to engage when users move the mouse pointer over them.

a. Start Flash, open the file FL G-8.fla from the location where you store your Data Files, then save it as **ibrobotz_actions.fla**.

b. Create a new layer named **actions** at the top of the Timeline.

FIGURE G-31

c. Give the initiate, halt, and contact buttons appropriate instance names.

d. Open the file ActionScript.as from the location where you store your Data Files, copy all the code in lines 3 to 28, then close the ActionScript.as file.

e. Make sure that frame 1 in the actions layer is selected in the ibrobotz_actions.fla document, paste the copied code, then using Figure G-31 as a guide, change the generic code so that the movie opens in a static state in frame 1 (except for the movie clip playing in the frame), the initiate button plays the movie when the user moves the mouse pointer over it, the halt button stops the movie when the user moves the mouse pointer over it, and the contact button opens the Web site of your choice when the user clicks the mouse. (*Hint*: Substitute the instance names you created in Step c.)

```
1  stop();
2
3
4  //When the user moves the mouse pointer over the initiate button, the
   movie will play.
5  initiateBtn.addEventListener(MouseEvent.MOUSE_OVER, onOverPlay);
6
7  function onOverPlay(event:MouseEvent):void
8  {
9      play();
10 }
11
12
13 //When the user moves the mouse pointer over the halt button, the
   movie will stop.
14 haltBtn.addEventListener(MouseEvent.MOUSE_OVER, onOverStop);
15
16 function onOverStop(event:MouseEvent):void
17 {
18     stop();
19 }
20
21
22 //When the user clicks the contact button, the Course Technology Web
   site will open.
23 contactBtn.addEventListener(MouseEvent.CLICK, goToSite);
24
25 function goToSite(Event:MouseEvent):void
26 {
27     var courseURL:URLRequest = new
28     URLRequest('http://www.course.com');
29     navigateToURL(courseURL);
30 }
```

f. Add comments of your choice above each button's code in the Actions panel, then remove blanks lines if desired.

g. Test the movie, test the buttons, then view the Web page in your browser.

h. Close your browser, then close the Flash Player.

i. Save the document.

Advanced Challenge Exercise

- Place the mouse pointer at the end of the stop(); line of code on line 18, add a new line, create a trace statement of your choice, test the movie, mouse over the halt button, then view the message in the Output panel.

j. Exit Flash.

Real Life Independent Challenge

This Independent Challenge will continue to build on the personal movie that you have been developing since Unit B. Here, you add a button to the movie.

a. Start Flash, open the file myproject.fla, then save it as **myproject_actions.fla**.

b. Use the skills you learned in this unit to add interactivity to your movie, including buttons.

c. Add code in the Actions panel so a button stops or plays a movie. Add comments where appropriate.

d. Test the movie and the buttons.

e. Save and close the document myproject_actions.fla, then exit Flash.

Visual Workshop

Visiting Web sites is a great way to get inspired for your own projects. Figure G-32 shows the monoface showcase Web page from the branding agency mono-1.com. Go to http://mono-1.com/monoface/main.html, click the "what do i do?" link, then follow the instructions to build a face. Answer the questions below. For each question, include why or how you reached a conclusion. You can open a word processor or use the Text Tool in Flash to complete this exercise. When you are finished, write down the URL of the Web page you select in Step d, add your name to the document, save it, print it, then close the word processor or exit Flash.

a. Identify the actions associated with the buttons and links at the monoface site.

b. What actions are associated with the text buttons and areas of the face?

c. Click the shuffle face and view gallery links, then briefly describe the action associated with those functions.

d. Go to one of the following Web sites, view several sites, then select one for the purpose of answering the following questions. Be sure to look for sections or links dedicated to Flash sites.

- www.thefwa.com/
- www.coolwebawards.com/?go=Nothing_but_flash

e. For each site you visited, including the site in Step d, what is the Web site's purpose and goal?

f. Who is the target audience? How does the design (look and feel) of the Web site fit the target audience?

g. What kinds of actions are associated with buttons?

h. Looking at the animation in the introduction and on the home page:

- What is animated on this page? Can you guess the kind of animation used?
- How is sound used?
- How many animations occur simultaneously?
- What is your overall opinion of the design, organization, and function of this page? How would you improve it?

i. Close your browser.

FIGURE G-32

UNIT
H
Flash CS5

Integrating Flash with Other Programs

STOP *This unit assumes you have Fireworks CS5, Photoshop CS5, and Dreamweaver CS5 installed on your computer, and that the file association for PNG files is set to Fireworks.*

When you create a Flash movie, you often work with a team using media in different programs. In this unit, you'll see how Flash interacts with other programs in the Adobe Creative Suite 5, specifically Adobe Fireworks, Adobe Photoshop, and Adobe Dreamweaver, to create animations and Web pages. You will also explore the issue of copyright law and publicly available material. The marketing team at GreenWinds Eco-Cruise wants to explore how they can use other Adobe products with their movie. You'll first review the concept of integration, import and edit media from Fireworks and Photoshop, insert and edit the GreenWinds movie from Dreamweaver, and then review concepts related to copyright law.

OBJECTIVES

Understand Flash integration

Import a Fireworks PNG file into Flash

Use roundtrip editing

Import a Photoshop PSD file into Flash

Edit a Photoshop image from Flash

Insert a Flash movie into Dreamweaver

Edit a Flash movie from Dreamweaver

Understand copyright

Understanding Flash Integration

As you have seen from your own projects and from exploring the Web throughout this book, Flash movies rarely stand alone; they usually rely on the other Adobe Creative Suite 5 programs to supply them with graphic objects and give them context. Flash animations consist of graphics in various formats and are usually part of a larger Web page.  Vanessa asks you for an overview of how she can integrate Flash movies with other Adobe Creative Suite 5 products.

DETAILS

When you use Flash movies with other Adobe programs, you should understand how to:

- **Integrate files**

  To create and use Flash movies effectively, you should know how Adobe Creative Suite 5 (CS5) program files can work together to create powerful visual experiences for your users. **Integration** is the process of combining suite components into Flash and incorporating Flash animations into Web pages. Figure H-1 shows a NASA Web site about the Hubble Telescope that incorporates objects created in Fireworks, Flash, Dreamweaver, and other programs in CS5, including Adobe Premiere, Flex, Flex Builder, Illustrator, and Bridge.

- **Use Adobe programs together**

  You can create graphics and illustrations for your Flash movies in conjunction with the following programs, as shown in Figure H-2:

  - **Adobe Fireworks** lets you create and edit bitmap and vector images as well as create Web page prototypes, which are models of what a Web page should look like. You can import animated Fireworks elements into Flash so that the layers are editable, or you can import layered Fireworks graphics so that the image is a noneditable bitmap image in Flash.
  - **Adobe Illustrator** lets you design and edit vector graphics, which are best for detailed graphic designs, illustrations, logos—any graphic that needs to be resized and still maintain its clarity.
  - **Adobe Photoshop** lets you create bitmap images in which you can manipulate practically every aspect of their appearance. After you customize an image, you can import the layered Photoshop PSD file into Flash, where you can specify how you want it to appear.
  - **Adobe Dreamweaver** lets you create Web pages in HTML format. You can place a Flash animation on a Dreamweaver Web page or save it as its own HTML document, as you did in Unit E.

  To create original art and manipulate photos in these Adobe programs, you would need to know how to use each one. But even if you only understand Flash basics, you can still import and edit objects that were created using those programs.

  - **Adobe Flash Catalyst** is a design tool that lets you combine content from other programs and experience interaction and interactivity without having to code any component.

- **Use roundtrip editing**

  You may find that after you create an object such as a graphic or an animation and place it in another program, you then want to change the original. Instead of deleting the imported object, changing it in its original application, and reimporting it, you can use **roundtrip editing**, meaning that you can edit the imported item within Flash using the tools of the program that created it. Because editing is a frequent and usual part of creating animations and Web pages, roundtrip editing can save you considerable time during the course of a project.

QUICK TIP

For photographs, JPEG files work best; GIF and PNG files are best for large solid blocks of color, and PSD and AI files are preferred when importing art to use as source files for Flash projects.

QUICK TIP

If you want to include ActionScript with an imported Fireworks graphic, it is much easier to import it as a movie clip instead of converting the image and layers to a movie clip in Flash later.

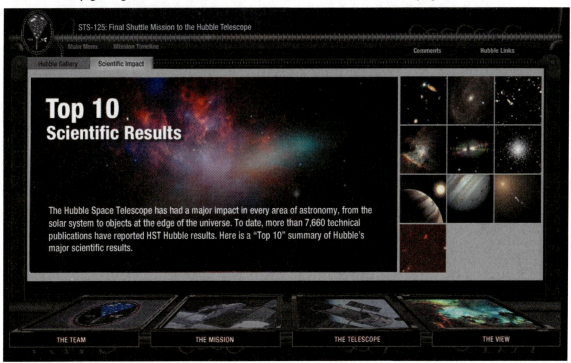

Courtesy NASA and STScI

FIGURE H-2: How you can integrate CS5 programs

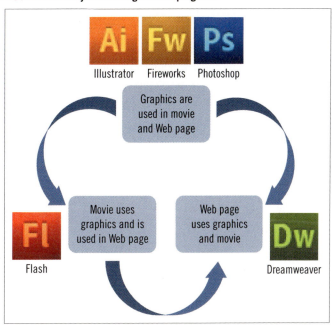

Understanding usability testing

Despite your best efforts to build a successful Flash project for your users, you'll need to understand what it's like to interact with your project as a new user. A best practice is to analyze feedback from how real users in your target audience interact with your Web site or interactive Flash project. Often, usability testing involves a user performing several tasks while sitting down with a trained observer who may takes notes, but not explain how to do something. A typical test plan involves developing a plan, identifying the user audience, obtaining test participants, testing, analyzing results, and finally, implementing the results into your project. Test results can show you what is or is not working, how easy it is for users to perform tasks, how they use interactive elements, even how they feel while interacting with your project. Users' feedback, which can be recorded as a video or completed through a questionnaire, provides invaluable information you can use to improve the user interface, and thus interest and approval from your target audience.

Importing a Fireworks PNG File into Flash

Designers often use Fireworks PNG files in Flash documents. You can choose whether you want to be able to edit the image with layers in Flash, or import the image as a single **flattened bitmap**, which compresses all layers into a single layer.  Vanessa has an image in the PNG format she'd like you to import into a new movie in Flash. You're not sure if she wants to be able to edit it in Flash or Fireworks, so you first import the image with layers editable in Flash.

STEPS

QUICK TIP
You can also click ActionScript 3.0 in the Create New section of the Welcome Screen.

1. **Start Flash, click File on the Application bar, point to New, click OK, then save the document as seahorse_FW_layers.fla in the location where you store your Data Files**

2. **Click File on the Application bar, point to Import, click Import to Stage, navigate to the location where you store your Data Files, click seahorse.png, then click Open**

   The Import Fireworks Document dialog box opens, as shown in Figure H-3. Here you can select whether to import the image with layers or as a flattened bitmap. A **page** in Fireworks stores all the layers in a document, or you can create new pages that store only certain layers, which is useful when you want to view different versions of a design or Web page. In the Into section, if you select Current frame as movie clip, Flash imports all of the PNG layers as new layers in the Timeline. If you select New Layer, Flash imports the page as a new layer in the Timeline.

QUICK TIP
You can also press [Ctrl][R] (Win) or [⌘][R] (Mac) to open the Import dialog box.

3. **Make sure the check box is not selected, click the Into arrow, click New Layer, click OK to import the image, then click Layer 1 in the Timeline**

   The seahorse.png file is imported into its own folder and layer in the Timeline, and a folder named Fireworks Objects appears in the Library panel, as shown in Figure H-4. The small red flag in frame 1 of the Page 1 layer indicates that a frame label, or name, was carried over from Fireworks. Because the layers were imported with the image, you can easily edit the object.

4. **Double-click the green rectangle on the Stage, click the Stroke color box on the Properties panel, then change the color to #000000**

   Flash inserts a black stroke around the rectangle. You have edited the imported Fireworks graphic in Flash.

5. **Return to the main movie, click the Pasteboard, then compare your screen to Figure H-5**

   The green rectangle has a stroke.

6. **Save and close the document**

Importing an Illustrator AI file

You can set default options for how you want Flash to import Illustrator AI files by opening the Preferences dialog box. To set Preferences for importing Illustrator files, click Edit (Win) or Flash (Mac) on the Application bar, click Preferences, then click the AI File Importer Category. Here you can select default options for text, paths, and their images, groups, and layers. The process for importing an Illustrator AI file is the same as with other Adobe programs: Click File on the Application bar, click Import, then click either Import to Stage or Import to Library. In the Import to Stage dialog box, you can select whether to import layers and their individual elements as a bitmap or movie clip, and how you want to convert layers: to Flash layers, keyframes, or a single Flash layer. You can also click the Incompatibility Report button to view incompatibilities with Flash. For example, a common incompatibility might be the color mode. Because Illustrator is used for print projects, where the color mode is always set to CMYK (cyan, magenta, yellow, black) instead of RGB (red, green blue), the color mode used for computers, mobile phones, and similar screens.

FIGURE H-3: Import dialog box

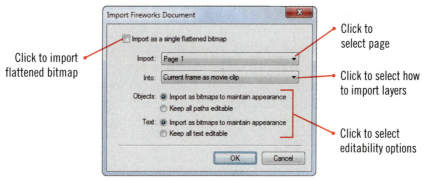

Click to import flattened bitmap

Click to select page

Click to select how to import layers

Click to select editability options

FIGURE H-4: Viewing an image and layers imported from Fireworks

Imported image

Imported image folder in Library panel

Imported layers in Timeline

FIGURE H-5: Viewing imported image edited in Flash

Stroke added to rectangle

Integrating Flash with Other Programs

Using Roundtrip Editing

As you have seen, when you import a layered image from Fireworks, you can edit it in Flash. However, if you import it as a flattened bitmap image, you cannot edit it in Flash; you must instead edit it in Fireworks using the roundtrip editing feature. Roundtrip editing lets you select a file you've inserted in one application, edit that file in its native environment, then seamlessly return to the open program to view the edited object. Vanessa plans to edit the seahorse graphic more extensively in Fireworks and asks you to demonstrate roundtrip editing.

TROUBLE

If you decide to redo this lesson, be sure to make a copy of the Data File; otherwise, you will modify the file permanently as you complete these steps.

1. **Open the file management utility for your computer, navigate to the location where you store your Data Files, click the file seahorse.png, copy and paste a copy of the file in the Data Files folder, then rename the copied file seahorse_roundtrip.png**

    You work with a copy of the Data File so you can preserve the original.

2. **Show Flash, click ActionScript 3.0 in the Create New section of the Welcome Screen, then save the new file as seahorse_FW_roundtrip.fla**

3. **Click File on the Application bar, point to Import, click Import to Stage, navigate to the location where you store your Data Files if necessary, click seahorse_roundtrip.png, then click Open**

    The Import Fireworks Document dialog box opens.

TROUBLE

If the Edit button is dimmed, right-click the image in the Library panel, click Edit with, navigate to where you store your Adobe program files, click the Adobe Fireworks CS5 program folder, then double-click Fireworks.exe.

4. **Click the Import as a single flattened bitmap check box, then click OK to import the image**

    The seahorse_roundtrip.png file is imported into Layer 1 on the Timeline, and you can see a single image listed in the Library panel. Data in the PNG file tells Flash that it was created in Fireworks. You decide to edit the file using roundtrip editing to open a Fireworks editing window.

5. **Click the image on the Stage to select it, show the Properties panel if necessary, then click the Edit button on the Properties panel**

    The image opens in a Fireworks editing window, as shown in Figure H-6. The Fireworks interface has features similar to Flash. You change the color of the rectangle using tools on the Fireworks Properties panel at the bottom of the screen.

QUICK TIP

The Pointer tool in Fireworks operates similar to the Selection tool in Flash.

6. **Make sure the Pointer tool is selected on the Fireworks Tools panel, click the green rectangle, click the Fill color box on the Fireworks Properties panel, double-click (Win) or click (Mac) the value in the hexadecimal text box, type #F5952D, then press [Enter] (Win) or [return] (Mac)**

    The rectangle fill color changes to orange, as shown in Figure H-7.

7. **Click the Done button at the top of the Editing from Flash window to close the Fireworks editing window and return to Flash**

    The image in Flash displays the edits you made to the rectangle fill, as shown in Figure H-8. Because you edited the source seahorse_roundtrip.png file directly in Fireworks, it, too, has been updated. Fireworks remains open, so you close it.

8. **Show Fireworks, exit Fireworks, show Flash, then save and close the document**

FIGURE H-6: Viewing the roundtrip editing window in Fireworks

Pointer tool

Roundtrip editing window features

Properties panel

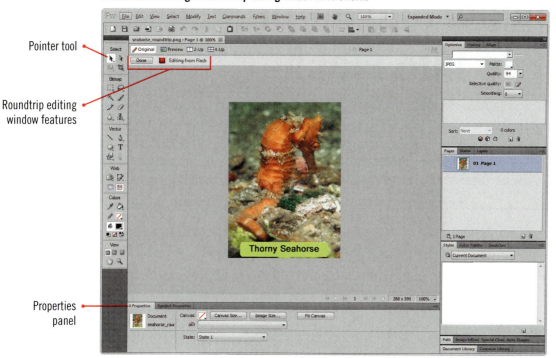

FIGURE H-7: Modifying the fill color of an object in Fireworks

Done button

New fill color

Fill color box

FIGURE H-8: Viewing the Fireworks-edited image in Flash

Updated image

Flash CS5

Importing a Photoshop PSD File into Flash

When you need to include photographs in your projects, you can easily incorporate Photoshop images. When you import a Photoshop PSD file into Flash, you can choose which layers to include and whether the layers will be editable in Flash. You can also set import preferences for Photoshop files in the Preferences dialog box. 🎨 The marketing department is beginning a new campaign for river cruises. Vanessa wants to edit the GreenWinds logo, so you keep that layer editable when you import the file into Flash.

STEPS

1. **Click ActionScript 3.0 in the Create New section of the Welcome Screen, then save the new file as china_rivers_PS.fla in the location where you store your Data Files**

QUICK TIP

To set Preferences for importing Photoshop documents, click Edit (Win) or Flash (Mac) on the Application bar, click Preferences, click the PSD File Importer Category, then select how you want Flash to import images, text, and shapes.

2. **Click File on the Application bar, point to Import, click Import to Stage, navigate to the location where you store your Data Files if necessary, click china_rivers.psd, then click Open**

The Import to Stage dialog box for Photoshop opens and lists the objects in the PSD file, as shown in Figure H-9. The name of the file you're importing appears in the title bar. Here you can select which layers to import and specific options for each layer type. You can choose whether the Photoshop layers are imported as layers or keyframes in Flash, and whether the Stage should resize to the size of the Photoshop image. You view the options for different layers.

3. **Click each layer and view the options for each one**

Each graphic layer is set to be imported as a flattened bitmap image, which is what Vanessa wants.

TROUBLE

Adjust the zoom as necessary.

4. **Select the Set stage size to resize to same size as Photoshop canvas check box at the bottom of the dialog box, click OK to import the image, show the Library, then click the Pasteboard**

The china_rivers.psd file is imported into several layers in the Timeline, and a folder named china_rivers.psd Assets appears in the Library panel, as shown in Figure H-10. Because you chose not to retain editability by importing each layer of the image as a flattened bitmap, you can delete two layers from the imported image and the original Layer 1 layer as they no longer affect the appearance of the object.

5. **Click the MASK layer in the Timeline, press and hold [Ctrl] (Win) or [⌘] (Mac), click the Shape 5 layer, click Layer 1, then click the Delete button 🗑 at the bottom of the Timeline**

6. **Click the Expand folder icon ▶ next to the china_rivers.psd Assets folder in the Library, then click ▶ next to the Dragon mask folder**

All objects in the Library panel are visible.

7. **Press and hold [Ctrl] (Win) or [⌘] (Mac), click the MASK and Shape 5 objects, then click 🗑 at the bottom of the Library panel**

The document no longer contains extraneous objects that may increase file size, as shown in Figure H-11.

8. **Save and close the document**

Design Matters

Animating bitmap images

Animating a bitmap image is as easy as animating a vector image, but beginning Flash animators should always remember the effect an animated bitmap image has on the movie's performance. Even after you optimize a bitmap image, and the movie's overall file size seems acceptable, performance can suffer because of the data load in individual frames. As you learned in Unit E, it's good practice to experiment with the compression settings for JPEG images to understand the trade-off between quality and performance.

Click name to view
layer import options

Click to exclude layer
from importing

Click to reset
Stage size to
image size

Click to
select how
layers import

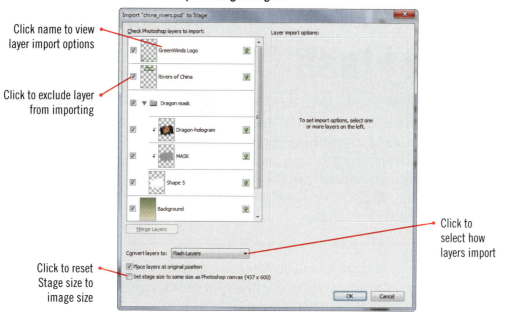

FIGURE H-10: Viewing an image and layers imported from Photoshop

Imported image

Imported
folder in
Library Panel

Imported layers
in Timeline

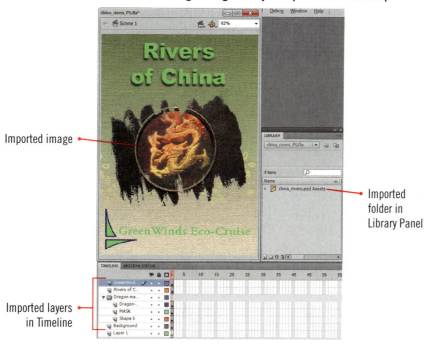

FIGURE H-11: Viewing imported image edited in Flash

Objects
deleted from
folder in the
Library

Layers deleted
from the
Timeline

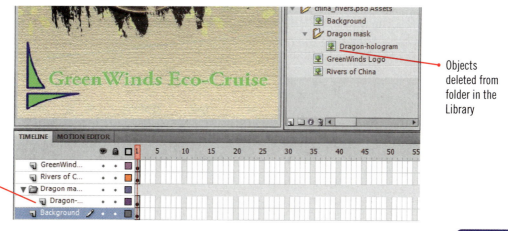

Integrating Flash with Other Programs

Flash CS5

Editing a Photoshop Image from Flash

Roundtrip editing from Flash to Photoshop is slightly different than from Flash to Fireworks. You can import an image file, such as a JPEG file, that was created in Photoshop into Flash and then edit it in Photoshop, but the file does not open in a roundtrip-specific editing window in Photoshop; it opens in a Photoshop editing window. So, instead of clicking the Done button, as you do in Fireworks, you must save and close the document in Photoshop. Flash updates the changes automatically in the image when you continue working on the movie in Flash.  Vanessa would like you to insert a new background image for the GreenWinds movie and then edit it in Photoshop.

STEPS

TROUBLE

If you decide to redo this lesson, be sure to make a copy of the Data File; otherwise, you will edit the file permanently as you complete these steps.

1. **Open the file management utility for your computer, navigate to the location where you store your Data Files, create a copy of the file ocean.jpg in the same folder, then rename the copied file ocean-roundtrip.jpg**

   You work with a copy of the Data File so you can preserve the original.

2. **Show Flash, open the file FL H-1.fla from the location where you store your Data Files, save it as GreenWinds_imports.fla, then click frame 1 in the ocean layer in the Timeline**

3. **Click File on the Application bar, point to Import, click Import to Stage, navigate to the location where you store your Data Files, click ocean-roundtrip.jpg, then click Open**

   The ocean image is imported directly to the Stage, but it is not aligned properly.

4. **Show the Properties panel, click the image on the Stage, then set the X value to 0 and the Y value to 0 in the Position and Size section of the Properties panel**

   The ocean image aligns perfectly on the Stage, as shown in Figure H-12. You decide to edit the file using roundtrip editing to open the file in Photoshop.

TROUBLE

You can also right-click an image in the Library, click Edit with, navigate to where the .exe file for the program is stored, then click Open to select a program with which to edit an image, if necessary.

5. **Click the Edit button on the Properties panel**

   The image opens in a Photoshop editing window, as shown in Figure H-13. The Photoshop interface has some features similar to Flash. You decide to blur the image to remove some of its graininess.

6. **Click Filter on the Application bar, point to Blur, then click Blur More**

   Photoshop blurs the image slightly. Photoshop does not have a roundtrip editing window, so you save and close the file.

7. **Click File on the Application bar, click Close, click Yes (Win) or Save (Mac) to save your changes, then exit Photoshop**

   You don't want to lose any more quality in the image, so you set the quality to maximum. Photoshop closes, and the changes to the image appear in Flash.

8. **Test the movie, click the Start button, compare your screen to Figure H-14, close the Flash Player, then save the document**

FIGURE H-12: Viewing imported and aligned image

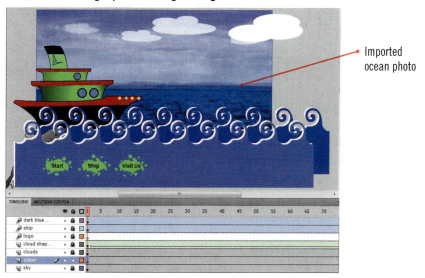

Imported
ocean photo

FIGURE H-13: Viewing image in Photoshop

Application
bar (Win)

Filter menu

FIGURE H-14: Viewing Photoshop-edited image in Flash

Edited image
with blur filter

Integrating Flash with Other Programs

Inserting a Flash Movie into Dreamweaver

As you use Dreamweaver to design Web pages, you will often want to include Flash movies. You can insert a Flash movie in a Dreamweaver document as part of an existing HTML document or as its own Web page in an HTML document. You need to publish the Flash movie to an SWF file before you insert it in Dreamweaver.  Vanessa wants to show management how versatile Flash movies can be in Dreamweaver. She asks you to insert the GreenWinds movie in a Dreamweaver Web page.

STEPS

1. **Click File on the Application bar, click Publish Settings, deselect every check box except the Flash (.swf) check box, click Publish, click OK to close the Publish Settings dialog box, then save and close the document**

   You published the SWF file, so it is ready to be inserted into a Dreamweaver Web page.

2. **Start Dreamweaver, open the file FL H-2.html from the location where you store your Data Files, then save it as GreenWinds_DW.html**

   An HTML document opens with a blue background, as shown in Figure H-15. You set the insertion point where you want to insert the GreenWinds movie in the document, which in this document is already set to the top center.

3. **Click Insert on the Application bar, point to Media, then click SWF, navigate to the location where you store your Data Files, click GreenWinds_imports.swf, then click OK (Win) or Choose (Mac)**

> **QUICK TIP**
> The Property inspector in Dreamweaver is similar to the Properties panel in Flash.

4. **Type GreenWinds Flash Movie in the Title text box in the Object Tag Accessibility Attributes dialog box, then click OK to close the dialog box**

   Screen readers will be able to read this object title. Also, the title text will appear in your browser when a user moves the mouse pointer over any part of the movie. A placeholder for the SWF file appears in the document, and options and information specific to the placeholder appear on the Property inspector, as shown in Figure H-16. You can play the Flash movie in Dreamweaver using controls on the Property inspector.

5. **Click the Play button on the Properties panel, click the Start button in the movie, watch the movie for a few seconds, then click the Stop button on the Property inspector**

   Clicking the Play button on the Property inspector opens the Flash Player in Dreamweaver. It doesn't play the movie if buttons have ActionScript to control that action. Similarly, clicking the Stop button on the Properties panel closes the Flash Player. The movie plays with fully functional buttons in the HTML document. Next, you save and preview the movie.

> **QUICK TIP**
> You must also include dependent files when uploading an HTML file to a server that contains a Flash movie.

6. **Click File on the Application bar, click Save, then click OK in the Copy Dependent Files dialog box**

   Flash saves the two dependent files, expressInstall.swf and swfobject_modified.js, to a Scripts folder in the location where you store your Data Files.

> **TROUBLE**
> If you are previewing the page in Internet Explorer 8, click the Information bar, click Allow Blocked Content, then click Yes to close the Security Warning dialog box.

7. **Click File on the Application bar, point to Preview in Browser, then click your default browser**

   The Web page opens in your browser, as shown in Figure H-17. If you point to the movie, a ScreenTip appears, showing the title you assigned to the movie in Step 4 above.

8. **Click the Start button, click the Stop button, then close your browser**

FIGURE H-15: Viewing an HTML document in Dreamweaver

Your path will differ

Flash movie will be inserted here

Blank HTML document

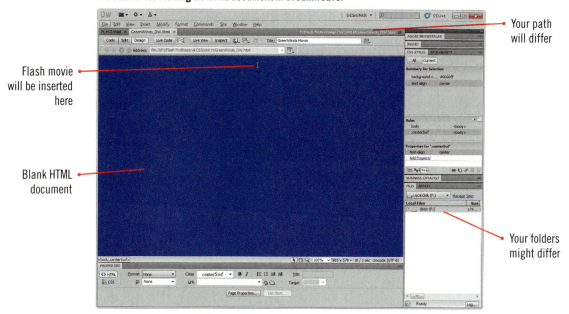

Your folders might differ

FIGURE H-16: Viewing a selected Flash placeholder

Insert menu

Selected Flash movie placeholder

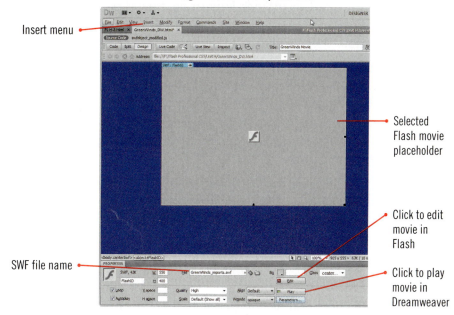

Click to edit movie in Flash

SWF file name

Click to play movie in Dreamweaver

FIGURE H-17: Previewing a Flash movie in a Web page

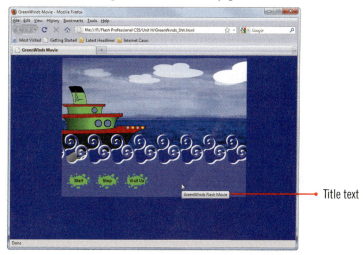

Title text

Integrating Flash with Other Programs

Editing a Flash Movie from Dreamweaver

Once you've inserted a Flash movie into Dreamweaver, you can edit it using Flash tools from within Dreamweaver. Flash and Dreamweaver have the same roundtrip editing integration functions as Flash and Fireworks. In Dreamweaver, you insert a published SWF file; so to edit the movie, you first locate the source FLA file to open it in Flash. Dreamweaver automatically republishes the movie as an SWF file.  Although the new ocean background is interesting, Vanessa wants you to modify the image so it is more stylized. You'll use the trace bitmap feature to accomplish this.

STEPS

1. **Make sure that GreenWinds_DW.html is open in Dreamweaver, then click the placeholder on the Stage to select it**
    Options for the placeholder appear on the Property inspector. You want to edit the movie in Flash, so you use the roundtrip editing feature.

2. **Click the Edit button on the Property inspector, navigate to the location where you store your Data Files, click GreenWinds_imports.fla, then click Open**
    The movie opens in a roundtrip editing window in Flash, as shown in Figure H-19. You decide to edit the ocean image to make it less realistic.

> **TROUBLE**
> Depending on the size of the image, rendering a bitmap image to a vector image requires significant processing power from your computer.

3. **Click the ocean image on the Stage, move to frame 1 in the Timeline if necessary, click Modify on the Application bar, point to Bitmap, click Trace Bitmap, click OK to accept the default settings, then click the Pasteboard**
    Flash converts the ocean bitmap image to a vector image, which matches the overall design, as shown in Figure H-20. You're satisfied with its appearance and are ready to return to Dreamweaver to preview the Web page in a browser.

4. **Click the Done button at the top of the Editing from Dreamweaver roundtrip editing window, click the movie placeholder in Dreamweaver, click the Play button in the Property inspector, click the Start button, then click the Stop button on the movie**
    Flash automatically republished the SWF movie.

5. **Click File on the Application bar, point to Preview in Browser, click your default browser, click the Start button, compare your screen to Figure H-21, then close all open browser windows**

6. **Close GreenWinds_DW.html and FL H-2.html in Dreamweaver, then exit Dreamweaver**

7. **Exit Flash**

Swapping a bitmap image

If you have two or more images or symbols in a document, you can swap one image or symbol (technically, its instance) for another right on the Stage. Swapping substitutes a new image or instance in the same location along with its attributes, such as size, color, or button states. If you have applied an animation to one instance and then swap it with another, the swapped-out instance has the animation applied to it, instead. To swap an object, select it on the Stage, then click the Swap button on the Properties panel. The Swap Symbol or Swap Bitmap dialog box opens, shown in Figure H-18, depending on the object selected. You can swap an object with any other similar object in the Library: a symbol with a symbol (either graphic, button,

or movie), or a bitmap image with another bitmap image. You can also duplicate a symbol in the Swap Symbol dialog box, which is a great time-saver if you need to modify the same symbol many times in a movie.

FIGURE H-18: Swap Bitmap dialog box

FIGURE H-19: Viewing the Flash roundtrip editing window

Roundtrip editing window features

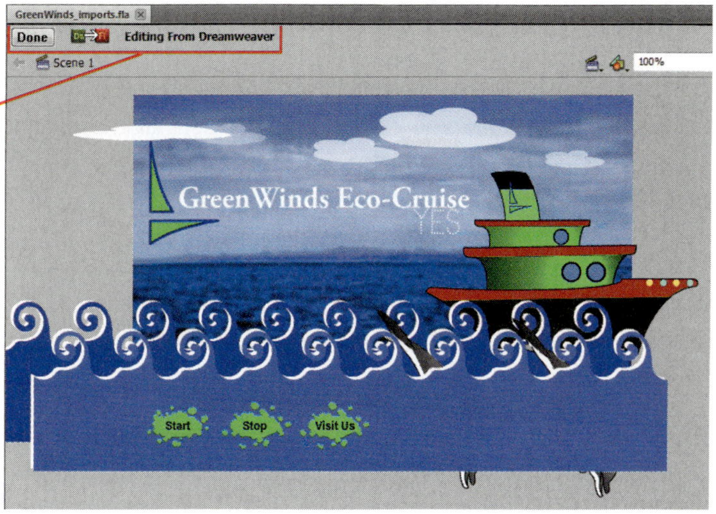

FIGURE H-20: Viewing results of Trace Bitmap command

Modify menu

Ocean bitmap converted to vector shapes

FIGURE H-21: Previewing edited Flash movie in a Web page

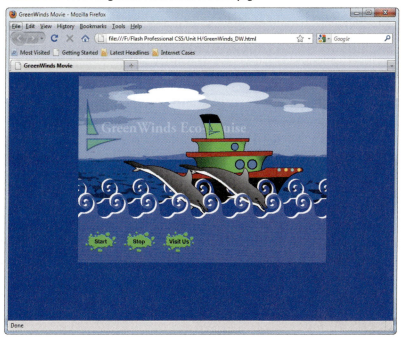

Understanding Copyright

The Web is full of engaging video, photos, and music, but can anyone use them however they wish? What about protecting your own work? The answers lie in understanding copyright law. Copyright law is a category of intellectual property. You can think of **intellectual property** as an idea or creation from a human mind that also has the potential for commercial value. Working at GreenWinds Eco-Cruise will require that you use material from many sources, so you familiarize yourself with the basics of copyright law.

Understanding copyright protection involves the following concepts:

- ### Copyright's purpose and what is copyrightable

  Copyright is a form of legal protection for authors of original works, whether those works are published or unpublished. The word **author** refers to any creator of a copyrighted work—composer, photographer, writer, or Flash animator. Copyright law gives authors exclusive rights to control how their work can be used, and it protects literary works, music, books, movies, art, dance, and computer code, among others.

  Purpose. The purpose of copyright law is to balance the interests of authors with the interests of the public. Copyright law gives authors a monopoly on their work for a set amount of time, but the law also dissolves that monopoly by eventually allowing the work to be accessed by the public, which presumably would build upon and improve the work for the progress of society.

  Copyright law defines copyrighted works as "original works of authorship fixed in any tangible medium of expression." In other words, the result is something created by you that someone else can experience. The major components of copyright consist of:
  - Originality: An independent creation with a small amount of creativity; doesn't have to be unique.
  - Fixation: Established in a tangible medium; this is the defining aspect of a work being copyrightable. The work exists, and it can be experienced, from a full-length movie to a digital work stored for a nanosecond in computer RAM.
  - Expression: A person's unique output or take on an idea. An idea is not protected (taking a photo on the beach at sunset), but the expression of that idea is (clicking a camera at a particular moment).

- ### Copyright protection

  Start and duration. A work acquires copyright protection *as soon as* you create it. Generally, for an individual, copyright lasts the life of the author plus 70 years. You don't have to register your work with the U.S. Copyright Office, shown in Figure H-22, to prove your copyright or use the copyright symbol (©), but you establish your strongest legal position when you do (the cost is $35 for an online submission at the time of this book's printing).

  Your rights. Copyright law protects your work by giving you the right to reproduce a work, create a new work based on the original (known as a **derivative work**), distribute copies, and perform or display a work publicly and digitally. Cropping and altering a photo would be considered making a derivative work.

- ### Public domain, flexible licensing, and permissions

  You should assume that every text and media file (audio, video, image) on the Internet has copyright protection or protection under another category of intellectual property law. Works no longer protected by some form of intellectual property law are in the **public domain**; therefore, no one owns them or controls their use. You can use and modify public domain content however you wish. Even if a work is protected, you can obtain written permission from the owner, thus ensuring your ability to use the work. To retain some of your rights but share the work so others may build upon it, learn about Creative Commons copyright licenses, shown in Figure H-23. You should cite Web sites and media you download from the Internet, although attribution is never a substitute for permission. Common citation styles include APA, MLA, and Chicago. For an example, visit www.apastyle.org, then click a link, such as Learning APA Style.

FIGURE H-22: The U.S. Copyright Office home page—www.copyright.gov

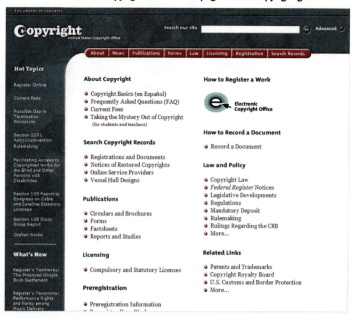

FIGURE H-23: The Creative Commons home page

Courtesy Creative Commons (http://creativecommons.org)

Understanding copyright infringement and fair use

Copyright infringement is the unauthorized use of one or more of the rights of a copyright holder. The penalty per infringement of a registered copyright can be tens of thousands of dollars. Even accidental infringement can lead to penalties. The assumptions and burdens of proof governing copyright infringement are based on civil law, which has broader rules of evidence. Civil law does not require proof of infringement beyond a reasonable doubt. The court's assumption may be that you are guilty, and the burden of proof is on you to prove that you're not.

The **Fair Use Doctrine** is a built-in limitation to copyright protection that allows users to copy all or part of a copyrighted work in support of their First Amendment and other rights. You do not need to ask permission from the copyright holder for a fair use of the work. For example, you could excerpt short passages of a protected film or song, or parody a television show, even though your use may have commercial value. Determining whether fair use applies to a work depends on the purpose of its use, the nature of the copyrighted work, the amount you want to copy, and the effect on the salability or value of the work. Fair use is used as the defense in many copyright-infringement cases, but it is always decided on a case-by-case basis—there is no set legal formula.

Practice

Concepts Review

For current SAM information, including versions and content details, visit SAM Central (http://www.cengage.com/samcentral). If you have a SAM user profile, you may have access to hands-on instruction, practice, and assessment of the skills covered in this unit. Since various versions of SAM are supported throughout the life of this text, check with your instructor for the correct instructions and URL/Web site for accessing assignments.

Label the elements of the screen shown in Figure H-24.

FIGURE H-24

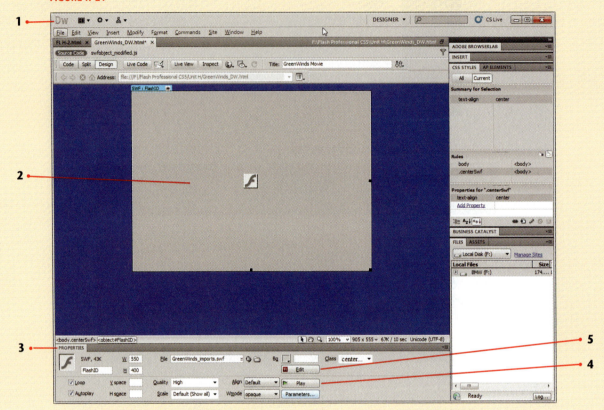

1. _____   4. _____
2. _____   5. _____
3. _____

Match each term with the statement that best describes it.

6. **Single flattened bitmap**
7. **How an SWF file appears in a Dreamweaver document**
8. **Copyright infringement**
9. **Roundtrip editing**
10. **Intellectual property**

a. Allows you to edit a file in its native program and return immediately to another program
b. An idea or creation from a human mind
c. A placeholder
d. Is imported into the selected layer in Flash
e. The unauthorized use of a work in violation of someone's copyright

Select the best answer from the list of choices.

11. In Flash, on which panel do you find the Edit button?
- **a.** Library
- **b.** Roundtrip edit
- **c.** Info
- **d.** Properties

12. What are the built-in exceptions to copyright law known as?
- **a.** Copyright infringement
- **b.** Fair use
- **c.** Open access
- **d.** Public domain

13. What is the native file format for a Fireworks document?
- **a.** PSD
- **b.** PNG
- **c.** PHP
- **d.** FLA

14. Before inserting a Flash movie in Dreamweaver, what action should you perform in Flash?
- **a.** Publish the document as an HTML file.
- **b.** Publish the document as a JPEG file.
- **c.** Publish the document as an SWF file.
- **d.** Do not publish the document.

Skills Review

1. Understand Flash integration.
- **a.** Describe how integration can work in the Adobe Creative Suite 5.
- **b.** List two programs commonly used to create source bitmap or vector artwork for your projects.
- **c.** Describe how roundtrip editing works.

2. Import a Fireworks PNG file into Flash.
- **a.** Start Flash, then open a new file and save it as **recycling_art_FW_layers.fla** in the location where you store your Data Files.
- **b.** Use a command on the File menu to import to the Stage the file **recycling_art.png** as a new layer with paths and text editable.
- **c.** Select just the text in the text object on the Stage, then change the Style in the Character section of the Properties panel to bold italic.
- **d.** Deselect the text object, then save and close the document.

3. Use roundtrip editing.
- **a.** Use the file management utility on your computer to navigate to the location where you store your Data Files, create a copy of the file recycling_art.png, then rename the copy **recycling_art-roundtrip.png**.
- **b.** In Flash, create a new file and save it as **recycling_art_FW_roundtrip.fla**.
- **c.** Use a command on the File menu to import to the Stage the file **recycling_art-roundtrip.png** as a single flattened bitmap image.
- **d.** Select the image on the Stage, then use a button on the Properties panel to edit the image in Fireworks. (*Hint:* Depending on the file associations set up for your computer, you might need to right-click the image on the Stage, click Edit with, then select Fireworks.exe.)
- **e.** In Fireworks, click the text object on the canvas (Stage) to select the text, click the Fill color box on the Properties panel to open the color pop-up window, double-click (Win) or click (Mac) the hexadecimal value, type **#660000**, then press [Enter] (Win) or [return] (Mac) to close the color pop-up window.
- **f.** Click the Bold button on the Properties panel, then click the Done button in the Editing from Flash roundtrip window to return to Flash.
- **g.** Deselect the image, resize and center the image on the Stage, compare your screen to Figure H-25, then save and close the document.
- **h.** Show Fireworks, then exit Fireworks.

FIGURE H-25

The possibilities are endless

4. Import a Photoshop PSD file into Flash.

  a. In Flash, create a new file, then save it as **recycling_puzzle_PS.fla** in the location where you store your Data Files.

  b. Use a command on the File menu to import to the Stage the file **recycling_puzzle.psd** from the location where you store your Data Files, then in the Import to Stage dialog box, make sure each individual layer will be imported as a flattened bitmap image if that option is available. Select Flash Layers as the convert layers type if necessary, then set the stage size to be the same as the Photoshop canvas.

  c. Click the Pasteboard, then delete the Layer 1, Mask, and Shape 3 layers in the Timeline, then delete the MASK and Shape 3 objects in the Library.

  d. Compare your screen to Figure H-26, then save and close the document.

FIGURE H-26

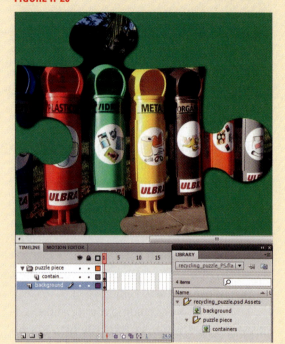

5. Edit a Photoshop image from Flash.

  a. Use the file management utility on your computer to navigate to the location where you store your Data Files, create a copy of the file lightfoot_texture.jpg, then rename the file **lightfoot_texture-roundtrip.jpg**.

  b. In Flash, open the file FL H-3.fla from the location where you store your Data Files, then save it as **LightFootRecycling_imports.fla** in the location where you store your Data Files.

  c. Use a command on the File menu to import the file copy you renamed to the Stage, then set its X value to **0** and Y value to **0** in the Position and Size section of the Properties panel.

  d. Use a button on the Properties panel to open the image in Photoshop for editing. (*Hint*: Depending on the file associations set up for your computer, you might need to right-click the image on the Stage, click Edit with, then select Photoshop.exe.)

  e. In Photoshop, click Filter on the Application bar, point to Stylize, click Wind, click Blast in the Method section, click From the Left in the Direction section, then click OK to close the Wind dialog box.

  f. Click File on the Application bar, click Close, save your changes, exit Photoshop, then show Flash, if necessary.

  g. Test the movie, click the Start and Stop buttons, close the Flash Player, then save the document.

6. Insert a Flash movie into Dreamweaver.

  a. Publish the LightFootRecycling_imports.fla file as Flash (.swf) only, then save and close the document.

  b. Start Dreamweaver, open the file FL H-4.html from the location where you store your Data Files, then save it as **LightFootRecycling_DW.html**.

  c. Click Insert on the Application bar, point to Media, click SWF, navigate to the location where you store your Data Files if necessary, click LightFootRecycling_imports.swf, then import the movie.

  d. Type **LightFoot Flash Movie** as the title text, then click OK.

  e. Use a button on the Property inspector panel to play the movie, play and stop the animation in the HTML file window, then use a button on the Property inspector to stop the movie.

  f. Save the document, then use commands on the File menu to preview the Web page in your browser.

  g. Use the buttons to start and stop the movie, then close your browser.

7. Edit a Flash movie from Dreamweaver.

  a. In Dreamweaver, click the placeholder on the Stage, use a button on the Property inspector to edit the movie in Flash, navigate to the location where you store your Data Files, then select and open the file LightFootRecycling_imports.fla.

  b. In the Timeline, click frame 160 in the actions layer (the top layer), press and hold [Shift], click frame 160 in the light foot texture layer (the bottom layer), then use a command on the Insert menu to insert a keyframe in those layers. (*Hint*: Extending the Timeline will make the movie play longer before it moves back to frame 1.)

Skills Review (continued)

c. Click the Done button in the Editing from Dreamweaver roundtrip editing window to return to Dreamweaver. (*Hint:* Move to Dreamweaver, if necessary.)

d. Save the file, use a command on the File menu to preview the Web page in your browser, click buttons, compare your screen to Figure H-27, then close your browser.

e. Close FL H-4.html and LightFootRecycling_DW.html, exit Dreamweaver, then exit Flash.

8. Understand copyright.

a. Describe the purpose of copyright.

b. Discuss when copyright protection is attached to a work and the kinds of work copyright protects.

c. Describe how a work can enter the public domain.

d. Describe two ways you can ensure you are using a work properly.

Independent Challenge 1

You work at CoasterWoop, an online source of news by, for, and about roller coaster enthusiasts. Your boss wants you to create a new Flash document with a unique image, and then add a background image to the CoasterWoop movie.

a. Open your file management utility, navigate to the location where you store your Data Files, copy the file one_long_drop .png, rename it **one_long_drop_FW.png**, copy the file amusementPark.jpg, then rename it **amusementPark_PS.jpg**.

b. Start Flash, create a new file and save it as **coaster_fantasy_FW.fla** in the location where you store your Data Files, import to the Stage the file one_long_drop_FW.png as a single flattened bitmap, then make sure the X and Y values are 0.

c. Edit the image in Fireworks, select the Text tool on the Tools panel, select the text object on the canvas, select the text, change the text to the color of your choice, then return to Flash. (*Hint:* Click the Layers panel tab in the Pages panel group to view objects on layers.)

FIGURE H-28

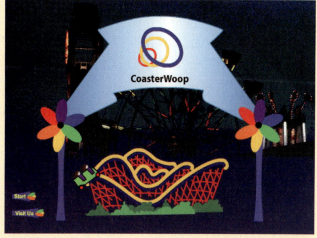

d. Save and close the document, then exit Fireworks.

e. In Flash, open the file FL H-5.fla from the location where you store your Data Files, save it as **CoasterWoop_imports.fla**, then import to the Stage the file amusementPark_PS.jpg as a flattened bitmap. (*Hint:* Depending on the file associations set up for your computer, the image may simply import to the Stage.)

f. Edit the image in Photoshop, click Image on the Application bar, point to Adjustments, click Posterize, type **6** in the Levels text box, click OK, save and close the file, exit Photoshop, then show Flash. (*Hint:* Depending on the file associations set up for your computer, you might need to right-click the image on the Stage, click Edit with, navigate to the location where you store your Adobe program files, click the Photoshop folder, then double-click Photoshop.exe.)

g. Test the movie, compare your screen to Figure H-28, then close the Flash Player.

h. Save and close the document, then exit Flash.

Independent Challenge 2

As the new Program Director at Lingoroots, an educational Web site specializing in linguistics, you're constantly looking for exciting ways to engage new visitors. For the next Web site feature, you'll compare the evolution of written Chinese across its 4,000-year history. The earliest written Chinese characters were pictures and evolved to a more stylized and artistic writing form. You want to show how Chinese calligraphy has changed over time and you decide to create a new Flash document. You add a background image to the existing Flash movie, then insert the movie in a Web page.

a. Open the file management utility on your computer, navigate to the location where you store your Data Files, copy the file calligraphy.jpg, then rename it **calligraphy_PS.jpg**.

b. Start Flash, open the file FL H-6.fla from the location where you store your Data Files, save it as **lingoroots_imports.fla**, then click the calligraphy layer to select it, if necessary.

c. Import to the Stage the file calligraphy_PS.jpg, make sure the X and Y values are 0, then open it for editing in Photoshop.

d. In Photoshop, click Filter on the Application bar, point to Blur, click Blur More, save and close the file, exit Photoshop, then show Flash.

e. Publish the document as a Flash (.swf) file only, then save and close the document.

f. Start Dreamweaver, open the file FL H-7.html, then save it as **lingoroots_DW.html** in the location where you store your Data Files.

g. Insert the SWF file, then type the title text of your choice.

h. Use buttons on the Property inspector to play, stop, and edit the movie, then select the file lingoroots_imports.fla to open in Flash.

i. In Flash, extend the length of the movie by inserting a key-frame in frame 180 on all the layers in the Timeline, then return to Dreamweaver.

j. Save the document, use a command on the File menu to preview the Web page in your browser, click buttons, compare your screen to Figure H-29, then close your browser.

k. In Dreamweaver, close FL H-7.html and lingoroots_DW.html, then exit Dreamweaver.

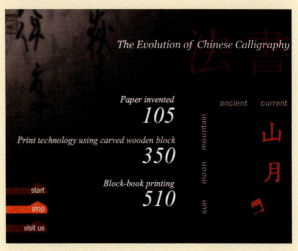

FIGURE H-29

Advanced Challenge Exercise

- Open the file management utility on your computer, navigate to the location where you store your Data Files, copy the file calligraphy_brushes.png, then rename it **calligraphy_brushes_FW.png**.
- In Flash, open a new file and save it as **calligraphy_brushesACE.fla** in the location where you store your Data Files, import to the Stage the file calligraphy_brushes_FW.png as a single flattened bitmap, make sure the X and Y values are 0, then open it for editing in Fireworks.
- In Fireworks, click Commands on the Application bar, point to Creative, click Add Picture Frame, click the Select a pattern list arrow, click Dark Flower, double-click the Frame Size text box, type **12**, then click OK.
- Return to Flash, then save and close the file.

l. Exit Flash.

Independent Challenge 3

You work for ibRobotz, an online entertainment site. Users can download ibRobotz characters or create their own to insert in stories. Your boss wants you to add an image to the movie, then insert the movie in a Web page.

a. Open the file management utility on your computer, navigate to the location where you store your Data Files, copy the file ibancestralbot.png, then rename it **ibancestralbot_FW.png**.

Independent Challenge 3 (continued)

b. Start Flash, open the file FL H-8.fla from the location where you store your Data Files, then save it as **ibrobotz_imports.fla**.

c. Import to the Stage the file ibancestralbot_FW.png as a single flattened bitmap, set the X value to **445**, set the Y value to **135**, then open it for editing in Fireworks.

d. In Fireworks, click Filters on the Application bar, point to Sharpen, click Sharpen, then return to Flash.

e. Publish the document as a Flash (.swf) file only, then save and close the document.

FIGURE H-30

f. Start Dreamweaver, open the file FL H-9.html, then save it as **ibrobotz_DW.html** in the location where you store your Data Files.

g. Import the SWF file, then type the title text of your choice.

h. Use buttons on the Property inspector to play and stop the movie, then edit the file by selecting the file ibrobotz_imports.fla to open in Flash.

i. In Flash, select the ancestor robot on the Stage, use the Free Transform tool to move and transform or edit it as you wish, then return to Dreamweaver.

j. Save the document, preview the Web page in your browser, mouse over the buttons, compare your screen to Figure H-30, then close your browser.

Advanced Challenge Exercise

- In Flash, open ibrobotz_imports.fla, save it as **ibrobotz_importsACE.fla**, publish the document as a Flash (.swf) file only, then save and close the document.
- In Dreamweaver, save the document as **ibrobotz_DW_ACE.html**, delete the placeholder, insert the ibrobotz_importsACE.swf file, then enter title text as desired.
- Edit the movie in Flash, import the file silhouette.png as a single flattened bitmap, then resize and move it as desired. (*Hint*: Depending on where you want the silhouette to appear, you may need to move the silhouette image to a new layer and move it up in the Timeline.)
- Return to Dreamweaver, play the movie, save and view it in your browser, then close your browser and the document.

k. Close all files, exit Dreamweaver, then exit Flash.

Real Life Independent Challenge

This Independent Challenge will continue to build on the personal movie that you have been developing since Unit B. Here, you import images and edit them in their native programs, and insert the movie into a Dreamweaver document.

a. Start Flash, open the file myproject.fla, then save it as **myproject_imports.fla**.

b. Obtain images for your movie. You can obtain images from your computer, the Internet, a digital camera, or scanned media. When downloading from the Internet, you should always assume the work is protected by copyright. Be sure to check the Web site's terms of use to determine if you can use the work for educational, personal, or noncommercial purposes.

c. Use the skills you learned in this unit to import and edit images, and insert a movie into a Dreamweaver document. (*Hint*: If you are not familiar with Dreamweaver, open one of the .html Data Files you used in this unit, then save it as **myprojectDW.html**. To change the background color, click the Page Properties button on the Property inspector, click the Background color swatch, then select a new color.)

d. Test the movie and the buttons.

e. Save and close the document myproject_imports.fla, then exit Flash, Dreamweaver, and either Fireworks or Photoshop.

Visual Workshop

You want to learn more about how to share your content with others while keeping some, but not all of the rights granted under copyright law, and how to find work you can use. Figure H-31 shows the Licenses Web page from the nonprofit organization Creative Commons. Go to http://creativecommons.org, click The Licenses in the Information section on the right, scroll down, then read the information about licenses. Next, click the About link on the navigation bar, then watch the video. Answer the following questions. For each question, include why or how you reached a conclusion. You can open a word processor or use the Text tool in Flash to complete this exercise. When you are finished, add your name to the document, save it, print it, then close the word processor or exit Flash. You decide to learn more about Creative Commons and gather ideas on how to manage copyright policies for works you create.

a. Creative Commons allows you to search for public domain and open access work, and attach copyright to your own work based on which rights you want to keep and which you want to waive so that others may use your work. Which license, if any, would you be interested in using for your work?

b. Have you tried to find work you can use for your projects? If so, were you sure you could use the work legally?

c. Have you given much thought to how you want to avoid copyright infringement? Does it vary depending on where you sit in the copyright scenario—as a user of protected work or as a creator of protected work?

d. How do you think using media from various sources could complicate your use of them and how you license your own work?

e. Identify the advantages and disadvantages to having a body of work available to the public for free and legal sharing, use, repurposing, and remixing. What is your personal opinion?

f. Close your browser.

FIGURE H-31

Courtesy Creative Commons (http://creativecommons.org)

Glossary

ActionScript The programming language in Flash that lets you control interactivity and actions in a movie or Web site.

Additive primary colors The primary colors red, green, and blue that combine to form all other colors in light.

Adobe Dreamweaver An Adobe CS5 program you use to create Web pages in HTML format.

Adobe Fireworks An Adobe CS5 program you use to create and edit bitmap and vector images as well as create Web page prototypes.

Adobe Flash Catalyst An Adobe CS5 design tool for combining interactive content from other programs without entering code.

Adobe Illustrator An Adobe CS5 program you use to design and edit vector graphics.

Adobe Photoshop An Adobe CS5 program you use to create bitmap images in which you can manipulate practically every aspect of their appearance.

Align panel The panel used to size, align, or distribute multiple objects to the Stage or to each other.

Alpha The transparency of an object.

Anchor points Squares on a vector object used to manipulate its path.

Animation The illusion of movement created by rapidly displaying a sequence of images.

Application bar An interface element located at the top of the workspace containing Flash commands on the left and workspace and Help options on the right.

Assistive technologies The types of technologies that allow persons with disabilities to interact with and perform tasks in a Flash document.

Author The creator and owner of a copyrighted work.

Authoring tool A program that creators use to develop and package content for users.

Bitmap graphic Displays a picture image as a matrix of dots, or pixels, on a grid. Also called raster image.

Blank keyframe A timeline element that does not contain artwork.

Breadcrumb trail A navigation aid used to track an element's location in the document.

Button symbol A symbol that responds to users clicking or rolling over it, which activates a different part of the movie, such as playing a movie clip.

Code hints A tooltip or pop-up menu that lists possible ActionScript elements.

Color panel Contains features for adjusting an object's stroke and fill colors.

Comments Lines of text in the Actions panel that ActionScript programmers use to document their code; Flash ignores comments when running the code.

Copyright A form of legal protection for authors of original works to control its use.

Copyright infringement The unauthorized use of one or more rights of a copyright holder.

Deliverable A tangible product delivered as part of a project.

Derivative work A new work based on an original work.

Documents Projects created in Flash.

Down A button state after the user clicks and holds down the button with the mouse pointer.

Dynamic text The Classic Text type used for displays that constantly update.

Easing A control on the Properties panel that speeds up or slows down the start or end of an animation.

Editable A TLF text type that allows users to select and edit text.

Elements of Design The basic ingredients used to produce artistic imagery.

Event handler ActionScript 3.0 code that tells Flash what event to listen for and then what to do once it hears the event.

Fair Use Doctrine A limited exception in copyright law that allows use of copyright material without permission of the copyright holder.

Fixed-width text A text type whose width is limited by the size of the text block.

FLA The native Flash file type; file extension for a Flash file is .fla.

Flash Player Plug-in A program used to play an SWF in a Web page.

Flash Video (FLV) The name of a file format used to deliver video over the Internet using Flash Player.

Flattened bitmap A bitmap image whose layers are compressed into a single layer.

FLV *See* Flash Video.

Font The entire array of letters, numbers, and symbols created in the same shape, known as a typeface. Also called a font family.

Fps Frames per second; measurement of video-playing speed.

Frame An element of the Timeline that represents a single point in a movie.

Frame-by-frame animation Animates an object gradually over several consecutive frames.

Frame labels Frames associated with a text name that ActionScript references when running the code.

Frame rate A measurement of video-playing speed, expressed in frames per second (fps).

Frame span A group of frames in the Timeline.

GIF Graphics Interchange Format; a still image file format best for creating drawings and line art; can support transparency.

Graphic symbol A static object usually used to create an animation spanning across frames in the Timeline.

Grid An alignment guide consisting of lines forming a grid of small squares on the Stage.

Group A command that manipulates multiple shapes or objects as one.

Guide Alignment guides dragged from the ruler onto the Stage.

Guide layer A layer that contains a shape used to trace or align objects, or to create a motion path for an animated object.

Hexadecimal An alphanumeric system for defining color on the Web that designates each color using a set of six numbers and/or letters.

Hit area The active clickable area of the button that corresponds to the button object in either the Over or Down states.

Hovering A mouse action in which the user moves over or points to a button; also called rolling over.

Iconic view Collapsed panels that display only an identifying icon.

Info panel Shows information based on where the pointer is on the Stage, such as the color beneath the pointer, and the size, location, and color of a selected object.

Input text The Classic Text type used for obtaining and processing user information.

Instance A reusable copy of a symbol on the Stage.

Integration The process of combining suite components into Flash and incorporating Flash animations into Web pages.

Intellectual property An idea or creation from a human mind that also has the potential for commercial value; the areas of law that govern creative expressions of ideas.

Interactive content Content that accepts and responds to human actions using multimedia elements.

Interactivity In a Web page or Flash movie, an element's response to a user's mouse pointer action.

JavaScript A programming language used to add interactive and dynamic features to Web pages.

JPEG Joint Photographic Experts Group; a still image file format that is versatile and often used for photographs and gradients.

Layers Individual rows in the Timeline that contain content in a Flash project.

Library panel Contains the media used in a project, including video, sound, photos, and other graphics.

Loop A setting that instructs a movie to play repeatedly.

Mask An object used to expose the content of the layer beneath it.

Menu bar A Flash interface element containing Flash menu commands on the left and workspace and Help options on the right.

Merge Drawing mode A tool setting that combines objects' paths.

Morph How a shape tween animation changes from its starting shape into a different ending shape.

Motion Editor A Flash panel that provides detailed control over properties in every keyframe in a motion tween.

Motion tweens Animate movement on the Stage as an instance moves from one position to another or changes properties such as color, size, or rotation.

Movie clip symbol A mini-movie or animation within a Flash movie that has its own Timeline and plays independently of the main movie's Timeline.

Multimedia Content such as text, graphics, video, animation, and sound that is integrated into technological expression.

Navigational components Icons, menus, and similar items that help users navigate a Web page or another application.

Nested symbol A symbol placed inside another symbol.

Object Drawing mode A tool setting that treats the shapes as separate objects.

Object-oriented language A programming language that uses a modular approach to programming, including reusing elements.

Onion skinning Displays frames before or after the current frame so you can see the content.

Optimize To modify file attributes to eliminate bottlenecks in a given frame during downloading.

Over A button state after the user rolls the mouse pointer over the button.

Page A feature in Fireworks that stores some or all the layers in a document.

Panel group A group of related panels that open as one.

Panels Individual windows that control crucial aspects of a project and display context-sensitive information and options.

Pasteboard An interface element where you can place or store objects that do not yet appear in the movie.

Path Straight or curved line segments.

Persistence of vision The capacity of the eye to retain an image for a short period, creating an illusion of continuous motion in film and video.

Pixel The smallest square of color used to display an image on a computer screen.

Playhead A Timeline element consisting of a red translucent square that moves through the frames as a movie plays in Flash.

PNG Portable Network Graphics; a still image file format that is the native file format in Adobe Fireworks. It supports higher-resolution images and transparency.

Pose To adjust the configuration of the joints in an inverse kinematics animation.

Principles of Design The concepts used to determine how the Elements of Design are used in a work.

Project The source FLA file containing content.

Projector A stand-alone application that plays a movie without using a computer's browser software or (for Flash projectors) Flash Player.

Properties panel Displays the attributes and available options for the selected element on the Stage or in the Timeline.

Property keyframes The motion tween keyframes in the Timeline that contain the specific property values that change in that frame: position, scale, skew, rotation, color, or filter.

PSD Photoshop document; the native Photoshop Element file format.

Psychoacoustics The study of how the brain interprets audio.

Public domain Works no longer protected by any form of intellectual property law; you can use public domain works as you wish.

Publish Instructs Flash to create the files necessary to display it on the Web or to use in other situations.

Publish profile A file in XML format that Flash creates in the Publish Settings dialog box and uses when it exports data.

QuickTime A popular export format that plays animation on both Macintosh and PC computers.

Raster image Another name for a bitmap image.

Read Only A TLF text type that prevents users from selecting or editing text.

Registration point Appears as a small plus sign and is the default point that positions an object on the Stage.

Resolution Describes the degree of clarity, detail, and sharpness of a displayed or printed image.

RGB Red, green, blue; a color model for color produced by emitted light, such as computer monitors.

RIA *See* Rich Internet Applications.

Rich Internet Applications (RIA) Web applications that function like desktop applications.

Rolling over A mouse action in which the user moves over or points to a button; also called hovering.

Roundtrip editing Adobe CS5 Creative Suite feature that lets you select a file you've inserted in one application, edit that file in its native program environment, and then seamlessly return to the open application to view the edited object.

Rulers Alignment tools that appear along the top and left sides of the Stage using pixels as their unit of measurement.

Sample To select a color by picking up a color in an image.

Scripting language A programming language used to interpret and execute user actions and tasks; Flash CS5 uses ActionScript 3.0 as its scripting language.

Scrubbing Manually dragging the playhead in the Timeline to play a group of frames on the Stage.

Selectable A TLF text type that allows users to select but not edit text.

Shape hints In shape tween animation, a feature that marks specific points on the beginning and ending shapes that Flash uses to transition one area into another.

Shape tween An animation that changes one shape to another, in a process known as morphing.

Skin The playback interface for a Flash video.

Snap ring An alignment aid that appears as you reshape an object on the Stage; becomes larger as it approaches a snapping point.

Sort To rearrange elements on the Library panel in ascending or descending order.

Stage An interface element that contains the movie's elements—text, images, graphics, drawings, and video.

State The appearance of a Flash button that corresponds to user actions, such as Up, Over, or Down.

Statement A complete sentence in ActionScript.

Static text The Classic Text default text type best used for basic content.

Storyboard A visual script containing captions to describe the action in keyframes in a movie; used to plan animations.

Streaming An online method of playing media before it has downloaded completely.

String Text, including letters, numbers, and punctuation, that is enclosed in quotation marks in ActionScript.

Stroke A border around a path or object.

Swatches panel Contains colors from the active color palette, or set, of available colors.

SWF (Shockwave Format) A published output file from Flash program; used to play movies in a browser. File extension is .swf.

Symbol A copy of an object, such as a graphic or button, that can be used more than once in a movie.

Syntax The order, structure, and use of words in a sentence of code.

Tags The building blocks of XML and HTML used to describe the data and create a document.

Text block An object containing text that you can move and modify.

Text Layout Framework (TLF) The default text option that provides flexible formatting features and can accommodate advanced typographic requirements.

Timeline Controls and organizes movie elements by using layers and frames.

TLF *See* Text Layout Framework.

Tools panel A Flash interface element containing tools to draw, select, modify, and view graphics and text.

Trace statement An ActionScript function that makes a message appear in the Output panel when users perform an action.

Transform Reconfigures an object by scaling, rotating, skewing, and distorting it.

Transformation point A small circle that appears on an object when it is selected, which Flash uses to orient the object every time you transform or animate it.

Transform panel Performs the functions of the Free Transform Tool, and more precise modifications.

Tweened animation An animation with defined starting and ending keyframes where Flash automatically creates the animation between the two keyframes.

Tween span The frame span in a tweened animation.

Typeface A font family created in the same shape or style.

Up The default button state, not affected by any mouse movement.

User interface The design and appearance of a Web page or other Flash content to users.

Variable-width text A text type in which the text block continues to expand as long as you type.

Vector graphic A mathematically calculated object that can be resized without losing image quality.

Vlog A video blog.

Waveform A graphical representation of sound in the Library and the Timeline.

Web-safe color palette A set of 216 colors that appear consistent across Web browsers and computer platforms.

Workspace The Flash program interface area where you work with documents; consists of panels, Timeline, and Document window.

Workspace switcher Application bar feature that switches to a different preset workspace configuration.

XML eXtensible Markup Language file; an Internet file format similar to HTML that describes information and data.

XMP eXtensible Metadata Platform file; metadata embedded in a Flash file that is able to be indexed by search engines.

Index

Note: Page numbers in boldface indicate key terms.